a usable past ?

a usable past?

a story of living and thinking vocationally at the margins

Paul Peachey

Foreword by George F. McLean

DreamSeeker Books
TELFORD, PENNSYLVANIA

an imprint of
Cascadia Publishing House

Copublished with
Herald Press
Scottdale, Pennsylvania

Cascadia Publishing House orders, information, reprint permissions:
contact@CascadiaPublishingHouse.com
1-215-723-9125
126 Klingerman Road, Telford PA 18969
www.CascadiaPublishingHouse.com

A Usable Past?
Copyright © 2008 by Cascadia Publishing House LLC,
Telford, PA 18969
All rights reserved.
DreamSeeker Books is an imprint of Cascadia Publishing House LLC
Copublished with Herald Press, Scottdale, PA
Library of Congress Catalog Number: 2007047885
ISBN-13: 978-1-931038-48-5; **ISBN 10:** 1-931038-48-1
Book design by Cascadia Publishing House
Cover design by Dawn Ranck

The paper used in this publication is recycled and meets the minimum requirements of American National Standard for Information Sciences—Permanence of Paper for Printed Library Materials, ANSI Z39.48-1984.

All Bible quotations are used by permission, all rights reserved and unless otherwise noted are from The New Revised Standard Version of the Bible, copyright 1989, by the Division of Christian Education of the National Council of the Churches of Christ in the USA; KJV from the King James Version of the Bible.

Library of Congress Cataloguing-in-Publication Data
Peachey, Paul, 1918-
  A usable past? : a story of living and thinking vocationally at the margins / Paul Peachey ; foreword by George F. McLean.
     p. cm.
  ISBN-13: 978-1-931038-48-5 (alk. paper)
  ISBN-10: 1-931038-48-1 (alk. paper)
  1. Peachey, Paul, 1918- 2. Mennonites--United States--Biography. I. Title.
  BX8143.P43A3 2008
  289.7092--dc22
  [B]
                    2007047885

16 15 14 13 12 11 10 09 08   10 9 8 7 6 5 4 3 2 1

To my parents:
Shem Yoder Peachey
Saloma Bender Peachey
and their legacy of humanity and faith

CONTENTS

Foreword: A Man Before His Time, by George F. McLean   9
Acknowledgments   13
Introduction—My Autobiographical Narrative   15

PART ONE
1 A Walk in the Woods • 21
2 Cradled Between Two Mountains and Two Wars • 31

PART TWO
3 The European Aftermath of World War II • 47
4 Reentering the Mennonite Enclave • 63
5 An Awakening to Peacemaking • 76
6 A Sally into the Orient • 87
7 Jousting with the Legacy of Christendom • 105
8 A Midlife Fork in My Road • 119

PART THREE
9 A Churchman's European Journey • 133
10 The Wealth and Poverty of Sociology • 143
11 Cold War Bridge-Building • 155
12 Retreat in a Wilderness • 169
    Excursus

PART FOUR
13 The Creation/Salvation Symbiosis • 187
14 *Ekklesia* and Diaspora • 205
15 The Sacralizing/Secularizing Duet • 218
16 Being Human/Christian in This Postmodern World • 233

Epilogue   248
The Author   253

Foreword:
A Man Before His Time

For many years before 1989, I had worked carefully with the Academies of Sciences in Central and Eastern Europe. Carefully, I say, meaning in part avoiding any contact with the peace movements or agencies strongly supported by the Soviet government. During these years occasionally I met in passing a professor from the sociology department of my own university, the Catholic University of America in Washington, D.C. In contrast to my practice, he was leading teams to Eastern Europe and working precisely with the Soviet-sponsored peace academies there.

I was conscious at the time that the professor, Paul Peachey, was a member of a peace church and hence could engage the Soviets without being suspected of being complicit in the Cold War. Where the old saying held that "fools rush in where angels fear to tread," I felt that for Paul it was just the opposite: "Angels could go in where fools feared to tread." This book explains in depth not only his theory, which could still be incomplete, but his life, which moved bravely ahead.

Professor Peachey grew out of a rigorous, classically rural Mennonite family background and was tested by the great call to militarism which was World War II. Even great religious leaders committed to nonviolence would conclude then that the evil of the times was an imperative for a military response. Yet Paul remained a stalwart conscientious objector (CO). Nevertheless, sensitive to the moral question this posed to his own sincerity, he willingly went off to serve in refugee work in Germany, followed by mission work in Japan.

Passing the test of personal sincerity and now prepared by university studies in sociology, he was ready for a lifetime of work in the religious peace movement, which included reaching out to those on the other side of the Iron Curtain.

Had he left it at that, this book would be the story of a rich and wonderfully dedicated life in the service of God and of peace on earth. The text goes further, however, to probe the deepest issues of religion and particularly of Christianity. These he confronts both historically and theoretically. Historically, he traces the education of Judaism, from temple as dwelling place of God and of sacrifices to synagogue as meeting place for the reading of the Scriptures and for prayer. He traces parallels in the history of the Christian church from the original coming of the Spirit upon the apostles at the first Pentecost to the achievement of state status with Constantine and again in the Reformation churches, then to the original meeting of the Anabaptist brethren to reestablish the pentecostal character of the church.

Theologically, he articulates this in broader strokes as, on the one hand, the basic theme of creation and hence the development of the church as a natural social body. This meant its building as the ethically good community, which politically would be Christendom. On the other hand, he would note the fallen character of human freedom and hence the need for redemption and salvation by grace, seeing this not in political but in the personal terms of the free church tradition.

In this context he would locate his own Mennonite community as an attempt to escape the characteristics of Christendom as renewed by the Reformation churches and their engagement in the responsibilities of state and power. He finds in Luther traces of a desire for a church that would be more clearly non-state but also a sense that this would require a level of holiness not yet experienced by a sufficient number of people. In this light it could be said that if there was a mistake in the Mennonite initiative to found a church in the spirit of redemptive grace and salvation, it lay not in being misguided but in being premature.

Yet Professor Peachey may take us further. A contrast between creation and salvation and thus between Christendom and the Pentecostal or believers church would appear to move to the margins of human social life not only the conscientious objectors of the believers church but the work of the Spirit as well. Thus he does not call for the substitution of one by the other, but for a transcendence of both, thereby pointing beyond to a church for which we can long but in which we cannot yet live.

Others have tried to bring the two more closely together. Thus, for example, Paul Tillich would see human nature, here understood in terms of creation, as subject to the Fall. What is here attributed to "salvation" or "redemption" as a response beyond human capabilities is hence a matter of grace. Humanity and philosophy, in other words, can constitute the question, but only God can provide the response. This would be his way of assimilating Luther's interpretation of the term *sola fide* in Paul's letter to the Romans.

The Catholic communion would calibrate this even more closely by seeing the Fall not as corrupting but only as weakening human nature. In this case the continued study of society and its dynamics could yet provide a real ethic for human life, which in turn could help with the human effort to live its divine vocation and mission in this world.

It will take more time to work out the deep theological issues with which Paul Peachey has grappled throughout his life and which he reflects in this work. Perhaps in God's providence his work of creation and salvation are closer together than Luther thought. In any case he certainly was correct that those who would follow the path of Christ in reuniting both are too few in numbers. Paul Peachey, I feel, is one—a man before his time.

—George F. McLean, Director
 Center for the Study of Culture and Values
 The Catholic University of America
 Washington, D.C.

Acknowledgments

This book, the story of my selected life experiences, serves as an autobiographical treatise. While emerging from a scholarly career, it deals more with lived experience than with academic data or theory. Properly understood, such a claim, far from being exalting, is humbling instead. For the quality of Christian callings far exceeds the quality of our frail human responses. And the grace of God, communicated to us individually, flows as well through the presence and ministry of our fellow humans.

With deep appreciation I acknowledge such friendship through a long and varied life, though for the most part anonymously. I will name only my parents, plus a few mentors at boundaries of transition into the wider world, and finally those who helped in various ways in the writing of this book. None of the persons named can held accountable for flaws in the pages that follow.

First, I applaud with gratitude the great company of people who deeply befriended me and my family over the years, who by now increasingly are shrouded in anonymity. The price of modern mobility is the disruption of the bonds of time and place. Repeatedly after deep immersion in rising streams I found myself taken elsewhere, unable to continue all "the ties that bind," and thereupon entered into new ones. Yet without the contributions made by earlier colleagues, those subsequent engagements could not have blossomed.

Foundationally, of course, my greatest debt is to my parents, Shem Yoder Peachey (1889-1973) and Saloma Bender Peachey (1896-1972), and the legacy of lived humanity and faith they forwarded to their children. Though differing, that legacy was then conjoined and reaffirmed by my own spouse, Ellen Shenk Peachey (and our children and grandchildren). At the boundary between the limited world of youth and the wider domains I eventually entered, I once listed four mentors: Harold S. Bender and C. F. Klassen, who pioneered the journeys outward, and A. J. Muste and John Oliver Nelson, persons "out there," congenial to me as a newcomer. From here the lapse into anonymity.

One further exception remains: persons who were involved to one degree or another in helping me shape this book. I hereby thank Myron S. Augsburger, Lois Bowman, Bonnie Bowser, George Brunk III, John Fairfield, Harold Huber, Irvin B. Horst, Vernon Jantzi, Laban Peachey, Mark Thiessen Nation, Calvin Redekop, Gerald Shenk, Linford L. Stutzman, Carroll Yoder, and Nathan E. Yoder.

Three due special mention are John and Kathryn Fairfield, who subsidized the editing; and George F. McLean, a Catholic University of America colleague and collaborator for more than two decades, who wrote the foreword. I also thank the two editors who assisted me on this project: Dan Shenk during the preliminary work on the manuscript and Paul M. Schrock during the final stage of my writing.

—*Paul Peachey*
Harrisonburg, Virginia

Introduction: An Autobiographical Narrative

This book is a personalized account of my believers church odyssey, within our crumbling Christendom, during the second half of the twentieth century. Being fully human—at once a member of society generally and of the distinctly Christian faith community particularly—remains irreducibly paradoxical. Absence of that tension signifies not the triumph of Christianity in society but more likely its dissolution. According to the biblical story, salvation, begun here and now, will be realized fully only at the end of the present age: "Then comes the end, when he [Christ] hands over the kingdom to God the Father . . . " (1 Cor. 15:24). What that fulfillment entails is beyond present human comprehension.

Medieval Christendom, to which legacy our American saga is deeply indebted, mistakenly assumed otherwise. During that era, human affairs rested on the ostensible belief that in the fourth and fifth centuries the imperial political order had accepted, and thereupon been incorporated into, the reign of Christ. Efforts by the sixteenth-century Protestant Reformation fundamentally to disengage the two domains were abruptly aborted. Only at the persecuted margins did the believers free-church project survive.

In the eighteenth-century American context, however, church and state, both constitutionally and institutionally, once more separated. But the reasons for that separation were merely practical, not fundamental. As a result, the ambience of Christendom remains comfortably embedded in the American ethos, even though formally church and state now are separate. Despite the United States constitutional separation of church and state, our nation was deeply involved in the two World Wars that emerged among the peoples of Christendom, for the most part with Christian (and church) support on both sides. Despite all this, the forces of secularization long advanced.

That advance permitted in the twentieth century, for the first time, the free and full publication of the sixteenth-century Anabaptist (believers church) writings, along with the legal records of their political prosecution. With the collaboration of European and North American scholars, that publication project peaked during the mid-twentieth century, even as the alternatives for conscientious objectors to military service were being fleshed out fully for the first time. Though these two developments unfolded independently, they became mutually reinforcing, particularly for the military draft-age generation during and after World War II.

Only after that war ended formally was service abroad for conscientious objectors permitted. Given the importance of the pacifist commitment in sixteenth-century Anabaptism—(for example, "the sword is an ordering of God, outside the perfection of Christ," as Amabaptists put it at Schleitheim in 1527)—the publication of the early documents during the World War II era had a bracing effect at that time and even more later, as we will see in pages that follow.

While these interactive influences affected the churches of Anabaptist descent generally, both church leaders and young draftees were most directly stimulated by the publishing of these historical materials. Not surprisingly, however, differences of reading also emerged between the older and younger generations. Church leaders looked to those publications for renewing support for prevalent modes of faith and practice in their communities. The younger generation, thrown abruptly into new alternative service experiences, whether at home or abroad, was more attuned to new challenges than to older customs. Those differing experiences added to the normal intergenerational ferment.

Born in 1918, I grew up in a conservative Anabaptist enclave in Pennsylvania. By early adolescence, I had become a personally committed Christian. After delayed college, some graduate school at home and abroad, and five years of Mennonite Central Committee (MCC) relief and service in Europe, in the early 1950s I completed a doctoral dissertation at the University of Zurich, Switzerland. Written in German, it was published in Germany in 1954. The topic was a sociological study of the original Swiss Anabaptists, 1525-1540. The primary data were the court records of some eight hundred Swiss people, mostly men but also women, arrested during that period in Switzerland for joining this illegal movement.

For me, the impact of that study became life-changing. It caused me to concentrate on my own century rather than to pursue a career in sixteenth-century studies. The return to contemporary denominational contexts led in the course of the next decade to a midlife career change. That change was occasioned not by disillusionment with my faith but by the deepening that the explorations of earlier roots had brought. In keeping with the physicians' Hippocratic Oath, "First do no harm," I chose to continue explorations in wider contexts. This autobiographical account tells that story and the discoveries resulting from that career change.

The possibility of confusion is inherent in the mode of writing here described as an autobiographical account. The intent and design is not that of a complete autobiography. Until part 4, the narrative is autobiographical, hence chronological. But interpretive cross-referencing sometimes intrudes. Suddenly there may be mention of an earlier or later event or concept than the date of the immediate chapter. At times this approach leads to repeated citings of examples as agenda treated in one context reappears in another context or stage. If the reader is aware of the design at the outset, this will hopefully minimize any difficulties.

Observe also that notes as well as index have been avoided. I intend to keep the reader's focus on the emerging thread of insights in their event-settings, mostly leaving pertinent literature aside for the moment. There is little attempt to cite or assess current literature on the many issues that emerge in the course of the pages that follow. While a listing of acknowledgements precedes this introduction, it does not include the pool of contributors, named and unnamed, to whom I am indebted in the experiences here sketched. Nor do the chapters that follow presume fully to name or account for all the events that impinged on my life journey.

A Summary Outline

As the contents page indicates, this narrative-based account falls into four parts:

Part 1 consists of an introductory chapter, followed by a second one that briefly sketches my family history and upbringing until I came of age.

Part 2 treats what can be regarded as an overview of the first half of my adult life: college (which came late after age twenty-one); wartime and postwar experiences; graduate training; early college teaching; and involvement in peace/war discussions in Europe, Japan, and America. The last two chapters in Part Two summarize the development of those experiences and their unfolding in a midlife career change.

Part 3 is a descriptive account of the second half of my life, including retirement. It begins in chapter 9 with the story of how that repositioning emerged: my appointment at the Catholic University of America; my extracurricular involvement in bridge-building into the Soviet world during the Cold War; and finally my post-retirement participation in a wilderness haven for study, dialogue, and retreat.

Part 4 summarizes the findings of the redirected portion of my life. These chapters take the form of essays. Yet even so they are based more on living experience than theoretical abstraction, at times more attentive to *both/and* tensions, than to *either/or* oversimplifications. Listening respectively to the grandeur and misery of both life and abstraction, and to the informing and judging Word transcending both, is hardly part of the professional canon—or of an outwardly successful career.

PART ONE

Chapter 1

A Walk in the Woods

Life can only be understood backwards; but it must be lived forwards.
—Soren Kierkegaard (1813-55)

Learning how to spell the meaning of life-experiences backwards,
some of us discover how the scattered syllables form a single phrase.
—Abraham Joshua Heschel

Moral knowing and being arise from doing, from experience rather than
thinking alone.
—Cynthia Moe-Lobeda

It was a bright spring morning in 1998 at the Rolling Ridge Study Retreat Community on the west slope of the Blue Ridge Mountain south of Harpers Ferry, West Virginia. My wife, Ellen Shenk Peachey, and I had lived and worked there since 1986, after retiring from the second half of our careers in Washington, D.C. I was on my daily walk on one of the local trails—daily, that is, when no physical task, like gardening or firewood cutting, clamored more for attention. I crossed the footbridge across the stream in the ravine between the staff community cottages and the retreat buildings. To my right lay the rotting trunk of a huge oak tree that must have been a vigorous sapling when George Washington, late in his teens, helped Lord Fairfax's surveying team prospect this mountainside and the adjoining valley. Though once cut over and farmed, this slope had long since returned to wilderness.

After passing the fallen tree and climbing the hill on the far side of the stream, I encountered a young woman from a Washington, D.C., inner-city ministry. As a newcomer to this retreat, she asked what this project was about. Its brief history was hardly self-evident, yet that history was inseparable from the reason for its existence—to become a haven for contemplation and dialogue.

This retreat, located on a land lease from a private nature preserve, is held in perpetual trust by the Rolling Ridge Foundation. The entire preserve of some 1,400 acres was also coming under a scenic easement of the Appalachian Trail Conference. Lying some sixty miles northwest of the nation's capital, this spot is readily accessible to its residents yet safely beyond the often futile noise of that metropolis. This particular study retreat serves both its sponsoring association and a number of partner church groups from the Washington, D.C., region.

Newly constituted in the early 1970s, the foundation holding this large tract had offered a cost-free lease to a small emerging informal group in northwest Washington, D.C., in which my wife Ellen and I participated. We dreamt of creating a semi-communal center for study and retreat, serving the greater Washington region.

With a tentative agreement with the foundation, by summer 1976 we began, with a week-long tenting retreat onsite (chapter 12). For the next decade, until 1986, we proceeded with mere brief summer camping events. At summer's end, 1986, Ellen and I moved onsite, into our newly built house, as the first resident staff members. A year later (1987) came my retirement from the Catholic University of America. Both of us then continued as full-time volunteers at Rolling Ridge until 2001, when we moved to a retirement community at Harrisonburg, Virginia.

Meanwhile, over the years, several others settled there as well. There were utopian hints in the dream that brought us there. The resident staff community, we fancied originally, might carry the individual members to the very end of their life journeys. By now, two decades later (after the 1976 beginning), it was becoming evident that remaining indefinitely would not be feasible. At the time of the above conversation, we had begun vaguely to consider a possible move to a retirement community. But such a move still lay in a misty future.

Details of the origin of this retreat, however, were of less interest to my young conversation partner than its purpose and future direction. What is the Rolling Ridge Study Retreat Community about? What are we trying to accomplish? What do we offer? Suddenly I found myself a bit on the defensive. Now eighty years old, how could I speak for the future, something of which I would not be a part?

I sensed, but vaguely, that just as two paths in space had intersected in this conversation, so likewise two lines in time, past and future, were somehow converging. As the conversation faltered, I found myself muttering something about my task now having more to do with shaping a *usable past* than with creating a *livable future*. The "usable past" phrase, however, was not of my own coining. Somewhere I had picked it up (as I did the title of this chapter), and it lay dormant in my memory, waiting to be activated in just such a moment as this.

Our conversation ended and we went our separate ways. But something had happened within me. I had been brought face to face with the fact that the future course of the Rolling Ridge Study Retreat Community was now beyond me, and that looking back into the twentieth century, contributing thereby to the shaping of a "usable past," was now emerging as my task instead. Some days later this vocational shift was reinforced by my encounter with the prayer in Psalm 71:17-18:

Oh God, from my youth you have
Taught me,
And I still proclaim your wondrous deeds.
So even to old age and gray hairs,
O God, do not forsake me,
Until I proclaim your might
To all the generations to come.

Here is the testimony that building a usable past, a celebration of the mercies of God experienced in the past, is the divinely ordered vocation in the final stage of the human life course! I typed a copy of this passage and taped it to my study door above a few other maxims. Retirement, it now appeared, is storytelling time, human experiences as divinely informed.

A Usable Past—What's That?

Initially the notion of building a usable past came like a breath of fresh air, an inspiring, even liberating, moment. Suddenly there was something to fill the gap that would come with retirement. But this optimism was short-lived. Once I started to think more concretely about what this might entail, I began to feel overwhelmed. Time, time past, history, memory—what are they? How can they be made usable? All my adult life I had worked at constructing futures. When things didn't quite succeed, there was always another day. Shaping the future, the specifics of day-to-day action, suddenly appeared much easier than making sense out of the receding past. And even if I figured out what this past entailed, how could I make it usable? The future belonged somehow to the generation of the young woman I had encountered—without me.

As these questions began to percolate, doubts deepened. I soon recalled a conversation I had some fifty years earlier, when I was at the young end of the age spectrum. In spring 1946, shortly after the end of World War II, I was helping to set up a clothing distribution by the Mennonite Central Committee (MCC) in Liege, a city in eastern Belgium. There I called on a retired Lutheran pastor, living in a riverbank apartment. As he trotted out an old photo album, he spoke fondly of his student years at Heidelberg University in Germany before World War I. To me, he seemed locked up in those memories, somehow disconnected from the realities that we now faced. I left that visit impressed with the quaintness of old age.

Now, in a similar conversation more than fifty years later, I had become the quaint old man, challenged by an optimistic youth. That graybeard, long ago in Liege—had he learned something in life that I have meanwhile missed? Maybe I should simply revel in my memories and forget about trying to shape a usable past? May not an effort to construct a usable past be merely a disguised effort to control the future, or worse yet, mere ego-tripping? And there are the practical questions, the fact that the past is often experienced as heavy-handed, as irrelevant to the future in this rapidly changing society. Admittedly, for that very reason, I had left behind some of the traditions that had shaped my life. In fact, doing so led to a career change in midlife, which I thought at the time might deserve an eventual recounting.

So Now a Deeper Challenge

The seed of a life story lay dormant in a career-change I had undergone at midlife, germinated in that walk in the woods that morning in 1998. But to tell my life story I had to address not only the general questions just cited but also a host of questions particular to my own experience. Front and center of those particularities lay my mid-career course-change. Telling that story would require an account of the first half of my life as backdrop for what emerged in the second half.

The midlife course change, however, had to do not with the *what* of my life but with the *how*. By early adulthood I had come to understand my life as Christian calling. The change in course meant not the abandonment of that calling but rather a shift in its route of travel. Life calling in some traditions is read, possibly misread, as prefabricated blueprint. For me it came to mean acting in terms of the already given, while awaiting further instructions along the way. "For we walk by faith, not by sight" (2 Cor. 5:7).

My midlife career shift set me unexpectedly on an uncharted path, "a road less taken." Problems had arisen in the context in which I earlier found myself, problems requiring wider perspectives and investigation than the situation afforded. Eventually I sensed that my earlier training and experience prepared me more for further investigation than for coping in that earlier context. Confronting that enigma, I took note of the Hippocratic oath axiomatic among physicians that the first consideration, before bodily intervention in an ailing patient, is to do no harm. I sensed a call to step outside the context for further experience and investigation, while remaining deeply rooted in my spiritual tradition, thus doing no harm. If travel along this uncharted route yielded new options, opportunity would arise in due time to report accordingly. This walk in the woods dramatized for me that the time to report was now upon me.

The psalmist's prayer cited above sheds light on this process. Where life is seen as divinely formed and informed, so likewise is history. History (the stream of generations disclosed in the biblical story) is the arena of divine-human discourse. The psalmist sensed that in the divine purpose life culminates in recounting God's wondrous deeds from generation to generation. Having lived my life, however imperfectly, as a focused vocation, I have glimpsed something of those "wondrous deeds." Yes, there are "deeds" to "proclaim," but precisely what and how?

Three years after the above walk in the woods, my wife and I moved to the Virginia Mennonite Retirement Community at the edge of Harrisonburg, Virginia, in 2001. By that time I had begun to wrestle with the problem of tempering my academic writing habits with real-life idioms. There a widely experienced colleague and friend of many decades, Calvin Redekop, invited me to join him in auditing a course in creative writing at nearby Eastern Mennonite University. This greatly stimulated my further probing, though as a former academic, I can't pretend fully to have popularized my style of writing in this narrative!

The Current Vogue of Storytelling

Narration, storytelling, and memoir-writing have become popular in our time, an era frequently characterized as postmodern. But Jonathan Yardley, a *Washington Post* literary critic, complains that writers of memoirs today tend to be obsessed with self—and thus are uninteresting. The reader is "left with the feeling that what is taking place is a bravura performance (Look at me!) rather than an effort to tell a story that will help us see the world in a new light" (*Washington Post Book World,* July 14, 2002, p. 3). Postmoderns tend to discount all claims beyond material reality. In the eyes of many we are left with nothing but our own stories, what Yardley calls "obsession with self," a trait long since labeled as narcissism.

In *Telling God's Story: Bible, Church and Narrative Theology* (Cambridge University Press, 1996), Gerard Loughlin, a contemporary English scholar, calls for "realistic narrative" (p. 70). He adapts the concept of Yale theologian Hans Frei for narrative in which "character, circumstance and theme are nothing without each other and become themselves only in their mutual reaction." Not only can character be known only as "engagement with the vicissitudes of life"—the words of Loughlin—but likewise, the deeper meaning emerges only in actual engagement with life circumstances. That form seems implicit in Yardley's assertion that the purpose of memoir writing is to help the reader to "see the world in a new light."

The psalm quoted above takes us a step further. In the end, the new light at stake here is God's wondrous deed that with old age and gray hair we are called to proclaim. Undertaking this task continues to be profoundly humbling. In the words of the epigraphs heading this chapter, viewing life backwards, with syllables thereby becoming phrases, results in awesome discoveries. What is worth reporting came about not through my own accomplishment but despite its limitations.

I resonate ever more deeply with the Pauline experience, wherein Christ's power is made perfect in Paul's weakness (2 Cor. 12:9). His human frailty, whatever that may have been, underscored that the abiding reality that emerged in his ministry was due to God's redeeming grace and not the product of Paul's own genius. As he increasingly learned in the school of hard knocks, Paul experienced a freedom and a joy previously unknown to him.

A Preview of My "Autobiographical Treatise"

While benefiting here from the Frei-Loughlin formula and the rich history behind it, I now offer my story as an "autobiographical treatise." I was reared in a relatively isolated Anabaptist enclave in rural Pennsylvania. "Anabaptist" was the label attached to the believers church movement that emerged in Europe north of the Alps in the 1520s, partly in the bosom of the Protestant Reformation. Originally the Reformation sought to correct the abuses that had crept into the sacramentally and politically enforced Christendom of medieval Europe. But soon questions arose about the underlying structure of Christendom as such. System reform—the Protestant Reformation—quickly and unexpectedly led to separation from the head of papal Christendom in Rome. The resulting uncertainty added to the unrest before a new church order could be established. So the reformers quickly turned over external church affairs—buildings, finances, liturgies—to political authorities. This arrested both rioting and renewal from within the churches.

Scattered groups from both the reforming and the old church emerged acknowledging only the authority of Christ in their gatherings (cf. Matt. 18:20). That movement, interpreted by the religious and political establishments as both sacrilegious and criminal, was hounded and suppressed, producing many hundreds of martyrs in the course of some decades. All this was beset by the diversity of spontaneity and circumstance.

Outwardly speaking, this "sectarian" episode was but a blip on the wide screen of Western history. Yet history has now moved far in that direction—governments ruling without direct church participation. For the most part, however, the separation of church and state comes about for practical reasons. Fundamental grounding for that disengagement is still wanting in the Western ethos, even in this new millennium. Confusion persists to our day within the legacy of Christendom regarding the relation of nature and grace—God's action as Creator and subsequently as Savior, a problem to which I return later.

Marginally, and principally in three variations, the sixteenth century believers church movement has survived into our own era: the Hutterites (named for sixteenth-century leader Jacob Hutter), who in Moravia included community of goods in the faith community; the Amish (named for seventeenth-century leader Jacob Amman), who culturally codify their separation from society; and the Mennonites (named for sixteenth-century Dutch leader, former Catholic priest Menno Simons), today more readily assimilated into society than the other two. Variously these groups serve as prototypical reminders to both society and mainline Christianity that according to the gospel we serve the world by being other than the world. To this day, the widespread yet aborted sixteenth-century Protestant reform remains incomplete.

Anabaptism Today

Meanwhile these Anabaptist groups, marginalized and introverted over nearly five centuries of their history, have their own flaws that stifle their contribution to the challenges of this new millennium.

Anabaptism, though intrinsically a product of urban ferment, survived largely in rural enclaves, tolerated and at times welcomed as rural energy in Europe and North America. I grew up on a small Pennsylvania farm, happily expecting to be a farmer. I was blissfully unaware that in my early twenties several unexpected events would bring me to Eastern Mennonite School (EMS) in the Shenandoah Valley of Virginia. Founded a year before I was born, EMS had meanwhile been certified as a high school and a junior college and was an uncertified four-year Bible college. The motive in establishing this institution was to improve the education of church leaders in ways that would reinforce the teachings of the traditions.

Anabaptism, however, was essentially a lay movement without trained professional leadership. Conservative impulses within the communities viewed the establishment of such institutions with suspicion, and not without reason. No sooner had several such institutions been founded than professionalization of the ministry set in. This tended to alter the inner character of spiritual life within these communities.

In any event, the founding of EMS to improve leadership education simply replicated what had happened in mainline church institutions a century or more earlier—training institutes for church leaders evolved into the American graduate university system (see chapter 4). EMS became an accredited liberal arts college in 1948 and by century's end had developed graduate programs and a regular seminary, thereby eventually becoming Eastern Mennonite University.

By my early twenties I understood Christian calling as a life to be lived in the world rather than an occupational withdrawal from the world in Christian service. "World" in this context, however, was an ambiguous term—on the one hand positive, referring to God's creation; on the other hand negative, in reference to flawed human constructions. Yet grasping that distinction is bewildering, evident in our efforts to come to terms with its real-life consequences. Basically these questions arose for me through my participation in the institutional changes I here question. Critics might well accuse me of "biting the hand that fed me."

By the time I began my senior year in college Bible at EMS, I commented to a few student colleagues, "Theology may reach to heaven, but I'm quite sure it doesn't well reach the earth; I will also have to study sociology." Eventually I found myself living at the interface of those two disciplines, theology and sociology, whether in graduate study or in "real world" activity. Arising from that ambiguity was an ever more baffling one, the tension between two opposing readings of the Christian story that came into sharp focus in the sixteenth-century Reformation—the polarization between the state church and the independent believers church.

THE BELIEVERS CHURCH
CONCEPT OF THE HUMAN STORY

Wrestling with definitions of world and church led to ferment among Mennonites. This was partly triggered by the draft-age generation of World War II. I was privileged to spend the better part of the immediate postwar decade in Europe, first in emergency relief activity, then in rehabilitation services, and finally in completing graduate study. Perspectives that emerged for me there were hard to articulate back home. Beginning a teaching career at my alma mater, formerly Eastern Mennonite School (EMS) but by then Eastern Mennonite College (EMC), a full-blown liberal arts college, I became involved in the postwar ferment in the Mennonite churches.

Four years later, I took a three-year leave of absence from my teaching position for an unexpected church and mission assignment in Japan. I experienced a growing sense of call to listen further at the interface of the Christendom and believers church configurations. The issues that our churches and society faced at mid-century were far from clear, and the solutions with which we sparred even less so. Switching to a listening posture, I could work as a sociologist in "secular" terms, both learning and contributing. Whereas during the period from 1945-1960 I responded to church callings outwardly, institutionally this emerging vocation was secular in character.

I reached the decision to decline further church assignments without knowing where the alternative would lead me. Aware that this was a hazardous course of action, especially for a young husband and father, I could not foresee what would follow. In looking back today, I'm reminded of the three career stages of urban craftsmen in medieval Europe: first apprentice, then journeyman, and finally master. After training as apprentice, many workers set out on journeys from town to town to gain experience under varied masters. Only then were they qualified to become independent masters, exercising their own trade. Effectively, my listening and working, working and listening posture at several intersections, both historical and academic, made me a journeyman for life, without my ever becoming fully a master in a particular craft.

Having done a dissertation in primary sixteenth-century historical data, I might well have continued as a specialist in that arena. The Radical Reformation in fact became an expanding field of historical, sociological, political, and theological study during the second half of the twentieth century, career-wise a promising option. Instead, what I learned in my dissertation and the issues of that era catapulted me back into my own era. Had I done a second doctorate, this might well have been appropriate. But that was not an option.

Practically my course of action was an instance of mixing apples and oranges. The decision to turn from my sociological study of a sixteenth-century phenomenon to my own twentieth-century faith commitment resulted in a confusion of categories, a direct invasion of empirical analysis with a leap of faith.

Chapter 2

Cradled Between Two Mountains and Two Wars

Look to the . . . quarry from which you were dug.
—Isaiah 51:1

What you inherit from your fathers, embrace to possess.
—German Proverb (translation of German proverb)
 (From an etching in my study of a stooped farmer following a plow pulled by two horses, purchased from a store in an Alpine village, reminiscent of what I did during my teen years.)

Come on now, all you young men. . . .
"The earth is yours and the fullness thereof."
Enter upon your inheritance, accept your responsibilities.
—G. K. Chesterton

In my infancy and youth I was cradled between the two World Wars that dominated the twentieth century. Born a month and a day before the end of World War I, I came of age (at twenty-one) a month and a week after the outbreak of World War II. The latter war was triggered by Hitler Germany's invasion of Poland on September 1, 1939. World War I indirectly, and World War II directly, framed the course of my life.

The same was true for millions of young men sent into World War II, many thousands of whom perished. For me, however, the consequences of these two wars were exceptional rather than typical. As a conscientious objector, I did not participate directly. Though I was spared from direct military service, World War II triggered the sequence of events that shaped the rest of my life.

Obviously I cannot recall World War I, but I do remember its echoes during my early childhood. And at the opposite end of my youth came the forebodings of an approaching new war. Yet both the memories of the war past and the forebodings of the one to come seemed remote from the daily realities shaping my childhood and youth. Not only did I grow up in rural isolation but also in what was widely regarded as sectarian withdrawal from the general society.

All this set the stage for a midmorning episode on Monday, September 2, 1939. My father and I were in a hayfield, harvesting a late second cutting of clover. John B. Meyer, our livestock dealer from Meyersdale, about ten miles away, came driving his small truck into our field. My father had inquired about the availability of some shoats (young pigs) to supplement a shortfall in that season's baby pig "crop" on our farm. Meyer, with fourteen sleek shoats aboard, exited from his truck with the announcement, "You can't go wrong on them; there's a war on this morning." Nazi forces had invaded Poland, he told us. Without radios and daily papers, we were blissfully unaware of what had taken place the previous day.

More than sixty years later, this scene remains seared in my mind. Why? This announcement quickly triggered memories that followed World War I—occasionally seeing someone in uniform, elementary school classmates bringing war souvenirs from their fathers, once in a while passing the home of a veteran whose sleep reportedly was disrupted by recalling frontline trauma. Above all, there were stories of difficulties that conscientious objectors had experienced.

Now, a few weeks short of my turning twenty-one, the announcement, "There's a war on this morning," struck home. I was about to be summoned by the military. The wider world for the first time was breaking directly into my experience. For the moment, the shoats were what we needed, and the deal was quickly closed. Meanwhile I'm sure the livestock dealer's sales pitch—there's a war on this morning—had no influence on the transaction!

And the Two Mountains?

Just as the two wars located my infancy and youth in time, the stretch between two mountain ranges located my childhood in space. These ranges, named Allegheny and Negro respectively, were part of the Appalachian chain, mapped politically as Elk Lick Township in Somerset County, Pennsylvania, reaching across the Mason-Dixon Line into Garrett County, Maryland. The area between the two mountain ranges was a hilly plateau that permitted farming interspersed by wooded areas. My great-grandfather, Wilhelm Bender, a young immigrant from Germany, acquired a tract of land there in 1841, bordering on the Mason-Dixon Line. This tract later was subdivided into several farms. The portion of that larger tract on which I grew up was one farm removed from the Mason-Dixon Line and the parallel short stretch of country road.

Some twenty miles to the north lay the national highway, Route 30, skirting the town of Somerset, our county seat. Far more defining for us was the national east-west highway, Route 40, some two miles to the south across the Mason-Dixon Line. By that route we traveled east to Cumberland and west to Oakland, both in Maryland. I vaguely remember a glimpse of "hunger marchers" on Route 40 straggling home after the march on Washington during the Great Depression in the early 1930s.

This was also the corridor for early airplane flights (between Baltimore and Pittsburgh) which we often heard and saw to our south. Once a small, single-propeller plane made a forced landing in a field near Grantsville. My father took my older brother and me for the first time to see a plane on the ground. Thus, though we were relatively isolated, Route 40 and the flight path afforded hints of a wider world.

My Parents and Their Family

My father grew up in the Kishacoquillas ("Big") Valley in an Amish family. While I know nothing of the details, his particular Amish home congregation was in disarray. Possibly for this reason, in 1911 or 1912 as a twenty-one-year-old, he headed west to follow the wheat harvest north through Kansas and the Dakotas. During that odyssey, he learned of a small and young church-related college in Hesston, Kansas, and toyed with the possibility of seeking enrollment there. That fall, however, his sister (two years older) was to be married, and he had to return home for the occasion. Once there, his mother said to him (in Pennsylvania Dutch, the native dialect), "Now Shem-boy, you're staying home."

Stay home he did. Between the lines, I gather that his mother was the family pacesetter. But about two years later "Shem-boy" headed south to Somerset County during the maple sugar season (February-March) to earn a bit of money and possibly a breath of fresh air. There he met a beautiful young zither-playing blond named Saloma Bender, in an Amish Mennonite community that had broken away from the

Old Order Amish. An attractive young blond in a progressive community? As the saying goes, the rest is history. Less than two years later, on January 2, 1916, they were married, across the line in the state of Maryland.

Newly married, my parents first settled on a small rented farm, some five miles to the north of the Wilhelm Bender tract, right on the Pennsylvania side of the Mason Dixon Line. The farm, newly created by a subdivision of a larger holding, included a vestigial one-room log cabin in which they lived while new farm buildings were being constructed. As the second child in this young family, I was born in that log cabin in 1918, merely months before we moved into the new house. Then early in 1923 my parents bought my mother's homeplace from her five siblings, who with her had inherited it from their parents, Enoch and Mary Bender. Enoch was the son of Wilhelm. This farm had been part of Wilhelm's original tract.

The farm our family thus acquired totaled 137 acres, with barely fifty acres tillable. While I was growing up we cleared a few more acres at the fringes. Our day-to-day "community" crossed the Mason-Dixon Line south into Garrett County. We engaged in mixed farming, with rotating crops, to feed cattle, poultry, and pigs (plus sheep in the early years). We wholesaled and retailed dairy, poultry, and pork products in nearby towns: Meyersdale, Pennsylvania; Frostburg and Cumberland, Maryland. A team of horses and a farm tractor provided mobile power on the farm. Threshing and silo-filling were cooperative events with half a dozen nearby farmers.

Eventually we were a family of ten children, six girls and four boys. I was second oldest. My older brother had already left home by the time the youngest of our siblings, a sister, was born. We lived a mile from a village called Springs (originally Chestnut Springs), named for the spring at the foot of a hill around which a settlement began. We walked to and from the two-room public school, partly through the woods of our farm, partly along unpaved public roads. High school, however, was not part of our way of life. A little country store with a post office had been built next to the spring, where we both shopped and picked up our mail. A treasured childhood memory is my riding by horseback to fetch the mail, perhaps along with buying a small grocery item.

During those early years the larger society was merely a distant horizon, for both geographic and technological reasons. A long winding and hilly lane through the neighbor's farm connected us to the public county road, which lay beyond our view. Our farm house was constructed next to a spring, with its water-flow piped into the cellar and through the cellar into the farmyard into a trough for the livestock. Hand pumps drawing from open tanks in the cellar brought water to the kitchen and the dining room. There was only an outdoor toilet, no electricity as yet, and of course no radio or daily newspaper. A local party-line telephone system linked several dozen farmers. When the phone rang, everyone on the system heard it and anyone could listen to any conversation!

We did subscribe to a biweekly farm newspaper, the *Pennsylvania Farmer*. I recall Charles A. Lindbergh's 1927 first transatlantic flight from reading a poster in our nearby village machine shop. I remember as well Herbert Hoover's presidential election in 1928 that as a ten-year old I heard about at school. Four years later, younger siblings brought news of Franklin D. Roosevelt's election home from public school, the school from which I had graduated the previous spring. It was a gloomy November day and, in this Republican country, ominous. It was rumored that FDR was communist-tainted!

If this were a full family history, much more could be told. My Peachey ancestor came directly from Switzerland in 1767, some sixty years before my mother's Bender ancestor. I will say more later about my father, my most important mentor, sixth-generation descendant from that original immigrant, Peter Bitsche (as then spelled).

THE QUARRY FROM WHICH I WAS DUG

In keeping with the epigraph at the beginning of this chapter, I turn next to the theme of the quarry from which I was dug. I was reared in the pacifist Anabaptist tradition. At the age of about eleven, rather young in the Anabaptist tradition, I had experienced Christian conversion. By early adulthood I knew where I stood spiritually.

In part, my story exemplifies the force of the family farm in American history. The yearning of the common people to escape from serfdom was an important impulse in European history and the immigrants who left it behind. The landed aristocracy in Europe possessed freedoms beyond the reach of the peasantry. Though less severe than slavery, the territorial attachment of peasants to manorial estates sharply limited their human freedom and development.

Between these two social strata, especially in England, a limited number of independent "free-holding" farmers emerged, farmers who owned and worked their own land without feudal intervention. Characterized as yeomen, these farmers came to be regarded by some historians as the backbone of the English nation. But contrary to the European story, apart from the slavery chapter, America had no peasants. Somewhat like the yeoman farmer in England, the independent family farmer in the early generations could be viewed as the backbone of the emerging American nation.

But in my cradling, something more important was operative, namely the "sectarian" Anabaptist tradition. At age fifteen in 1830, Wilhelm Bender, my great-grandfather, sailed from Germany to America, leaving his native family behind. After a nearly two-month voyage he landed in Baltimore.

A rebellious youngster running from home? To the contrary, he was sent by his parents in the company of an older man. The Benders lived in a village near Wohra, some thirty miles southwest of Kassel in west-central Germany. Their Anabaptist Swiss ancestors had filtered northward into these forested hills and valleys after the Thirty Years War ended with the Peace of Westphalia in 1648. In that region feudal landholders sought to repopulate the estates devastated in that war. Anabaptists, still hassled by Swiss authorities, were known in this region of Germany as upright, hardworking farmers. Whatever regional restrictions against sectarianism remained in German territories, these local feudal landholders had the leeway to develop working agreements with their immigrant renters.

While by the early nineteenth century there was a scattering of Benders among the resulting settlements in the Wohra region, that name had not appeared originally among these Swiss immigrants. Whether by direct conversion or as a result of intermarriage, Benders among these Anabaptists apparently were of German stock. Later, following the Congress of Vienna in 1815, the Prussian monarchy had been able to consolidate its power in regions of Germany to the west, including the above area. Men in the Prussian domains thereupon became subject to Prussian military mobilization.

The Anabaptist wing of the Protestant Reformation from its origins in the 1520s held, however, that "the sword is an ordering of God outside the perfection of Christ" (*The Schleitheim Confession*, trans. and ed. John Howard Yoder, Herald Press, 1977). These believers respected and obeyed political authorities, but for believers such obedience was nonetheless conditioned, indeed limited, by loyalty to Christ. This paradoxical formula again and again over the centuries has proven to be ambiguous.

Wilhelm, born August 22, 1815, was the first son of Daniel Bender and Elizabeth Bauman Bender. Daniel, widowed and remarried, already had three children in a previous marriage. According to family history, the immediate occasion for Wilhelm's departure to America in 1830, alone at the age of fifteen, was the family's Anabaptist pacifist faith. Otherwise, a few years later, young Wilhelm would have been recruited into Prussian military service.

But the hope that the entire family might eventually follow seems also to have been part of the picture. Four siblings followed Wilhelm, with Michael, the youngest, born shortly after Wilhelm left for America. Eventually, twelve years later, in 1842, the family followed Wilhelm to America, saddened, however, by the death of Daniel, the father, shortly before they set sail.

THE ANABAPTISTS—AN HISTORICAL FLASHBACK

During the long era of Western Christendom, the concept of the just war has tended to prevail in most Christian churches. This concept has two broad meanings. First, recourse to war is permissible only as a last resort. Second, a complex series of rules regulate the conduct of war. In medieval times, the inconsistency of warring activity with the Christian gospel was still honored in the exemption of clergy and monks from direct arms bearing. Moreover, persons in those callings were thought to constitute the church proper. All this evolved from the fourth-century claim, not foreseen in the gospel, that with the Emperor Constantine's ostensible conversion early in the fourth century, the Roman Empire was beginning to accept the lordship of Christ.

Given the corruption that followed, this whole scheme was challenged by the early sixteenth-century Reformation. And while the rule of both the Roman church and the Roman Empire were repudiated in various European territories north of the Alps, the related political unrest led to renewed and intensified state control of the sphere of churchly expression. Accordingly, efforts to establish "free" or "believers" churches, regarded as "sectarian" and labeled Anabaptist (rebaptizer), were quickly and ruthlessly suppressed. A few survived at the margins and served in some respects as prototypes of modern free church expressions. While commitment to peace and nonviolence became a hallmark of the Anabaptist movement, that movement was far more profound than mere pacifist protest.

Long hassled in Europe, by the late seventeenth century a few Anabaptists began to find a haven in the New World. Circumstances in the United States during the first half of the twentieth century, both around the groups and among them, served as a challenge and an opportunity for these communities. In later chapters I will say more about those developments. Here I merely note that I was caught up in that mid-century ferment. Given the interplay of wartime and postwar experiences, by the end of the 1940s the issues of peace and war became focused in my life, education, and work. Subsequently, however, by the mid-1960s a midlife redefinition was underway. I now confronted the deeper common confusions that underlay that polarity.

While I was unprepared for the pacifist/just war debates that emerged originally, I was even less prepared for the challenges I was to face in that redefinition.

Meanwhile, Back to the American Story

The Great Depression, next to the two wars noted above, was an important "cradling" impetus in my young life. That Depression, triggered by a stock-market crash in October 1929, followed a few years of economic turbulence after World War I, then a five-year period of relative prosperity. As I recall, my parents had some $80 in their bank checking account when the 1929 crash came. With the bank's sudden closing, that money now was inaccessible. It represented far more purchasing power than such an amount today. As an eleven-year-old in 1929, I still remember the visit of our small town banker from Salisbury, five miles away to help my parents figure out a way to cope with this crisis.

While by 1937 measures introduced by the feared Roosevelt administration had improved the overall economy somewhat, my adolescence was dominated by the Depression that persisted. As the two oldest children, my late brother and I worked hard to exploit our farm resources to enable the family to survive. This eventually included sharecropping neighboring farms temporarily available for such use. The 1930s provided a "make-do" education that for better and for worse followed me through life.

Military Conscription for World War II

In summer 1939, the United States Congress updated the Selective Service Act and the agency that drafted the country's able-bodied men, ages eighteen to forty-five. On February 6, 1941, President Roosevelt signed Executive Order 8675, providing for the first time in

American history a full legal provision for conscientious objection to war. Persons of demonstrable religious sincerity, whose conscience forbade the taking of human life, would be assigned to nonmilitary service in our society—forestry care, mental hospital staffing, "smoke jumping" in forest fires, and the like. Often these were programs that, due to the flow of manpower into the military, experienced manpower shortages. While support for conscientious objectors in alternative service would be provided, they were required to work without pay.

On the face of it, this was a remarkable development. Human cultures, from archaic to modern times, were grounded to some degree in war, whether defensive or offensive. Evasion or refusal of service was widely despised as a cop-out and defined as punishable. With the rising complexity of Western society and the corresponding growth of individualism, especially in England and the United States, reliance on the individual conscience likewise grew apace. Respect for conscientious objection to war became legally recognized in these countries.

In 1941, after the initial registration of draft-age men in the United States had been carried out, the first call-up of a limited number of men, selected by lottery, was issued. My name appeared in that first lottery. I had registered as a CO, and my status as a CO had been approved.

Meanwhile my future was unfolding at its own pace, and I was beginning to look beyond life on the farm. The United States had not yet entered the war, and I had not yet been summoned by Selective Service. In the fall of 1941 I enrolled in a college Bible course at Eastern Mennonite School (EMS) at Harrisonburg, Virginia.

This was several months before the Japanese attack on Pearl Harbor and the formal United States declaration of war it triggered. About two months after my enrolment at EMS came my Selective Service call for induction—a date and place where I was to appear for assignment to a Civilian Public Service (CPS) project. I reported this call to the dean of EMS. He had a surprise for me. He had just been notified that the four-year college Bible course at EMS was being classified by the Selective Service Authority as seminary-equivalent.

The Selective Service Act provided for a number of classifications for drafted men, ranging from 4-A for men qualified for active service to 4-F for those physically unqualified for service. A special classification, 4-D, was established for seminarians, persons studying for the Christian ministry or priesthood. These were deferred from military service, since the work of clergy was deemed essential in the national interest. Anabaptists, historically maintaining a lay ministry, had no seminaries. However, our colleges offered Bible majors that attracted people anticipating, or already active in, church ministries.

For me a vision of Christian calling and service was unfolding, though not in the form of clergy as profession. The ministry as a salaried profession or occupation was not part of our tradition. I had been admitted to a two-year Bible program at EMS, open to older students like me who had not been to high school. Meanwhile I had learned that Pennsylvania, my native state, offered "pre-professional examinations" that, if successfully passed, qualified candidates for college admission. (GED tests did not yet exist.) Thus an academic track was open to me after all. I had thirty-six hours to decide—either commitment to the four-year Bible-major program at EMS, or induction into CPS. What was an inexperienced Pennsylvania farm boy to do under this unconventional circumstance?

With the deadline upon me, the next evening I phoned the dean, still undecided. When he answered, I began to speak. As I vividly recall, I mumbled a rather tenuous, "I guess I'll stay in college." Thereby my die was cast. As it turned out, I spent the four years of World War II, 1941-1945, at Eastern Mennonite School. I do not regret that decision, though it brought mounting inner discomfort. During those years my sense of calling to a life of Christian service grew. In that respect my 4-D classification for Christian ministry was authentic. But whatever form my service would take, becoming a professional clergyman for me personally was not an option.

With my age peers in either military or CPS, spending precisely those four years sheltered in college was not easy. Moreover, by the time I began the final year in my program, a further complication arose. I had concluded, as I commented to a few fellow students, that while "theology may reach heaven, I'm not sure it reaches the earth." Therefore, after graduation I began graduate training in sociology. This did not mean the abandonment, but rather the enrichment, of my biblical and theological interest. And only now, by "understanding backward" (Kierkegaard), did I fully discover in that first sociological inkling the germ of much that was to come.

The population of my native community was entirely of European descent, mostly mainline Protestant—Methodist, Presbyterian, Lutheran, and the like—with a Catholic minority. Anabaptists (Mennonites and Amish) in that area came in five varieties, ranging from the most separated from the wider society to those most accommodated to it. I was born and raised in the middle group known as Amish Mennonite, midway between the two extremes. We had selective exchanges with the groups immediately above (a Mennonite church in Springs) and below (Beachy Amish). Our relations with those at the opposite extremes, Old Order Amish and General Conference Mennonites, were practically beyond religious and social fellowship.

The diversity among the Anabaptist groups was common in other parts of the country as well. These divisions were slightly tempered by the Mennonite Central Committee (MCC) that had been formed in 1917. As an agency for government contacts and emergencies, but not fully a "church" or denomination, MCC was informally and variously supported by the several Anabaptist groups. I mention this here merely to note that all this entailed "church politics" to which I would be introduced as my college years ended.

A Pivotal Year

My graduation coincided with the end of the European part of World War II in May 1945. A month later I married Ellen Elizabeth Shenk from Denbigh/Newport News, Virginia. We had met at Eastern Mennonite School. After a brief honeymoon, we moved temporarily to a Philadelphia suburb for my enrolment as a graduate student in sociology at the University of Pennsylvania. My bride worked in a men's clothing factory to support us, but only for the summer.

The draft was still in effect. While the pursuit of sociological training now was part of my own sense of calling, this hardly satisfied Selective Service. In any event, college and church leaders at Harrisonburg stressed the need for a course of action consistent with the Selective Service classification—preparation for "Christian service"—I had been accorded. Temporarily, then, I accepted two half-time church-related assignments back at Harrisonburg, Virginia, beginning in September 1945.

Meanwhile, two other larger, rather different but parallel developments were underway. The first was the now rapid implementation of the postwar relief program by Mennonite Central Committee (MCC), developed as the war unfolded. At that time Mennonites still lived mostly in rural areas. In the course of the war, they began to assemble food products and clothing for shipment abroad to countries devastated by war. Mostly young adults in our communities, ages twenty-four and up, were mobilized and briefly trained for managing distributions of food and clothing and eventually for reconstruction services, both physical and social. During the war itself, however, alternative service for conscientious objectors was limited by law to the domestic arena.

Second, by the 1940s an important project in sixteenth-century historical research was underway in Europe. This involved the first-time publishing of the legal records and related documents of the sixteenth-century Anabaptist believers church movement. Until then the story of that movement had been based primarily on the interpretations of the politically established Protestant and Catholic churches that sought to vilify and suppress it. The first-time publication of many important documents from the Anabaptists own readings reinforced the inspiration of Anabaptist COs—Amish, Hutterites, and Mennonites—during World War II.

That publication energized both the CPS program at home as alternative to military service during the war and the budding relief and reconstruction activities destined for war-torn areas abroad. Getting a fuller view of the origin of our movement inspired our church communities anew as we faced war-time and postwar challenges. Ellen and I, while distantly aware of these developments, were not yet directly engaged by them. No sooner had we entered our provisional assignment for the next academic year than these two converging programs, MCC postwar relief and the publication of sixteenth-century Anabaptist records, suddenly entered our life at the very center. That change is the subject of the next chapter.

Coping with an Ambiguous Heritage

I have briefly noted how a devout, rurally isolated, self-sufficient farm family stamped my character. I responded positively to its Christian witness in my young conversion. At the same time, the self-containment of our family exacted an enormous price for me. Our rural isolation reinforced the church-versus-world dualism of the four centuries of negative stereotyping earlier expressed in outright persecution. That isolation and stereotyping reinforced my tendency to withdraw and turn inward as an introvert.

Nonetheless, there were two alleviating impulses. The first was the outreaching perspective of my father. With public and higher education denied, he pursued lifelong self-education. His ordination by lot as a minister in our congregation in 1931, before I reached age thirteen, intensified that process. In keeping with our rural ethos, I loved our rural life and took it for granted as my future. Quite unexpectedly, soon after I came of age, my life turned in other directions.

Of the other circumstance I became aware only retrospectively. While going to a public high school at that time was not an option, my older siblings and I attended the local two-room, two-story elementary public school. Almost half a century later our class of eight years gathered in a class reunion in a nearby church—the old wooden frame school building had long since disappeared. The re-encounter with public school comrades from my youth touched strands in my psyche long since buried. I suddenly realized the significance of those contacts in my early years outside the cultural ghetto in which I had grown up.

Tension between the inner core and the outer shell (ghetto) in our tradition was widely experienced and variously handled at mid-twentieth century. Some young adults, finding the shell oppressive, rebelled and turned elsewhere. In my instance I sensed instead the call and the opportunity to probe the inner core more deeply and to address the incongruities of the shell from that perspective. In the end, whether viewed spiritually or socially, the relation between core and shell in forming character remains paradoxical, to some degree an irreducible tension. The formation of the human person by communally grounded family matrix is analogous to the formation of the physical body in the mother's womb, the indispensable second stage.

Conclusion

The contingencies of time and space, however particularized, are always critical in the determination of character, beyond our control as we appear on the scene. For my parents this included World War I. Probably more decisive was their generation's proximity to the family's immigration and selective acculturation. My mother's grandfather, Wilhelm Bender, died in 1894 two years before her birth in 1896. My parents were children of their temporal and spatial contingencies as we, their offspring, were children of ours. The interaction of those two generations was important in our ongoing development. Both of my parents passed from the scene in the early 1970s, a year apart.

As noted earlier, the independent farm-based nuclear family was important as a character matrix in American history within the wider context of time and space. By definition the family process is paradoxical, at once sheltering from and generating its host society. In earlier times, this familial matrix was itself embedded informally in ties of kinship and locality.

More recently, this embedding has largely disappeared, at the expense of family stability and viability. In my self-understanding, I was profoundly shaped by this paradox. The strength of the bonding and piety of my parents shaped my character at the deepest level even as both the rural and the sectarian legacy permanently handicapped the young as well. For me happily the former outweighed the latter. My life agendas emerged from those tensions. As will become evident in later chapters, poor articulation of the biblical "metanarrative" underlies the dissonance between the believers church and Christendom legacies. That quandary became my life challenge.

PART TWO

Chapter 3

The European Aftermath of World War II

Whether we wish it or not we are involved in the world's problems, and all the winds of heaven blow through our land.
—Walter Lippmann (1913)

Older men declare war. But it is youth that must fight and die.
—Herbert Hoover (1944)

Sometime they'll give a war and nobody will come.
—Carl Sandburg (1937)

At summer's end of 1945, two church-related careers opened. One was a teaching position at a parochial school in Delaware, the other an editing post at Mennonite Publishing House in Scottdale, Pennsylvania. Instead I opted for something temporary to allow me more readily to continue my sociological quest in a still indefinite future. Ellen and I as newlyweds shared the faith assumptions on which such decisions rested but without any clear notion as to how they would unfold. We were distantly aware of the two developments in Europe—the emerging MCC postwar relief program and publication of sixteenth-century Anabaptist records as a potential for study. At the moment, these were not yet an active part of our calculus.

In late September, a few weeks after our return to Harrisonburg from Philadelphia to begin my half-time assignments while Ellen continued college, we made our first post-wedding visit to her family and her former home in Tidewater Virginia. During this weekend, we attended the Sunday service in her home church. Midway through the sermon, but unrelated to it, I suddenly and unmistakably knew that I was called to go to Europe under MCC. The agonizing uncertainty of many months suddenly lifted. The seeming conflict between service and further training was abruptly resolved. We returned to Harrisonburg later that day.

The next morning, I knocked on the door of the dean of EMS where I now was employed half-time. I asked to be released, simply on the basis of that Sunday morning epiphany.

"Didn't Brother Mumaw see you on Saturday? He was sent to ask you on Saturday to go to Belgium for MCC," he replied with a baffled look.

"No, I was away for the weekend."

Suddenly there was clarity. "The rest," as the saying goes, "is history," eight years of personal history. Logistics and red tape took several months. At last, on February 13, 1946, I set sail for Southampton, England, on the SS *Washington*, along with Wilson Hunsberger, a Canadian MCC volunteer likewise assigned to Belgium. By way of London, then Amsterdam, we were to join Cleo Mann, already in Brussels, to become a three-man, postwar MCC relief worker team in Belgium.

Nonetheless it was not all that simple. Ellen and I had been married less than four months, but I was being asked to go alone. The immediate postwar turmoil in Europe was such that MCC was not sending married couples. Moreover, twenty-four was the minimum age for appointed workers. Ellen was twenty-two. We needed time to reflect and to discuss, but our shared faith enabled us to resolve the matter amicably. After all, married draftees were not exempt from military assignment abroad merely for that reason. Happily, a year later, though only twenty-three, Ellen was permitted to join me. Married couples proved to be a stabilizing presence in the MCC teams of largely unattached young workers!

Thus an amazing new chapter began for us. Our life, as for countless others in our generation, took wholly unanticipated directions. For me, the convergence of "inner" and "outer" call described above became a lodestar for the rest of my life. It was never repeated in just this manner, yet that experience set the stage inwardly for me, and for us, as we continued to confront life's testing decisions.

As for our European sojourn, the assignment in Belgium, though valid in its own right, would be but an opening chapter. After twenty months there (eight for Ellen) we were transferred by MCC to Germany for three years. That work, eventually followed by graduate study at several European universities and a doctorate in sociology and history at the University of Zurich, occupied me until late summer 1953. Effectively, the four and a half years of postwar emergency relief and rehabilitation work under the Mennonite Central Committee served as internship, but preceding rather than following graduate training, as commonly occurs.

Postwar Europe

Mennonite Central Committee came into its own through the challenges leading to and following World War II. Formed in 1920 to respond to the plight of Mennonites in Russia in the communist revolution there, MCC barely survived thereafter. By the late 1930s, it was reenergized by the developments leading to what became known as World War II, specifically military conscription and the fate of conscientious objectors. MCC, with corresponding agencies of the Church of the Brethren and the Friends (Quakers), conversed with the federal agencies concerning provisions for conscientious objectors to war as the Selective Service Act was updated and reenacted.

Initially, MCC's postwar relief activity in Europe involved two broad areas of service: (1) emergency food and clothing distribution in war-stricken residential population centers, and (2) refugee resettlement. The latter applied primarily to Mennonites fleeing from the Soviet Union in the wake of the retreating German armies. The roots of these refugees were originally Dutch, but with generations of acculturated North German residence until late eighteenth-century emigration to Russia. Frequently, however, displaced persons from various countries were included in food and clothing distributions in many areas. In later stages a variety of rehabilitative services often emerged—neighborhood centers, reconstruction units, international work camps and conferences, student and church leader exchanges, and the like.

As indicated, our first assignments took us to Belgium, headquartered in Brussels. Belgium had suffered under Nazi German occupation along with limited wartime damage, except for the eastern part of the country, which had been shattered during the von Rundstedt westward offensive near the war's end.

Initially in Belgium we were a team of three workers. Cleo Mann, a middle-aged minister, had been sent earlier. Considerable time and energy were consumed in red-tape procedures as we began. Antwerp served as port of entry for the support of the American forces during the immediate postwar period. This sped the recovery of the Belgian economy. Working through church and social service agencies, we served small pockets of postwar needs, mostly refugees and other forms of poverty. We distributed food and clothing shipped from the United States by MCC to Antwerp.

Planning began later for a team of MCC volunteers to help rebuild a village in the heavily destroyed region to the east. Eventually a town named Bullange, east of Malmedy, was chosen. Additional personnel joined our staff, and eventually part of the Belgian team was transferred to a project begun in Poland. Ellen became matron at the Brussels center. During our final six months in Belgium (1947), I was assigned to work with Maurice LeClercq, a lay staff assistant at the Belgian Protestant chaplaincy.

The Belgian Ministry of Justice asked MCC to take food and clothing packages to families of men, called *inciviques* in French, imprisoned for having collaborated with the German occupation of the country during the war. Public assistance for families of imprisoned collaborators with occupying armies from abroad naturally was not part of the regular public welfare system! Mr. LeClercq had been imprisoned himself in that manner for a year. During that time he was converted and soon became a chaplain's assistant.

Meanwhile, the development of the Belgian relief project was affected quite early by the interest of a Mennonite mission agency that eventually replaced the MCC presence in Belgium. I had misgivings about the church politics of linking these two endeavors, each with its own rationale and objective. At the same time, two other perspectives began to converge on my horizon: my continuing interests in sociological study and in the publication project of sixteenth-century court records of government prosecution and persecution of Anabaptists in the early years of that movement.

A few months after my arrival in Europe in early 1946, I had chauffeured Harold S. Bender, dean of Goshen College, from our Brussels base to Zurich, Switzerland, to meet Fritz Blanke, a church historian at the University of Zurich. Bender served also as assistant executive secretary of Mennonite Central Committee. Both he and Professor Blanke were leading figures in the effort to publish systematically for the first time the Anabaptist side of the sixteenth-century story. Until then, most historians had drawn on the polemical writings, both religious and political, which sought to stigmatize and suppress that movement.

After Bender completed his business with Professor Blanke, I told Blanke of my interest in a sociological investigation of Anabaptist origins as a doctoral dissertation. He opened a drawer in his desk and showed me a sheet of paper on which he had noted exactly that idea as a possible dissertation topic for a student. By the time our visit ended, we agreed on my taking that assignment, though not anticipating that five years would pass before I got to it. That expectation influenced me from then on, including part-time graduate study terms in Frankfurt and Basel.

MEANWHILE GERMANY

In early fall 1947, eight months after Ellen arrived in Brussels, MCC transferred us to an assignment in the French occupation zone of southwest Germany. The MCC headquarter for that zone was located in Neustadt/Haardt, from which several small teams fanned out into surrounding localities. This region has been known historically as *die Pfalz*, the Palatinate. A team already had been at work there for some months, and the peak of the emergency food and clothing distributions there lay just ahead. Within a year, however, would come the merger of the three western zones in the postwar occupation—the British, the American, and the French—to form the Federal Republic of Germany. Related to this was money reform, followed by the Marshall Plan and the remarkably rapid economic recovery of Western Europe.

Meanwhile, from Neustadt, Ellen and I were assigned to Pirmasens, then a city of 37,000 near the German/French border. Pirmasens had been, and remains today, the shoe-manufacturing metropolis of Germany. That industry had begun in earlier times, when German frontier guards began to make shoes to while away their idle time while guarding the frontier! During World War II the central city was heavily bombed.

The winter of 1947-1948 turned out to be the most dramatic part of our European stay. Deprivation from the war remained widespread. German currency, the mark, at the time had little worth. City folk were bartering away their valuables in scrounging for food from the countryside. We saw people hauling scraps of fallen branches in hand wagons from wooded areas outside the city for heating fuel.

Our major task during winter 1947-1948 was a twice-weekly feeding of all the city's school children, soup and rolls made from flour and meat from American farms shipped in by MCC. There were additional programs for specific groups, such as bread distributions for the elderly, more specialized packages for famished prisoners of war returning from the Russian front or for mothers of newborn infants.

These programs were implemented collaboratively by the three welfare agencies in the city—Protestant, Catholic, and Socialist—under one or the other of which the entire population of the city was registered. At our request an administrative committee was formed in the city of Pirmasens, with representatives from the above agencies, chaired by an older respected couple with whom we became lifelong friends. In addition large clothing distributions were overseen by Ellen, while I organized a mass student feeding program at the new University of Mainz, a hundred kilometers to the north. Obviously, work of this nature and at such a scale was unprecedented in our youthful experience and education, and it was at once humbling and enriching.

On November 11, 1947, we had the first twice-weekly bread distribution. The above three agencies had identified 2,000 needy adults to be served. Five distribution centers, regionally located in the city were designated, mostly in school buildings. Loaves were Italian-style, oblong but with rounded ends and sides. Ellen's five-year diary has the following entry for that first day:

> I stayed in one school, Paul another. . . . Many people came at 1:00 (o'clock) when it was to start at 3:00! Waited long in a drizzle—poor things—acted like animals, pushing each other. Some people went to wrong place and there wasn't enough at my school. Some were very hungry, and as soon as receiving their loaf, got out the crowd, started to break the loaf and eat.

A week later, after the third distribution, Ellen wrote:

> City truck came to distribution centers late. Awful mess at Mittelbachschule—people crowded so badly. Paul finally (standing up in the window) told them they had to line up or we would close till morning. They lined up—in 20 or 30 minutes everyone was served.

Given the crippled nature of the economy in the three western zones, a number of foreign-service agencies like MCC were active. CRALOG (Council of Relief Agencies Licensed for Operation in Germany) coordinated the distribution of these agencies geographically and provided consulting services. Conditions varied from zone to zone, in part due to variations in the occupying regimes. Of the three, the French zone was poorest, France for a time having been Nazi-occupied. Initially, given the devastation of the German infrastructure, these relief agencies were made dependent on the logistics of the occupying forces. Thus, for example, in Pirmasens, during the work week Ellen and I stayed in the hotel occupied by French military officers. When an American military plane accidentally crashed in the nearby mountains, suddenly the hotel lobby was filled with a motley crowd of French and American officers.

THE GRIP OF THE RURAL LIFE PARADIGM

After Ellen and I had settled into the food and clothing distributions in progress there, I asked locally to be directed to a farm that had been held for some generations by a German Mennonite family living in that region. I was soon introduced to the Kaegi family and spent a weekend with them. On the basis of that visit I wrote an article entitled, "A Way of Life That Has Stood the Test." What was the test? The Kaegis family, then in its eighth generation, had made it through 265 often difficult years with this farm. "To them," I wrote, "farming is not a money-making scheme; it is a way of life that has stood the test."

Mailed back to the United States, the article was published in the March 1949 issue of *Mennonite Community* magazine. I noted that peaceful German highways wound through comparatively undisturbed country areas into pulverized cities. In these rural areas society continued to function more coherently, if not entirely normally, I pointed out, while in cities virtually every function of society had disintegrated or deteriorated. I admitted that the ills of the age could not be solved by moving everyone onto farms, even if it were possible. Yet I noted that certain basic communal and spiritual values were preserved through these terrible years in the natural environment of rural life, while these had long since disappeared in the now-ruined artificial world of man's own technological creation.

Initially my European sojourn seemed to confirm my rural life bias. Yet in retrospect clues in my experience already pointed to the upending of so limited an ideal. Cities, however vulnerable or perverted in practice, are essential in the unfolding of the human potential. Cities have been defined as an invention to overcome the friction of space. Only in proximate dwelling do specialization and exchange become possible in human development. And only in that process can kinship and place be transcended, thereby yielding greater human complexity and development.

I was brought up in the belief that Christian reality and loyalty effectively stood above all other relationships. Ironically, however, the Anabaptist tradition, ostensibly shaped by that claim, across generations and several centuries became heavily compounded with ethnic, and in this instance, rural cultural energies. That inconsistency would trouble me increasingly.

Another Unexpected Turn in the Road

By April 1948, my two-year term had been more than completed. I enrolled at the University of Basel, Switzerland, assuming that later I would transfer to Zurich. Among the professors whose lectures I attended were Karl Jaspers, the philosopher who had just moved there from Hamburg; Karl Barth, the theologian; and Oscar Cullmann, the church historian and New Testament scholar. I would later hear Cullmann again in Paris. During the semester in Basel I resided at the MCC European headquarters located there and continued to help MCC informally. Ellen meanwhile continued her two-year term of service in the MCC team at Neustadt. Once again we lived apart, but this time for little more than three months!

By that summer of 1948, fundamental changes were underway in West Germany. The new West German state, the Federal Republic of Germany, was being created, embracing the three Western military zones. This political change brought also money reform, the creation of a new German mark, currency that immediately became stable internationally.

My temporary university sojourn in Switzerland, the European country not directly touched by the war, along with reflection on my experiences in Belgium and Germany, inspired me anew. One day in the Basel MCC office I sensed a direct call—with Germany now starting to rebuild, this was not the time for Ellen and me to leave Europe. I reported this conviction to MCC administrators, and a plan began to take shape accordingly. After a brief, late summer furlough back home, Ellen and I would return to Germany for a new five-year term with MCC. The focus would be on activities related to cultural and spiritual renewal, with Frankfurt on-the-Main, in the former American zone, as the base. Meanwhile that five-year term would also allow me to complete my doctoral studies.

The assignment entailed a variety of ecumenical activities, student exchanges, and international voluntary work camps. These camps, while often including Americans, brought together European youth from countries that had been at war. Other MCC programs continued meanwhile, adapting to the changes under way. By the fall of 1949, I already had enrolled part-time for a semester at the University of Frankfurt, where an important school of sociological theory was taking shape. It quickly became clear, however, that part-time study under these circumstances was not feasible. My heart was in the challenges of renovation in Germany and Europe more widely, and these tasks demanded all my energy.

By the time another year had passed, a deeper problem had arisen. Both the program opportunities and the challenges that were emerging lay beyond my training and experience. For example, I was invited to address a conference of Protestant clergy, held at a new evangelical academy in the Ruhr area in Germany, on the early church and war. I soon discovered that these well-educated Lutheran ministers knew their early church history better than I did! It didn't take many such experiences for me to get the message—finishing my education was more important than trying to operate beyond my reach. After three years in Frankfurt, by the fall of 1951, with MCC agreement, Ellen and I terminated our service there. We moved to Zurich for me to enter the doctoral program at the university program as foreseen five years earlier.

An Ambiguous Augmentation

Orie O. Miller, the MCC executive, warmly supported and followed this new venture in Frankfurt, though not uncritically. Much of my work connected me to Mennonite, and less directly, to other Protestant churches. This included various speaking opportunities. Nearly a year into this new project Miller came with a proposal that I should be ordained to the ministry. Until then I had held firmly to the four-centuries-old Anabaptist view of the lay ministry as emerging in the life of the congregation. I had already experienced the incongruity between that conception and my wartime deferral from conscription, effectively as a trainee for the Christian ministry. Though I felt neither called nor opposed to the lay ministry, precisely as lay ministry, it was not something that I had had occasion to rule out for myself.

When Miller came with this proposal, I had not yet been exposed directly to the sixteenth-century story, an exposure that would begin two years later. Not only was the proposed ordination not congregationally rooted, but it was more professional than lay. Despite all this, we reached agreement in July 1949 to proceed with ordination. Scheduling problems delayed implementation until February 19, 1950. I was a member of a congregation back home in Virginia. The appropriate conference leader there requested that Amos Horst, a Mennonite bishop from Pennsylvania, officiate at my ordination on behalf of Virginia Mennonite Conference. Horst, returning from a church visit to Africa, was stopping over in Europe to visit MCC projects.

The ordination was built into a regular Sunday worship service at Thomashof, a German Mennonite church and conference center on the outskirts of the city of Karlsruhe, in southwest Germany. A large congregation gathered for the occasion, including a number of MCC colleagues from several areas. The ordination was preceded with a sermon by Christian Schneble, the German leader of the congregation and conference center. Amos Horst then led the ceremony, along with a visiting Mennonite minister from the General Conference Mennonite Church in the United States. As we knelt in prayer, they laid hands on both Ellen and me. Given the nature of the MCC venture emerging at the Frankfurt center, this ordination indeed was appropriate. But eventually, as we shall see, this entailed problems.

The "Grandeur and Misery" of Christendom

The unmasking of my rural dream was but part of a larger reorientation now emerging. The sectarian legacy that had stamped my character was sharply dualistic. At one level, World War II and the ruins it left ratified the principled renunciation of war rooted in that legacy. At a more general level, however, I was becoming increasingly aware of the depth and complexity of the Christian presence in the development of European civilization. The impact of Christianity on European culture is at once undeniable and amazing. Nonetheless, a direct embrace of Europe as "Christendom" is as indefensible as was its total rejection by our Mennonite dualism.

Scholars occasionally call attention to "the grandeur and misery" of the human condition. That contrast was vivid in postwar Europe, especially in Europe perceived as Christendom. That Christianity had impacted Europe as light, leaven, and salt over the centuries was undeniable. In his *Violence Unveiled: Humanity at the Crossroads* (Crossroad Publishing Co., 1995), contemporary American Catholic scholar named Gil Baillie has well written,

> In truth, however, what the (European) Enlightenment did was to secularize a wariness about religion that has its roots in the Old Testament prophets, the Gospels, and the letters of Paul. For

both the secularizing and rationalizing impulses it espoused were products of the Judeo-Christian tradition that the Enlightenment came into existence by underestimating and repudiating. (p. 12)

Yet despite the impact of biblical faith, the two world wars of the twentieth century originated among nations that together constituted Christendom. What Jesus initiated clearly was incompatible with nations at war, notwithstanding Constantine's militant banner of the cross. Something surely had gone amiss.

Already the sixteenth-century Protestant Reformation responded to that incongruity. It began on the premise that reform was both needed and could be achieved. Precisely because the roots of the problem were beyond reform, that reform effort and its target, Rome, the head of Christendom, responded by mutual excommunication between the papacy and the Reformers. The alternative that loomed, as the leading Reformers Luther and Zwingli quickly surmised, was to reconstitute churches as gatherings of believers independent of political rule.

But by then social and political unrest in northern Europe was spreading rapidly. With chaos threatening, the Reformation churches, now separated from Rome, quickly sought and were readily accorded regional political sponsorship. Thereby the believers church pregnancy was aborted.

Here and there, however, a few small gatherings implemented the radical believers church option. Though previously baptized as infants, they now were baptized on their adult confession of faith as commitment to follow Christ in life. Such "rebaptism" (Anabaptism) was seen by the political-religious establishments as illegal and sacrilegious, a violation of the sacrament already bestowed upon them as infants. Despite the sharp differences between Catholic and newly formed Protestant regimes otherwise, both regarded such independent action as a fundamental threat to the human order. Accordingly from the very outset, both Catholics and Protestants vigorously suppressed the Anabaptist movement.

Experiencing the grandeur and misery of European Christendom in life and work during those years (1946-1951) served as an invaluable apprenticeship for the dissertation I was privileged to undertake. I had become reasonably fluent in German and French, had taken Greek in college, and finally passed a minimal course in Latin at Zurich. In addition, once on vacation with two colleagues, one American the other German, I had traveled south through the Balkans and

58   A USABLE PAST?

east through Greece to Turkey (more in chapter 8). In Turkey, we moved as far south as the ruins of Ephesus and Smyrna (present-day Izmir). Thus I passed through much of territory of early New Testament history (see chapter 16). This also was my first exposure to Eastern Orthodoxy, with which the Western (Roman) church had broken in the eleventh century (1064). Decades later (see chapter 16), my contacts in those Eastern traditions would become more extensive and direct.

My Graduate School Odyssey

This practical exposure to the grandeur and misery of Christendom became an indispensable backdrop for the task that descended on me in Zurich, 1951-1953. I had had three semesters of graduate study, each at a different university (Pennsylvania, Basel, and Frankfurt). In the fall of 1952, Rene Koenig, my sociology professor at Zurich, sent me to the Sorbonne in Paris for a trimester to observe the sociological study of French Catholics, led there by Gabriel LeBras. Already well before 1950, and ever since, the events of the 1520s in Western Europe posed the question, Was the Anabaptist movement originally simply part of the general economic, social, and political upheaval for which that era is known? Or was it intrinsically religious, a primordial response to the Christian message?

Identifying the social status of the participants in that movement, it seemed, would shed important light on that question. The names and identity of a few early leaders were long since known. But how might the participants in that early movement be identified more broadly?

Until the twentieth century, church historians generally relied on critical accounts of the Anabaptist movement left by the established regimes of the sixteenth century and thereafter, both Catholic and Protestant. Given the advancing diversification in modern culture, by the late nineteenth and early twentieth centuries, the climate in this regard was beginning to change. Hence, by mid-century systematic efforts were underway to publish hitherto unpublished records, mostly legal, from the sixteenth-century beginnings of what became known variously as the Radical Reformation, or the free or believers church expressions.

My dissertation, written and published in German, was merely a small part of that effort. The sources were the records in government archives in Switzerland of arrests and prosecution of Anabaptists in that country, 1525-1540. I worked primarily with those records, mostly in older versions of German, only occasionally in Latin. They had been hand-copied, then typed in preparation for publication. Thus I had access to them in typescript. Occasionally I had to return to the original sixteenth-century handwritten archival documents. Combing these records, I ultimately compiled a list of some 800 arrested persons, sometimes unnamed, most minimally identifiable as to occupation and time and place of their appearance. Only several dozen of these, as it turned out, had been falsely charged.

On the one hand, that sixteenth-century movement inevitably was a child of its time. The Renaissance, the proliferation of the printing press, pamphleteering, translation of the Bible into the vernacular, the ferment of the Protestant Reformation generally, early beginnings of the nation-state, unrest among the peasants, and so on, set the stage. Spreading literacy and Bible-reading circles were particularly fertile soil for human renewal at the time. What came into sharp focus in this movement, however, was the personal encounter with, and response to, the biblical gospel in contrast to the moral hollowness of a sacramental and politically imposed religious regimen.

Initially, however important economic, social, and political conditioners may have been, Anabaptism was unmistakably a religious movement. Anabaptist leaders came from the educated circles in urban centers, both religious (priests and monks) and secular (university scholars), and literate craftsmen. Apprentices in the crafts often moved between cities and some became carriers of the vision. With persecution and exile, Swiss adherents to the movement sought refuge in villages and later in the mountains. Within a generation, participation in the urban intellectual ferment was greatly weakened and Anabaptists were exiled or hidden away in mountain recesses. In the north, principally in the Netherlands, degrees of toleration came earlier. Additional respite was found in pioneering settlements to the east, and still later in czarist Russia.

Lessons of Postwar Europe

As indicated in the opening chapter, World War II (1941-1945) and its aftermath had enormous consequences for the generation in the American population then moving into adulthood. Universal military conscription affected everyone. The life of those killed or permanently injured in action was totally altered. Most others found their futures modified in one way or another by their military interlude.

Similarly those deferred from service, whether for reasons of health, occupation, or conscience, found their career paths modified or changed. Conscientious objectors, assigned to alternative public service, though not facing the dangers of front-line action, at times found themselves in work not entirely risk-free.

COs faced their own peculiar difficulties. While persons sent off to war as soldiers were applauded as heroes, conscientious objectors at times were derided as yellow bellies, as duty-shirking cowards. Some who completed terms in alternative service during the war volunteered afterward to serve in relief and reconstruction work in war-torn areas under agencies like the Mennonite Central Committee. Their need to express the deeper motive for the refusal of war doubtless contributed to postwar efforts to bind up the wounds of war. Strong rural Mennonite communities in the United States and Canada at mid-century provided the resource base for the material aid program undertaken by MCC after the war in Europe and elsewhere. Numerous volunteers, mostly young adults, were sent to administer distributions of food and clothing and eventually to participate in reconstruction efforts.

Amsterdam, 1952, a Pivotal Meeting

The decade of the 1940s, the war and its aftermath, was a time of testing and sifting both at home and abroad. In April 1952, seven young Mennonite men, on various assignments in Europe, all graduate students, met for ten days at the Mennonite Central Committee center in Amsterdam, Holland. I was privileged to be one of them. We met to sort out our varied experiences in the course of the preceding decade. We chose Amsterdam as the meeting place partly to learn more about Dutch Mennonite history, important in the sixteenth-century origins of our faith tradition.

Postwar Europe had confronted us with great opportunities and challenges, but what it all meant for us was hardly self-evident. These experiences had profound consequences not only for us but also for the communities back home which had sent us there. During the first week we enjoyed lectures from scholars on Dutch Mennonite history. On the weekend we traveled north to Friesland to visit the site where Menno Simons (from whom Mennonites take their name) had begun his career as a Catholic parish priest and was later converted to this new movement. During the second week, we discussed matters among ourselves, along with evening guest speakers. We did not agree on what all this meant and simply decided to continue our conversations.

The following year we met again, in Zurich this time, for only a few days. Professor Emil Brunner was our guest speaker for one session. I had attended two of his lecture courses at the university there more than a year earlier. He challenged us with perspectives of the theological renewal which he, along with Karl Barth and others, was nurturing. The English translation of his radical new essay on the *ekklesia* (church), entitled *The Misunderstanding of the Church*, appeared two months later. Starting a new church or denomination was clearly not an option or even a desire for our group. Instead wider conversations in all our communities were needed if we were more effectively to meet the challenges of our era.

By the end of our second meeting we decided to publish "occasional papers" to stimulate discussions throughout Mennonite communities. We agreed to do this by way of an occasional journal titled *Concern*. The first of these was printed in 1954. Seventeen more followed, with the last in the series appearing in 1971. Obviously we could not foresee the consequences of these efforts (see more next chapter). As it turned out, a thread of emphasis on congregational renewal running through the series inspired younger generations. Some historians conclude, however, that the Concern project detracted from church leadership authority in the Mennonite church over the next generation.

REAL WORLD INTRODUCTION 101

Circumstances change with the flow of time, both gradually and abruptly, always at varying rates. Gradual and abrupt processes commingle, tipping variously toward one or the other pole. The foregoing eight-year story, 1945-1953, had life-changing consequences for me, flowing into the decades that followed. Ellen and I were poorly prepared for the challenges that confronted us, admittedly less drastic than those of our generational peers who died in battle by scores of thousands during the preceding War years. Ironically, the inner resources on which we basically drew were shaped by an ethos whose outer trappings accentuated our lack of preparation.

I, even more than Ellen, had been shaped by a separatist Anabaptist subculture. Without full participation in American society, how could I manage the cross-cultural engagement into which I was so abruptly plunged? I am still embarrassed by my article on the Swiss

German family farm (noted above). Even after more than two years in postwar Europe, I still equated the Anabaptist vision with the rural way of life. I remained oblivious to the inconsistency of that notion with the gospel, with the Anabaptist vision itself, and even with human history in general. The irony of the situation lay in the fact that my rural Anabaptist matrix had formed the character that sustained me in these times of testing.

Another major discovery of those earlier years, as I have noted earlier in this chapter, was what I came to call the "grandeur and misery" of Christendom, a phrase coined in another context by Georges Clemenceau (1841-1929), briefly the French premier after World War I. My Mennonite upbringing tended toward a mere dichotomy—our believers church legacy versus the rest of Christendom, which we viewed as scarcely distinguishable from "the world" otherwise. This outlook was reinforced by the sectarian onus that until then Christendom had perpetuated against us.

Living, working, and studying amid the ruins of World War II in Europe for the better part of the first postwar decade confirmed my legacy of nonviolence. But it confronted me inescapably as well with many ways in which Christianity had penetrated European culture during the millennium of Christendom (fifth to fifteenth century CE). Wrestling variously with the grandeur and misery of the anomaly that is now Christendom became part of my life agenda.

Chapter 4

Reentering the Mennonite Enclave

*We shall not cease from exploration
And the end of all our exploring
Will be to arrive at where we started
And know the place for the first time.*
—T. S. Eliot

My wife Ellen and I with our two daughters, ages four months and three years, left Zurich on July 23, 1953, to return to America. We traveled via Frankfurt to Paris for a final visit to our former MCC home. From there we would proceed to the port city of Le Havre for our ship to New York. By advance arrangement, we remained in Paris an extra day. On the evening of July 27 and the morning of July 28, I met with other representative of the historic peace churches (HPC). Together we put the finishing touches on a statement that was to be submitted to the World Council of Churches (WCC).

We met in the hotel room of M. R. Zigler, the director of the Brethren Service Commission, then based in Geneva, who had negotiated with the WCC in the first place. Zigler was an organizer, not a scholar. The four-statement pamphlet originally submitted—but rejected by the WCC—had been entitled, "War Is Contrary to the Will of God." The writers borrowed that title from the Council's own declaration in its founding document five years earlier.

As we labored editorially over our document around the small table, we eventually reached agreement on the text. But now what should we name it, since we couldn't use the previous title? Zigler, lying atop his bed with his shoes off, suddenly sat up, announcing, "I've got it: 'Peace Is the Will of God'!" We quickly agreed. In due time, the document was submitted to the WCC, triggering fruitful discussions that continued for a decade. The next day my family and I sailed for New York from Le Havre on the SS *Queen Elizabeth*.

As my original departure to Europe had been unexpected and pivotal, so too was this episode at the end of my stay. It soon became a benchmark of an era now ended for me, as well as the beginning of an uncertain and more sweeping new one. Supposedly I was returning now to a lifetime career at my alma mater at Harrisonburg, Virginia, that by then had become Eastern Mennonite College (EMC). The two dock hands in the New York harbor who helped us as we disembarked put that location into perspective for me. Seeing the address on our baggage, one asked the other where this was. He replied, "Oh, it's a wide place in the road down south somewhere."

Getting Started

For me, the return to Harrisonburg was at once purposeful and definitive. The mutual commitment between us and the college was firm enough that they had provided the loans I needed to complete my graduate work. Teaching sociology and Anabaptist-related studies at EMC now were to become my long-term career.

My firsthand experience in war-torn Christendom for nearly a decade, culminating in my encounter with raw data from the sixteenth-century Radical Reformation in my doctoral study at the University of Zurich, would energize my teaching and further research. Harold S. Bender's "recovery of the Anabaptist vision" was the informing paradigm as I now embarked on my long-anticipated career. I was deeply indebted to him, indeed to a people of faith, to an historical tradition, to a process whose trends I had been called to absorb and to critique.

My family and I had most of the month of August to get settled and to prepare for the fall semester beginning in early September 1953. MCC had fully supported us during our five years of service, but there was no salary or income otherwise. My graduate study had been financed by borrowed money. Thus we arrived home penniless, a young couple with two small daughters. Settling into an apartment with minimal furnishings put us at the mercy of help from family and friends.

Meanwhile EMC itself was a struggling young institution, as reflected in low faculty salaries combined with heavy teaching loads. Equally demanding was my academic preparation to meet classes at the beginning of the new semester. Although my years of work and study in Europe provided rich resources on which to draw, a great deal of repackaging was needed to connect to standard American undergraduate college courses! All in all, a full plate indeed, but it held excitement and promise.

Over the next few years I introduced a variety of undergraduate sociology courses: principles of sociology, modern social theory, marriage and the family, social change, and sociology of religion. Other faculty came on board, and sociology soon became one of many undergraduate majors offered at EMC. Meanwhile I also worked on sociological perspectives in Anabaptist-Mennonite history and life and taught some church history courses. These activities occasionally included field work with student involvement. A Mennonite historical and archival collection in the EMC library had already been begun, an effort in which I became involved marginally. That effort was developed much more extensively by others in succeeding years, notably Irvin B. Horst.

EMC IN IMMEDIATE CONTEXT

When we returned to Harrisonburg in 1953, EMC was a different institution than the Bible college (EMS) from which I had graduated eight years earlier, as were the students. The school had become a liberal arts undergraduate college, receiving state certification in November 1948, five years before my return. This shift from high school and Bible college to a full-blown liberal arts institution was an ambiguous endeavor. On the one hand it sought to defend and enhance the spiritual life of its founding constituency—Mennonite churches in Virginia and the eastern United States. On the other hand were the urges to break through cultural boundaries that still surrounded the school and its sponsoring constituency. An inner ferment within the institution and among its supporters was bubbling.

At that stage, EMC was a church college in a full sense of the term. It was not merely formally church-sponsored. There were numerous contacts with the congregations of the sponsoring denomination as well. Most of the students were members of these churches, and members of the faculty traveled variously to the supporting communities. My service in the relief and reconstruction program of MCC in Europe, and my training and teaching in church and society matters, quickly drew me into church-related conferences, committees, and writing assignments for denominational periodicals. These additional activities, though enriching in many respects, also took their toll in terms of overextension in time and energy.

My appointment as a lay minister for MCC work in Europe left me without a congregational base for such ministry when I returned. I had been ordained for MCC's purposes directly under the auspices of Virginia Mennonite Conference, which sponsored and oversaw mission outposts in the mountains to the west of the Shenandoah Valley. A conference office maintained a calendar of services to which ministers were assigned as they became available. During the first two and a half years after our return in 1953 I served mostly on that calendar. During the last fifteen months before departure to Japan, I was assigned to pastor a small mission congregation in a poor section of Harrisonburg, several miles from EMC.

As already noted, the postwar period into the 1950s was a time of ferment in Mennonite churches and their communities. The two world wars of the first half of the century, along with the Great Depression between them, intensified the changes already underway in the course of population and industrial growth. Corresponding institutional developments were in flux as well, along with denominational activity and authority among the churches. Numerous conferences were held, at times in local congregations, but also on regional or national levels. Topics dealt with social, economic, and political issues, as well as questions pertaining to church life and practice. I participated in many such events and was appointed to two denominational organizations. One was the Peace Problems Committee for which I served as secretary. The other was the Committee on Economic and Social Relations of which I was a member.

Scanning my paper trails of this brief period, 1953-1957, I'm impressed with the creative vibrancy of that time in our churches and their institutions. The outbreak of war, the war itself, and the immediate postwar era brought with them a swirling and commingling of disruption and renewal. On the one hand, a sturdy majority of Mennonite young men declined military service, in keeping with the tradition that had shaped them. But the experiences of that majority, whether in Civilian Public Service or subsequently in relief and reconstruction abroad, brought new perspectives and energies into the churches. Cross-fertilization with "the recovery of the Anabaptist vision" (the systematic publication of sixteenth-century court records and other documents in Europe during the middle decades of the twentieth century) further stimulated and enhanced these impulses.

Paradoxically, this ferment reduced the distance between Mennonites and the surrounding society and the sense of mission to or in that society. As my own paper trail indicates, I was partly at odds with these developments. With my exposure to European Christendom and then to the agonies of the sixteenth-century Reformation, my attention was focused on the need to reinvigorate the ekklesia (church) at its elementary level (Matt. 18:20; Luke 17:20-21). This eventually resulted in a paper, "Anabaptism and Church Organization," published in the *Mennonite Quarterly Review* (July 1956). In effect, by this fifteen-page, footnoted sketch, I pled for a reengagement with the primary, small-scale congregationalism that was the "essence" of Anabaptism. This publication, at a time when with our "churches" we were headed in an opposite direction, stirred up some discomfort in our circles, possibly due to some extent to imprudence on my part.

The fourth century CE saw the beginning of the political incorporation of Christianity into empire. That politicization led eventually to its sacralizing as well. The "church" became a politically authorized, sacramentally-endowed, and sacrament-dispensing institution that aided the unifying of political rule. Meanwhile those individuals in the populace "wishing to become Christian in earnest" (Luther's later formulation) were shunted aside in monasteries, likewise though differently subject to political rule. All this became a "top-down" hegemony, vulnerable to a variety of corruptions.

By the early sixteenth century, historical changes, especially the invention of the printing press and thereupon the beginning of translations of the biblical texts into the vernaculars, "bottom-up" ferment began. Martin Luther, the above-mentioned premier reformer in central Germany in that era, toyed with the possibility of forming a bottom-up new beginning, effectively a believers church. Quickly concluding that the time was not yet ripe for a radical new beginning, he sought instead reform within the existing system.

When those reforms became politically disruptive in various regions, Luther and reformers elsewhere quickly found support against the Roman imperial system among regional political rulers. Modern nation-states were aborning. That compromise effectively set the stage for the birth of the Radical Reformation, the believers church ecclesiology. Both fundamentally and pragmatically, theirs was a bottom up enterprise. Even in the United States, until late in the nineteenth century, among the Swiss-descended Anabaptists congregations remained autonomous. Meanwhile district conferences and the

Mennonite General Conference denominational stream were emerging in the U.S., along with other institutions and colleges.

This new institutional development included the Mennonite Central Committee, under whom I served in Europe during the early postwar years, and in the mid-1950s, Eastern Mennonite College, at which I was serving as professor when I wrote the *Mennonite Quarterly Review* article. In that article was I "biting the hand that served me"? Or, by my espousal of small group congregational autonomy, was I a "spiritualist," as reportedly was rumored?

MCC IN WIDER CONTEXT

While EMC was energized by its primary constituency, the wider educational and societal context contributed increasingly to the ferment. The story of higher education in the United States is one of the most fascinating chapters in the history of Christianity and society. New England Puritans established higher education as schools of training for the Christian ministry. These schools later evolved into liberal arts colleges, then theological seminaries, and finally graduate universities. Private church-inspired colleges, beginning with Harvard in 1636, led the way.

From this process, full-fledged secular graduate education emerged only late in the nineteenth century. Until then, German universities set the academic pace in the Western world. Only in 1900 did the Association of American Universities emerge—fourteen private institutions such as Harvard, Johns Hopkins, Stanford, and Yale. The only church-sponsored university remaining was Catholic University of America, under direct pontifical control until Vatican II in the mid-1960s. State colleges began in the nineteenth century, then quickly followed their private counterparts as graduate institutions in the course of the twentieth century.

A growing body of historical research tells the remarkable story of the original religious inspiration of higher education in the United States beginning in the seventeenth century, then followed by rapid secularization in the nineteenth and early twentieth centuries. Throughout most of the nineteenth century, Protestant clergy and lay leaders remained prominent in higher education institutions. (Interested readers may turn to George M. Marsden, *The Soul of the American University: From Protestant Establishment to Established Unbelief*, Oxford University Press, 1994.) Secularization of the American academe blossomed in the last four decades of the century just past.

Higher education establishments among European Anabaptist immigrants to the United States came late, though their first settlement began at Germantown (now part of Philadelphia), Pennsylvania, in 1683. Until mid-twentieth century, Mennonite church polity was congregational. Leaders emerged in the processes of congregational life and continued their secular occupations. Typically that meant farming. Initiatives in elementary education were widespread from the beginning, though standardized private church schools came much later.

By the early twentieth century, broader organizational activities began to emerge in Mennonite churches and communities. The first Mennonite college—Bethel College in Newton, Kansas—was founded in 1893 by Dutch-German Mennonite colonists from Russia who immigrated to the United States after 1870. The second Mennonite college was founded at Elkhart, Indiana, in 1894. Now known as Goshen College, it was named for the town to which it moved soon after. This college emerged from a slightly liberal wing of the older (eighteenth-century) Swiss, German, and Alsatian Mennonite immigrants. In part as a conservative reaction to the Goshen venture, Eastern Mennonite School was established in 1917 in the east under heavy influence by millennialist evangelicals in American Protestantism.

In important respects the founding of these Mennonite colleges can be seen as replays of the Protestant story just sketched. By the second quarter of the twentieth century, professionalization of the ministry among Mennonites was emerging. This change was both reflected and reinforced by the recognition of Bible majors as seminary equivalent by Selective Service conscription in World War II.

As long as the lay ministry prevailed among Mennonites and churches were predominantly rural, the urge toward higher education was minimal. The need for higher education and the professionalizing of the ministry unfolded reciprocally, much as had the beginning of higher education among Protestants already two centuries earlier.

The Wider World

Given the "quarry from which I was dug" (chapter 2), when I began teaching at EMC in 1953 I had had a far wider exposure to European society than to my native American context. During the nearly eight-year absence, I missed the early postwar assimilations underway at home. Returning now to an academic setting rather than to farm life, my sectarian legacy persisted. This had both positive and negative aspects.

I now joined several professional societies in sociology and church history and began to attend professional meetings. I participated enthusiastically in activities related to nonviolence and conflict, peace and war. I recall here the final episode of my years in Europe, helping finalize the statement submitted by the peace churches to the World Council of Churches. My participation in that project triggered an invitation to attend the inaugural conference called by the Church Peace Mission in Detroit, Michigan, in the fall of 1953.

In 1950, three years before my return from Europe, a national conference of peace groups in mainline Protestant churches in the United States, along with participants from the historic peace churches—Church of the Brethren, Friends (Quakers), and Mennonites—had been convened in Detroit. This was the first such occasion after World War II. The purpose was to critically address the accommodation of the churches to that war. That accommodation had been undergirded theologically by Reinhold Niebuhr (1892-1971), professor at Union Theological Seminary in New York. The Detroit conference initiated the Church Peace Mission to address anew the peacemaking impulse at the heart the Christian calling. During the remainder of the decade a number of regional and local events were sponsored to discuss pacifist/nonpacifist issues in the churches.

Soon after the 1953 event, I was named to a six-person interdenominational peace committee, three from the newly formed Church Peace Mission and three from Christian Action, an association of nonpacifist scholars, largely Niebuhrian in orientation. This joint committee was chaired by Christian Action's Edward LeRoy Long Jr., later an Oberlin College professor of Christian ethics, who had been mentored by Niebuhr. Our assignment, as we worked it out, was to invite comments from pacifist and just war scholars on "The Relationship of Agape, the Essential Christian Ethic, to the Social and Political Structure." These comments would serve as material from which a focus for a national scholarly conference could be derived.

But after some eighty replies were received and the committee did some preliminary planning, the cosponsoring Christian Action agency (for other reasons) was disbanded. Hence the project was never completed. Those papers, however, were archived at Union Theological Seminary in New York.

This dialogue with "liberal" Protestants further fueled the malaise that percolated in conservative Mennonite quarters over the contacts coordinated by MCC with liberal or secular circles during and after the war. That reaction is hardly surprising. To spiritual descendants of the sixteenth-century Anabaptists, collaboration with other groups, whether religious or secular, quickly appeared suspect.

My involvement in the joint committee paved the way for my appointment, less than a decade later, as the executive officer of the Church Peace Mission itself for six years (see chapter 5). Despite the discomfort such outreach aroused in some Anabaptist circles, it also reinforced my extracurricular involvement in focused peace efforts in our own denomination.

The other development that impinged on my four-year period at EMC was the civil rights movement that began in the mid-1950s. The well-known triggering event was the arrest of Rosa Parks for refusal to surrender the "for-whites-only" bus seat to a white male passenger in Montgomery, Alabama, on December 1, 1955. As a result, Martin Luther King Jr., newly arrived pastor of the Dexter Avenue Baptist church, together with Ralph Abernathy, organized the Montgomery bus boycott to protest discrimination generally.

King had just finished a doctorate in philosophy at Boston. He had already found inspiration in the life and writings of Mohandas Gandhi, the pioneer of nonviolent direct action on the road to independence of India from British colonial rule. Inspired to some degree by the Gandhi example, King and Abernathy subsequently formed the Southern Christian Leadership Conference. A later development was the formation of the Congress for Racial Equality.

Within a few months, by spring 1956, the Fellowship of Reconciliation (FOR) based in New York, established contact with the new movement. (More on FOR can be found in Paul Dekar's *Creating the Beloved Community: A Journey with the Fellowship of Reconciliation*, Cascadia, 2005.) Glenn Smiley, a prominent staff member of that organization for many years, met with King and his associates on a weekend in Montgomery, Alabama. Shortly before that, Smiley visited Harrisonburg. Apparently, because by then I was secretary of the denominational Mennonite Peace Problems Committee, I met him on that occasion. Since Smiley thought it important to enlist the peace churches in the civil rights movement, he invited me to accompany him to Montgomery. Although in later years I was present in several meetings where King appeared, if my memory is correct this was the only time that I met him personally.

As a newcomer to all this, I surely benefited more than I was able to contribute. The meeting ended midday Sunday, its third day. Unexpectedly a protest march was suddenly announced for that afternoon, and all those present were asked to join. It was expected that there would be arrests.

Such activity was beyond the pale of my conservative moorings. I had never engaged in such action and was frightened at the prospect. What should I do? But then, just as abruptly, the march was canceled. As I recall, the reason for cancellation of the march was never publicized. We were told informally that in the planning process for the march, agreement could not be reached on who should appear up front as its leader, and hence the one to be arrested, Martin Luther King Jr. or his father, King Sr., also a pastor. So the march was canceled for that day!

A year later, in May 1957, J. Harold Sherk, then executive secretary of the Peace Section of MCC, on behalf of his agency led a team of five, including me, on a study tour of civil rights developments in the South. We visited educational, church, and community leaders and institutions in the Carolinas, Georgia, and Alabama, seeking contact and response from both races. The depth and complexity of the problems and upheavals we experienced on that trip left a lasting impression. So did the great diversity of responses and perceptions among both races from region to region.

THE MENNONITE ENCLAVE

We come now directly to the theme of this chapter, the Mennonite enclave. As already noted, the sixteenth-century Anabaptist movement sought to restore church as a community of believers apart from general society. The antecedents for such faith communities stretch all the way back to Abraham, in some ways the focus of the entire biblical story. Abraham's call would give rise to a "great nation" (Gen. 12:2). The response to that call turned out to be a paradoxical enterprise. As a New Testament writer observed many centuries later, "Abraham believed God, and it was reckoned to him as righteousness" (Rom. 4:3). With his household, he left everything behind to roam as a desert wanderer toward an unknown destination.

That destination was to become a "great nation" among other nations on their behalf. But once Abraham's descendants became a nation, a monarchy, it imploded. In exile the identity of the Israelites, as they were then called, was reconstituted as *Diaspora* (dispersion). Eventually in many countries, the Israelites, now known as Jews, were scattered in pagan cities. They were confined forcibly to live in ghettoes, isolated pockets of Jews only. While in some respects this resulted in deprivation, ghettoes also served as hearths of human creativity enriching host societies.

Synagogues replaced temples and animal sacrifice as anchors of identity. Synagogues served as antecedents to what came to be the New Testament churches. Diaspora corresponded to the scattering and spread of early Christianity. And the embrace of Christianity by the Roman emperors, beginning in the fourth century CE, paralleled the era of monarchy in ancient Israel. Something of a replay of all this has occurred in Anabaptist history in various countries. Over generations, some Anabaptist faith communities through shared life and worship became isolated ethnic communities, effectively on the way to nationhood.

This potential unfolded to a remarkable degree with a group who migrated to Russia. Beginning in the latter part of the eighteenth century, a Russian czar invited colonies of Dutch-descended German Mennonites to pioneer the development of potentially rich agricultural lands in the Vistula River delta. There in several generations they became a self-governing settlement directly under the czar, effectively at once a political state as well as a faith community, a miniature Christendom. Eventually, a Reformation-like spiritual renewal movement broke out, leading to a church split, "Mennonite Brethren" vs. the *Kirchliche Mennisten* (churchly Mennonites). A similar dynamic has been underway in Paraguay in South America among Mennonite settlers who emigrated from Soviet Russia.

Once Christianity was politically established, top-down centralized church authority was theologically brokered (based on Matt. 16:13-20; note especially Bishop Augustine, 354-430 CE). After many turbulent centuries of Christendom, with top-down efforts trumping the bottom-up nature of primary individual faith responses (John 3:3; Matt. 18:20), reform broke out (Luther's Wittenberg ninety-five theses, 1517), an effort then quickly aborted. The few efforts to proceed directly on those bottom-up premises were likewise quickly suppressed. Negative stereotyping—heresy, sect, rebaptizer (Anabaptist)—followed. Over the next few decades many hundreds who rallied to the movement in Europe were martyred.

A PIVOTAL ANECDOTE

Near the end of the previous chapter, I briefly described a meeting in Amsterdam in April 1952 of seven young graduate students, then on various temporary assignments from several United States Mennonite agencies. Over the next few years, four of them returned to the States. With their graduate studies mostly completed, they had taken teaching assignments at one of three Mennonite colleges here. As they introduced the Concern dialogue in several settings, malaise began to develop. By June 1957, top leaders from four Mennonite agencies—Goshen College, Eastern Mennonite College, Mennonite Board of Education, and Mennonite Publishing House—convened a one-day meeting in Cumberland, Maryland, with the four returned Concern members, hopefully to calm the waters.

A total of fourteen invited men attended. The meeting was appropriate and cordial. The purpose of the gathering was outlined in the personal invitations as follows:

> To review the current state of the Mennonite Church, to evaluate it in the light of scriptural-Anabaptist ideals and the history of the church in America, and consider ways and means to strengthen the church for her own spiritual life and mission in the world.

A relatively informal agenda was laid out. Introductory presentations were made by several persons from both sides, consisting mostly of personal impressions of current situations. From these presentations, questions emerged that then were discussed in an orderly manner. Detailed notes of the meeting were kept, with copies subsequently mailed to the participants. This was not a formal, policy-making gathering, though the notes that were kept are richly informative.

A key leader in his introductory remarks emphasized that "the general church must take priority over the local church. All the churches have come out of the a priori church." With this and the three final suggestions of the conveners we Concern members resonated:

> (1) Go ahead and have your group but do not allow it to crystallize into a sect or a dividing group.
> (2) Keep on with your writings but keep a charitable attitude toward the existing church order.
> (3) Beware of any hybrid Quaker-Mennonite combinations such as seems to be developing.

With the first suggestion the Concern group was in fundamental agreement from the outset. We did not envision beginning a new church. Nor did we have any interest in a "hybrid combination" with the Quakers. The rub came in the second suggestion. Church order was for us a critical problem.

I accompanied several of the EMC representatives on the two-hour drive to Cumberland. The dynamics on the return drive—the meeting was totally ignored—simply reinforced for me the shock of the meeting, a shock in two directions. First, I came to appreciate and respect anew the commitment and legacy of our elders. Although they were sincere "brothers"—the language of the time—the assumptions intrinsic to their legacy and options differed from the experiences that were ours. Second, for the first time, profound doubts arose in me about the feasibility of my continued involvement at EMC. Arrangements were already well under way for me take a two-year leave of absence with my young family for a temporary assignment with MCC in Japan. Two months later we set sail accordingly.

Meanwhile, pressed with a trip to several meetings in Europe and preparation for the Japan departure, dealing with the Cumberland aftermath was beyond reach. As it turned out, the sojourn in Japan was a welcome breather. I had no inkling how things would turn out. The call to peacemaking, described in next chapter, served transitionally to mark time until my unknown second career would emerge.

Chapter 5

An Awakening to Peacemaking

*Calling themselves "defenseless Christians,"
the separatist Anabaptist pacifist groups contained the embryos
of modern ideas of church and state.*
—Charles Moskos

*In the end there is one thing I am sure of. . . .
No matter a war's outcome the soldier never wins. . . .
After the shooting stops, how does the soldier settle back
into society and modern civilization?*
—Andrew Exum

*I know myself now, and I feel within me
A peace above all earthly dignities,
A still and quiet conscience.*
—Shakespeare (A Cardinal in Henry VIII)

The century just past was war torn on a scale never seen before. Less evident was the beginning of a change in the understandings of peace and war. After five years in war-scarred Europe under Mennonite Central Committee, in the fall of 1951 I enrolled at the University of Zurich, Switzerland. It was there in the mid-1520s that the nonviolent "sectarian" Anabaptist movement had emerged near Baretswil. In the highlands some thirty kilometers east of the city is "Baptist Hollow," a cave where outlawed Anabaptists gathered secretly during the early years. As recently as the 1950s, local middle school civics classes were still being taken there on guided hiking tours to underscore the importance of civic responsibility. Though identified in modern times as a neutral country, at mid-twentieth century Switzerland still maintained a militia-based defense system. All able-bodied male citizens were required to serve as active reservists.

My dissertation topic at Zurich was a sociological study of the origin of Swiss Anabaptism, with my field of study defined as sociology and history. While there, I attended a lecture course in Christian ethics taught by Emil Brunner, a well-known Protestant on the theological faculty. Brunner was a leading figure in the theological movement of "neoorthodoxy," challenging the liberalism and optimism that had preceded World War I. The previous century had climaxed in liberal Western religious thought that human progress was leading ever onward and upward. Advances in science, technology, and history seemed to point in that direction. But World War I and what followed radically suggested otherwise. In response, neoorthodoxy once more took human depravity seriously as well as the transforming energy of the Christian gospel. Repentance, forgiveness, and spiritual rebirth were again seen as central to the biblical story.

Brunner's introductory lectures emphasized the good news of the gospel in contrast to our human strivings and perversions. But on the topics of government and the state, his accent shifted. While we are called to be Christian, a call that entails a radical personal change, we nonetheless must live in the world as it is, the professor argued. Sometimes war is inevitable—hence the just war doctrine that had evolved over the centuries. While affirming that tradition, Brunner noted the pacifist counterclaim that Jesus calls us to nonviolence and thus the repudiation of warfare. But that reading of the gospel he rejected out of hand. For Christians to espouse nonviolence and refuse military service, thus leaving the dirty work of war to others, presumably to non-Christians, to him appeared parasitic.

Brunner's presentation was formally to lecture with no class discussion. The professor stood behind the lectern, reading and speaking authoritatively from his well-prepared text. But at this juncture, Brunner stepped from behind the lectern, leaned toward his audience, hands on hips, and with a derisive accent on his final word, declared: "If there's anything I don't want to be it's a *Schmarotze*"—the rather colorful German word for parasite.

A Parasite?

What was I to make of that Brunner moment? This episode came at an appropriate time and form for my own development. The decade of war and its immediate implications had just passed. I had been shaped by the very pacifist ethos Professor Brunner derided. Fortunately for me, the setting was a lecture course—there would be no discussion. The war amid whose ruins I had lived and worked for more than five years had been a war within Christendom, between ostensibly "Christian" nations. Those experiences reinforced my lifelong settled conviction that war is totally innappropriate for Christians. But as yet, I was hardly prepared for a learned debate on the matter.

Brunner's declaration can be understood only against the backdrop of the story of Christendom in which the Swiss culture was embedded. In dealing with the military question, Brunner simply echoed the millennium-long tradition of Christendom that had emerged from the adoption of Christianity as the Roman imperial "religion" in the fourth century CE. But the Constantinian adoption of Christianity had resulted in a major mutation of biblical faith. The conjoining of sacramental and political establishments in Europe had replaced personal transformation and decision as the defining basis of Christian identity. To me this ran counter to the clear teachings of the New Testament. Nonetheless, Brunner's challenge is to be taken seriously and has engaged me ever since

My Dissertation

Soon after this episode I began direct work on my dissertation, a sociological study of the origin of Swiss Anabaptists during the second quarter of the sixteenth century. My primary data were the court records of those prosecuted in Switzerland between 1525 and 1540 for joining this illegal subversive "sect." The assigned question of my study was to shed light on the question of whether this movement was a radically new religious beginning or simply a social or political uprising.

It soon became clear to me that this era was truly an archetypal moment in the story of Christendom—and that the very foundation of state-established and -maintained "Christianity" was fatally erroneous. To begin anew, these sixteenth-century "rebaptizers" (Anabaptists) put their lives on the line. Twentieth-century circumstances differed greatly from the sixteenth-century, but nonetheless engagement with that story contributed importantly to the midlife change of direction that was about to emerge in my own life.

Revolution in the Twentieth Century

An important ecumenical conference held at Oxford, England, in 1937 shortly before World War II (1941-1945), for the first time after many centuries acknowledged that the renunciation of violence, and hence the refusal to bear arms, is an appropriate option for Christians. Then in 1948 the founding meeting of the World Council of Churches (WCC) included in its report a section entitled, "War Is Contrary to the Will of God." It listed three approaches to war found among Christians. Some, it observed, believe it is necessary to support the use of force in the absence of "impartial supra-national institutions." Others, though prepared to support the use of force in some circumstances, now concluded that weapons of mass destruction eliminate war as an option. Finally, it was noted, there are Christians who adhere to "an absolute witness against war and for peace." Persons espousing this last position had become known as conscientious objectors, or COs. Those opting for the middle option could be called "nuclear pacifists."

The weight of the earlier legacy of Christendom was evident on both sides in World War II. On the one hand, Hitler had succeeded in enlisting the silence or support of Germany's institutional Christianity, both Protestant and Catholic, though with important differences between the two. But during that time a "Confessing Church" (Protestant) emerged underground in Hitler's Germany, refusing support of Hitler, often resulting in imprisonment of clergy and others. Martin Niemoeller, an imprisoned Lutheran clergyman, became the most widely known spokesperson for that initiative.

On the other hand, on the American side, the Hitler enterprise appeared evil enough that churches in the United States tended to support the Allied war against it. Ironically, Reinhold Niebuhr, the most visible spokesperson in the United States for that church support, was himself a leading figure in the neoorthodox school of theology. But Niebuhr, at the same time, acknowledged the ultimacy of Christ's nonviolent challenge—and hence the validity of the radical Christian pacifist minority witness he himself had espoused earlier in life!

We cannot ignore the fact that both twentieth-century world wars, though in the end taking on wider dimensions, originated within nations long described as Christian. Retrospectively, the Oxford (1937) and Amsterdam (1948) conferences, in their recognition of the refusal to bear arms as an acceptable Christian option, signified the beginning of an historical turning point. However, this fact did not immediately change public opinion. Nor for that matter did I at this early stage in my story have any awareness of the Oxford conference or of what Amsterdam signified in this regard.

"Peace Is the Will of God"

A year after the above-noted Brunner lecture, in the fall of 1952, I was drawn directly into the ecumenical conversations on peace and war helped by the Oxford and Amsterdam conferences. Rene Koenig, my sociology professor at Zurich while I was writing my dissertation, had sent me to the Sorbonne in Paris for a term to observe a sociological study of French Catholics underway there. I had just been asked by the Continuation Committee of Historic Peace Churches to draft a statement on peace for presentation and discussion to the World Council of Churches. At a Sorbonne institute I meanwhile attended a lecture course by Dominican Fr. Ducatillion on the early church and war. I was able to consult him at the Dominican House of Studies in Paris on my peace church writing assignment.

After considerable editing, the statement was submitted by the committee of the historic peace churches to the WCC under the title, "Peace Is the Will of God," clearly a positive echo of the above-noted WCC declaration. This exchange triggered a decade-long series of ecumenical discussions among theological scholars in Europe known as the Puidoux Conferences (named for the Swiss town where the first conference in that series was held). A brief account of the final editing of that statement appeared at the beginning of the previous chapter.

With my young family, I returned to the United States and did not participate directly in those conversations. But in ways that I could not have anticipated, that brief entry into the war-peace debate in the churches in Europe largely set my life course for the next decade and a half. Beyond that, in secondary ways these questions continued to occupy me for the years that followed.

A New Chapter in History

As already suggested, significant shifts in Western history had already begun to unfold before World War II. Echoes of early Christian renunciation of violence and war had lingered at the edges throughout medieval times. Beginning with the Anabaptists in the sixteenth century, Christian pacifist renunciation of war reemerged in the modern era as a fundamental challenge to premises of Christendom. Until the twentieth century, however, polities showed little understanding and tolerance for pacifist dissent. But in the course of World War I, the British and the United States governments began to experiment with forms of alternative service for religious objectors to military service. Might conscientious objectors to war be assigned instead to other forms of public service?

Vestiges of those World War I adjustments lingered. Then during the 1930s as war loomed anew, Selective Service, the United States congressional conscription agency, set about to update the World War I conscription program. Quaker, Mennonite, and Brethren representatives began exploring with the agency appropriate provisions for COs. From that conversation a program emerged that came to be known as Civilian Public Service (CPS). While oriented to peace church members, religious objectors from other traditions were also included (and in the end were more numerous than peace church objectors). "Conscience," a more inclusive category, now trumped "religion" as the basis of exemption from military service.

Such broadening was appropriate. Membership in any of the peace churches did not guarantee that an eighteen-year-old draftee was truly a CO, nor was conscientious objection to military action a peace church or even a Christian monopoly. By 1970 the United States Supreme Court ruled that "ethical and moral beliefs" were as valid as religious convictions for objection to military participation.

And a further twist emerged. What about "selective conscientious objection" to a particular war? Significantly, selective objection was seen as political judgment, not immediately as exercise of conscience, and thus was excluded from the CO category!

Compromise on Both Sides

The provision for exemption from military service in exchange for nonmilitary voluntary public service was clearly a compromise by each of the partners in the agreement. The government, according to an unconfirmed story, reasoned that accommodating a small minority of conscientious objectors would be less disrupting publicly than continued prosecution and imprisonment. On the other hand, the agreement involved formal collaboration between church and state. Previously this would have been unacceptable to many Anabaptist groups. In fact, some Mennonite pacifist minorities refused this new arrangement.

During the later decades of the twentieth-century, provision for public service rapidly spread internationally. The operating rationale was no longer religious but humanistic. The focus was on conscience, effectively the innate dignity of the individual, and hence a human right. Military service in the United States became voluntary as well. At this stage of historical development, exemption from military service for reasons of conscience appeared only in countries whose polities are rooted in Western tradition. However, already in 1987 the Human Rights Commission of the United Nations adopted a resolution urging universal recognition of the right to conscientious objection to war.

A dramatic example of respect by the state for conscientious objection to war involved the Federal Republic of Germany, formed from the three western zones of the Allied military occupation of Germany in 1948, soon after the end of World War II. Article 4 of the Basic Law of this new German state stipulated that "no one shall be forced to do military service against his conscience." (Serving in the postwar program of the Mennonite Central Committee in Germany in the late 1940s, I enjoyed a small ringside glimpse into the proceedings that led to this formulation.) This formulation reflected a fundamental change in the German political and military institutions and culture. The German alternative *Zivildienst* (civil service) continued in the reunited republic. This is the most extensively developed alternative service for conscientious objection among all the nations.

The 1993 book *The New Conscientious Objection,* edited by military-sociologist Charles C. Moskos and John Whiteclay Chambers II (Oxford University Press), describes this twentieth-century transition from religion to conscience as ground for such objection. Following the controversy surrounding the war in Vietnam in the 1960s and 1970s, conscription was abandoned in the United States. Voluntary professional service was seen as more appropriate in this high-tech military era than universal limited-term mobilization.

But new questions arose regarding the civic education of the youth formerly provided by universal military training. At the same time, staff shortages in various social services were mounting. Religious and other agencies drew on voluntary programs for students in response to these shortages, with obvious potential for significant future development.

In their introduction to the above volume, the editors write, "Calling themselves 'defenseless Christians,' the separatist Anabaptist pacifist groups contained the embryos of modern ideas of church and state" (p. 10). While the Christian conscience objected to military participation in earlier settings, the Moskos and Chambers collection of papers, beginning with World War I, deals with a specific example that unfolded in the course of the twentieth century. They trace a dramatic example of the impact of moral values (in this instance of Christian witness) on human affairs. Respect for the human conscience, expressed strongly in and by the peace church minorities beginning in World War I and clearly elaborated in World War II, is now on a worldwide journey in broadly humanistic terms.

An Abortive Moment?

In 1953, the late Professor Blanke ended a semester-long seminar at the University of Zurich, in which we had analyzed original sixteenth-century Anabaptist texts, with a sobering insight. The only thing wrong about the Anabaptist (free church) movement, he said, was that historically it came prematurely. As noted in chapter 13, a few years later he published that assessment.

I have pondered this thesis ever since. Viewed in longer terms—economically, socially, politically, even technologically—this judgment appears profoundly true. Specialization of activity, exchange of products, social arrangements beyond kinship and local ties—all these and more had to develop to permit the rise of the individuation and individualism that the believers church implicitly presupposes. The Reformation both reflected, and contributed to, important historical advances in Europe, even as history still resisted the believers church paradigm that broke through in the Anabaptist movement.

"The Fullness of Time"

Without belaboring the relation of Christianity to Judaism, it is instructive to note the difference in the social ambiance of the two testaments comprising the biblical story. Already in early Old Testament times, expanded human settlements were emerging. However, the basic scheme of things remained tribal, local, and nomadic, heavily communal. Personal freedom was largely circumscribed. New Testament times, coming more than a millennium later, resonate far more with our own era. Cities, technology, commerce, and trade in the Mediterranean world were far more developed and pervasive than in early Israelite times.

The concept of "the fullness of time" appears in both parts of the Bible. It plays a special role in Paul's apostolic writings, notably in Galatians 4:4, 5: "But when the fullness of time had come, God sent his Son, born of a woman, born under the law ... so that we might receive adoption as children." This is properly read as a theological statement, but it is profoundly sociohistorical as well. Beginning already with the Jewish Diaspora and the era of the Old Testament prophets, the human story increasingly becomes communally personalized. Ties grounded primarily in the determinisms of nature are surmounted in the above Pauline text by "adoption," by individualized personal responses to God's enabling grace in the Christ event.

Cities, as already noted, have been described as an invention whereby we as humans overcome the friction of space. The golden age of the city in Western history came in the late-medieval, early-modern era. The Protestant Reformation arrived midpoint in that era. The Renaissance (the reencounter with the cultural epitome of the classic Mediterranean traditions) and the invention of the printing press were the important external factors in the Reformation. The parallels between the emergence of the printing press and our own electronic revolution nearly five centuries later are at once fascinating and instructive, despite the enormous differences in scale and complexity of these two technologies. The industrial revolution eventually led to the end of the city in its classic form. Continuing advances entail the urbanization (or more accurately the "technologizing") of rural life in our time beyond our own premonitions.

The Unfinished Task

In a previous chapter I noted that my theological interest needed sociological elucidation. Over time my academic path expanded accordingly, further enhanced by historical inquiry as well. Interestingly, my adult life span coincided with the second half of the tumultuous twentieth century, thus with the pluralizing, globalizing, and now the digitalizing of the human project. These developments are at once energized and throttled by the legacy of human history I have briefly outlined.

The lingering shadow of the flaw of Christendom is a continuing paradox dramatized vividly by the policies of the George W. Bush administration played out even as this is being written. The cultural legacy on which the administration draws is the ethos of Christendom, the surface of which was barely scratched by the constitutionally grounded separation of church and state in the United States.

The conversionist evangelical faith championed by President Bush segregates private faith from the public ethos. Subjectively changed believers thus can be mobilized to support public policy and actions contradictory to the very gospel they profess. The distorting spell of Christendom lingers unabated in a confession of faith intrinsically disavowed by it. Surmounting that legacy remains the unfinished task of the sixteenth-century Reformation.

Who Is the "Parasite"?

Let us return here to Professor Brunner's parasite imagery with which the present chapter begins. Considering the continuing legacy of Christendom, it may be helpful to ask, What if the Brunner parasite in fact appears on the other foot, that of the nonpacifist "Christian" majority? Is Christendom, the attachment of the adjective *Christian* to whole societies without conversion, a parasitic adoption of the Christian label? Perhaps sweeping claims in either the Christendom or the pacifist direction all too quickly become human hubris.

These issues came to engage me full time during the 1957 to 1967 decade. Without presuming to answer this question here as to which foot wears the parasite shoe, I recall the pacifist germ in the vision of Reinhold Niebuhr, the leading nonpacifist prophet in American Christianity during World War II. While he provided the theological underpinning for American Christian support in the military crusade against Hitler, Niebuhr meanwhile recognized the validity of the nonviolent Christian minority when authentically expressed. Why? Because that indeed is the final outcome of the reign of Christ.

Beginning in the mid-1950s, I served a two-year term as secretary of the Peace Problems Committee (Mennonite Church), which had some advisory responsibilities for the Mennonite component in the Civilian Public Service program for conscientious objectors. On several occasions I heard and met General Lewis B. Hershey, the director of Selective Service for the United States government. Without the theological finesse of Reinhold Niebuhr, his was a position similar to Niebuhr's. Sooner or later, the war system had to be abandoned. While the time was not yet ripe for that to occur, those working toward that end needed to be acknowledged. Thus absent in General Hershey was any trace of the cynicism or bitterness that an official in his position might well have felt toward the conscientious objectors he had to accommodate in his administration of the military draft.

Thus our reply to the question of which side is truly parasitic might be, "It depends!" Yes, conscientious objection is parasitic if it means mere acceptance of the toleration of a liberal society without

Christian commitment otherwise, or if it reduces to mere activism that ours is a better idea. But might it apply as well, though differently, to established "churchianity," if it appeals to Christian symbols to justify warring action contrary to the reign of Christ? The hard work for the Christian movement still lies ahead. Stay tuned.

Chapter 6

A Sally into the Orient

Japanese poetry has as its subject the human heart.
—Kamo Mabuchi

Avoid what is evil; do what is good; purify the mind—
this is the teaching of the Awakened One.
—The Pali Canon

In Japan, when we finally decide to go to church,
it's as if we were going to our death.
—Kochi Kurosaki

Mennonite Central Committee, the relief and service agency of several Anabaptist groupings in North America, expanded rapidly during the 1940s and 1950s. While the home office included some paid staff, field programs abroad depended on MCC-supported volunteers. Orie O. Miller, the MCC executive, himself had served in Europe under that emergency agency after World War I. Located in Akron, Pennsylvania, he had meanwhile become a successful shoe manufacturer. With that enterprise now employee-operated, he served in Akron as MCC's top executive. At that stage he improvised administratively, relying heavily on skills he spotted among volunteers. After I had drafted the statement submitted to the WCC by the peace churches (see chapter 3), he pigeonholed me as someone potentially useful for special peace-advocacy tasks.

Japan appeared as a particular challenge to the churches after World War II. While the postwar material aid programs of MCC were mostly Europe-directed, the mission agencies in the Mennonite constituencies were drawn to Japan. Suffering defeat, that country had to be reconstituted politically. The situation was further complicated by the unresolved trauma of the atomic bombings of Hiroshima and Nagasaki near the war's end, with devastation unique in human history. In addition, by the 1950s the nuclear weapons arms race between the Soviet and American spheres of influence was underway. This brought new fears to the Japanese people long before the pain of the past could be healed.

In 1955, MCC began a consultancy to the missions and churches in Japan on the problems of peace and war that were keenly felt there. Given the volume of work on behalf of conscientious objectors, MCC had long ago formed a semiautonomous Peace Section within its general structure. The peace consultancy in Japan fell under Peace Section guidance, while ultimately accountable to the MCC's general secretary, Orie Miller. Melvin Gingerich, a Goshen College history professor on leave, accepted the initial two-year assignment in Japan.

By late 1956 Miller wrote a letter inviting me, with my family, to succeed Gingerich when his term ended, likewise for a two-year term. Having moved twice since returning from Europe, we were in the final stages of building a house, hoping finally to settle in. Taking a leave of absence had never crossed our minds. We declined Miller's invitation. After some weeks, he wrote once more, then a third time.

Finally we yielded. On August 23, 1957, we set sail from San Francisco for Yokohama. Including a twenty-four-hour stop in Hawaii, it was a thirteen-day voyage. Eventually our two-year term was extended to five, only to be terminated late in our third year when a health problem of our oldest daughter became acute. We returned to the United States and, after professional consultations, moved for treatment to Washington, D.C. In the next chapter I will deal with the career changes associated with these developments.

Our Dip into the Orient

Apart from the congenital neural problem of our oldest daughter, the Tokyo sojourn for our family was a happy one. We went there with three children. During our final year a fourth, our second son, was born. While being a wife and mother in this very different world was a demanding task, Ellen found time to teach English to a women's Bible class and to attend some English lectures on Japanese history. She also took training in the *Sogetsu* school of Japanese flower arranging, which she sometimes taught a after we returned to the States.

Since our stay in Japan was short-term, we took only conversational language instruction. We had a native helper in the household, and I had a very competent interpreter-secretary in my professional work. In addition to traveling widely in Japan during our stay there, MCC sent me on briefer visits to Korea, India, and Vietnam as well.

Christianity was brought to Japan in three waves:

(1) Roman Catholics arrived in the sixteenth century in Nagasaki at the western tip of the main island, contributing to Japan's closing of itself to the Western world for two and a half centuries.

(2) Protestants, mostly American, came after the partly forced reopening of Japan to the West in the nineteenth century.

(3) American evangelical missions weighed in after World War II. Mennonite missions came only during this third era, with beginnings in the far west and north and two locations in the central region.

To this day, Christians in Japan remain numerically marginal, making up less than one per cent of the population. Christian influence, however, is significant. Both the reason and purpose of peace consultancy to missions and churches in Japan were clear and straightforward. The missionary overtures of each of the three historic Christian groups noted above followed economic and political incursions. Not only was Japan defeated in World War II, but the country was also traumatized by the atomic destruction of two of its cities, a devastation unique in human history. The Japanese were haunted by further advances in nuclear weapons technology and by the nuclear arms race between the two new superpowers.

All this profoundly challenged the missionary presence in Japan, particularly in its "peace church" version. Somehow Americans had brought war and destruction, yet ironically they were now preaching against it.

Assisting a clear understanding of that problem, and a corresponding articulation of the healing and conciliatory nature of the gospel, defined the peace consultancy task to be carried out within the missionary discourse. Programmatically, however, specifics were allowed to emerge, largely corresponding to the consultant's gifts, experience, and vision. From the Mennonite mission and church core, I worked outward in concentric circles: first to the Christian communities more generally, both prewar mainline Protestant and postwar evangelical; then to peace action initiatives in Japanese society; and finally to academic discourse generally.

I quickly perceived that the modest familiarity I had with the nonpacifist/pacifist polarity in the Western Christian tradition had little direct relevance in the non-Christian Japanese setting. I traveled to missions and churches, both Mennonite and other; visited educational institutions; and attended meetings, international conferences, and other gatherings. Frequently there were opportunities to speak. When I addressed Japanese or other-country audiences, I depended on interpreters.

Two important constituencies for me were the missionary and fraternal worker communities related to the Japanese churches. Missionaries were those who came after World War II, chiefly evangelical and American, establishing new churches. Fraternal workers were those associated with the Protestant churches established after Japan was forced to reopen its doors to the West during the second half of the nineteenth and the early twentieth centuries. Those denominations, as we shall see, had been forced to merge (1940) under the Japanese wartime military regime and became known as *Nihon Kirisuto Kyodan*, the United Church of Christ in Japan. Catholics had never totally disappeared; the Jesuits operated Jochi Daigaku (Sophia University) in Tokyo.

The original Roman Catholic wave had been driven underground already in the sixteenth century. In the nineteenth century, after Japan was forced to open its doors to the West, in 1868 came the Meiji Restoration of imperial rule over the military regimes in control until then. This included an imperial religion that ascribed divinity to the emperor and a divine calling to the nation. The Imperial Rescript on Education of 1890 declared a national polity that glorified the nation as divine and the emperor as a god, with an aggressive mission among the nations. This polity was propagated through the educational system.

This action can be seen retrospectively as anticipating the Religious Bodies Law of 1939 that empowered the Minister of Education, through local officials, to supervise all religious bodies. The process of incorporating Christianity had begun long before World War II. For example, the Apostles' Creed, widely used in the churches, was modified accordingly. As events moved toward World War II, the aggressive regime in control of Japan attempted to unify all Christian denominations in the Nihon Kirisuto Kyodan. Only a few of the prewar denominations refused to join the Kyodan, notably the Holiness and Seventh Day Adventist groups. The real challenge for Kyodan, the recovery of integrity in Christian identity, came in the postwar era.

Of all this, my knowledge was (and is) far too limited for what my assignment required. Informally, fraternal workers and missionaries were important links for me to the Japanese, both Christians and non-Christians. Another important constituency in my work were the Japanese associations formed around military matters—war victims, for example, and antinuclear weapon actions, including those of religious as well as of secular persuasion.

THE GENSUIKYO (AGAINST A AND H BOMBS)

In 1955, a decade after the war ended, a Japan Council Against A and H Bombs (JCAAHB, abbreviated in Japanese as *Gensuikyo*) emerged, an agency still active half a century later. This agency assumed three tasks: (1) prevention of nuclear war; (2) elimination of all nuclear weapons; and (3) the welfare of those traumatized by the Hiroshima and Nagasaki atomic bombings. A decade later, in 1965, the Japan Congress Against A and H Bombs (*Gensuikin*) would be formed but that was well after my time there. In addition to Gensuikyo objectives, Gensuikin opposes the use of nuclear energy. More importantly, there is also an ideological difference. Gensuikyo, the original group, has never fully escaped the Communist spell under which it fell in the late 1950s.

Early in our Japan stay, I became acquainted with the director of Gensuikyo, Kaoru Yasui, a professor at Hosei University. I still have notes from a lecture that he delivered before the Council for a Christian Peace Movement at a meeting at the Shinanomachi Church in Tokyo, November 23-24, 1957, only a few months after our arrival in Japan. He stated clearly both the perspective of Gensuikyo, which he represented, then his own personal view. Given the diversity of groups comprising the Council Against A and H Bombs, it would be difficult to define its consensus, he argued. But given the political reality of the world at the time, he hoped for "a concentration of all the energies of all nations to change the concepts of the ruling classes, to turn them toward ending all nuclear armaments. . . ." In every country, public opinion should be mobilized, "then governments can get together [accordingly]." As an example he noted that in the United States the scientist Linus Pauling had gathered 2,000 signatures of this sort. Kaoru Yasui was not a Christian and did not believe in "religious power." But "political movement needs Christian support," he said. Hence Christians should act and join mass movements.

Over the next few months, I was often in touch with Professor Yasui at the Gensuikyo headquarters. Plans were getting under way for the Fourth Annual Conference of Gensuikyo to be held in Tokyo

August 12-20, 1958. During the last two months of preparation for the event, I agreed to help the organizing team two mornings a week. Part of my contribution would be an effort to encourage Christian participation from abroad, especially among fraternal workers in the churches in Japan. The ambiance among the organizing staff and volunteers corresponded to the rationale outlined by Professor Yasui in the above-noted address. Procedures were low-keyed and flexible.

I cannot recall the population mix of the volunteers who helped in the planning. But in the final week, as the delegations from the Communist-inspired World Council of Peace arrived, the climate abruptly changed. Clearly a procedural strategy was at work. The intent of that strategy surfaced as the meeting got under way. The format was typical for gatherings of a certain kind. Two levels of leadership were presented on the platform. At a higher, more remote level, seated at a table facing the audience, were a few well-known public figures whose presence was thought to validate the meeting. At a lower-level table sat the moderator of the meeting with several associates who together actually "ran the show."

The plan was to seat the foreign dignitaries at the symbolic table. One of these was André Trocmé, the French Reformed pacifist pastor, formerly from the village of Le Chambon-sur-Lignon. Trocmé had led the nonviolent resistance of that village to the German occupation during World War II. Under his leadership, and with his associates, the village had successfully hidden Jews from the Gestapo, mystifying the occupying Germans who perceived an invisible spiritual force at work. He certainly would bring symbolic authenticity to the occasion. But Trocmé, familiar with the two-table symbolism, insisted on a seat at the lower table. And the leadership had to concede!

Though the plenary sessions of the conference were attended by as many as a thousand persons, the working sessions were divided into three groups, each with its own topic. In all, about six peace church and FOR (Fellowship of Reconciliation) representatives attended, including Trocmé, with whom I had become acquainted in Paris six years previously (1952). We scattered ourselves among the three working groups and kept in touch between sessions.

The strategy soon became clear. At the time, the United States was involved in a series of nuclear tests in the Pacific, while Soviet testing was in a recess. So it was clear who the aggressor was. With the villain thus identified, the conference had its work cut out! When this emerged, I found myself on the spot. Having accepted the claim that this was to be a universal gathering of peoples from everywhere, calling on all governments to renounce nuclear weapons, I had prevailed on a few other Christians to attend. As Professor Yasui, the president of Gensuikyo admitted to me later, in this 1958 meeting the organization lost its original neutrality. Neutrality now yielded to Communist dominance. Because of mounting tension between the Soviet and Chinese Communist camps, the Chinese stayed away. I was being courted (unsuccessfully) by the Soviet delegation. Now what should I do?

Finally, on the last day of the conference (Aug. 20), I published a lengthy letter (nearly 2,000 words) in the *Japan Times*, the daily English newspaper in Tokyo, describing how the conference was being manipulated. Here I cite one long sentence from that letter:

> But as an able Christian delegate has vigorously maintained throughout this convention, a peace movement that does not begin with repentance of one's own sins and those of one's nation, but which merely levels an accusatory self-righteous finger at the other fellow (who may not even be present), becomes instead a provocation to war.

My letter was too late to affect this particular occasion (the above unnamed Christian was André Trocmé), but I was subsequently excluded from Gensuikyo. And the preexisting local peace group in Hiroshima with which I had been in continuous dialogue was ordered to sever ties with me or it would have to leave the Gensuikyo. I solved that problem by discontinuing my contact with that group. The following year I did not try to attend the conference, though I arranged an interview with an American scientist who had. Shortly before we left Japan in 1960, Professor Yasui, with a few associates at Gensuikyo, received me once more and we had coffee together.

What am I to make of this entire episode? Is there a larger lesson to be drawn from it? Did I overstep? This occasion was my most direct political action, leaving unanswered questions for me.

A footnote to this project on the missionary side was a special issue of the *Japan Christian Quarterly* that I was invited to guest edit two months later (Oct. 1958). It included ten articles of varying lengths on peace matters, half by Japanese writers and half by fraternal workers from the churches. In the introduction, I reported briefly on the Gensuikyo conference just held.

Several commentators called summer 1958 the "Summer of Conferences." During the last days of July, the Fellowship of Christian Missionaries held its annual fellowship and devotional life gathering in Nojiri. The following day the Evangelical Missionaries Association started its meetings in Karuizawa. While the above Gensuikyo gathering was in progress, the fourteenth World Convention on Christian Education met in Tokyo August 7-14. In a few instances the Gensuikyo gathering benefited from overlapping participation in both events.

THE HAYAMA CONFERENCE (JANUARY 1960)

American church representatives, both women and men, who lived and worked in Japan, as indicated earlier, fell into two distinct categories. First were those associated as fraternal workers with churches forced by the government into the *Kyodan* (United Church) or otherwise severed from American or European church ties by the wartime regime. The second were the mostly non-mainline postwar evangelical missionaries, there to win converts into new churches of various persuasions.

Because Tokyo is a hot city during two summer months, the prewar missionaries built summer homes on the east slope of the first mountain west of Tokyo. With that area already settled, the postwar missionaries simply traveled a bit farther to the west slope of the mountains to erect their summer cottages. This simple accident of history illustrates that these were two relatively distinct groupings.

My assignment called for taking both communities seriously. Evangelical missionaries, resident in Tokyo, met in a weekly morning prayer meeting in a United States army chapel still in the city. Meetings of the other group were less regular. In one way or another, whatever their particular legacy, both had to deal sooner or later with the kinds of issues that Gensuikyo engaged. And a conference to deal with those questions seemed appropriate.

Given my being in contact with both, it seemed more appropriate to bring them together in such a colloquy than to mobilize two separate events. A conjoint engagement by these two communities would be enriching for both and would address the issues more fully. After months of informal conversation, by late 1959 it seemed that we were reaching agreement on such an occasion.

But then a problem emerged. Gordon Chapman, the senior leader in the evangelical group, found the pacifist/just war topic too risky. If we were to proceed, with him bowing out we would likely lose a major portion of the evangelicals. A conference on peace would lead to schism, albeit informally! So we softened our theme to an acceptable formulation: "Our Ministry of Reconciliation in a World of Conflict" (2 Cor. 5:18). The conference met successfully in January 1960, at Hayama, the resort town and conference center southwest of Tokyo. About fifty persons from these two fraternal worker and missionary communities participated.

Six months later my family and I returned to the United States. Meanwhile the conferees decided to meet again the following January with Chapman as convener. Chapman, as I learned only recently, had first arrived in Japan in 1921, though returning to the United States at later intervals. He became acquainted personally with Uchimura Kanzo (see below), whom he regarded as his mentor.

The topic of the second (1961) meeting was "The Church and the Missionary in Japan" (Phi. 2:5). Thereafter the Hayama Conference met annually for forty years, with its proceedings published. Conference themes included "Christian Discipleship in Japan" (1963); "The Christian's Responsibility in Political Affairs in Japan" (1970); "Can the Gospel Thrive in Japanese Soil: Guilt, Shame, and Grace in a Unique Culture" (1982); "The Church in Japan and the Missionary" (1995); and "Strategies for a Christian Witness in a Postmodern World" (2001).

Mukyokai: Christianity Without the Institutional Church

An astonishing, yet too little noted chapter in the Christian story in Japan, is the *Mukyokai* movement that emerged there at the dawn of the twentieth century. Half a century later, a statistical yearbook published by a Christian newspaper estimated that this movement might include as may as 50,000 Japanese. But as we shall see, by its very nature this movement is hardly countable. The clue to this puzzle is captured in the name by which the gatherings of these people are known: *Mu* (non)-*kyokai* (church). Deliberately they claimed to be churchless Christians. But how can there be Christians without churches?

My own contact with the Mukyokai movement remains marginal, yet even so sheds light on a problem of importance in my life and work otherwise. My readings of the Mukyokai story are heavily shaped by my experiences at the interface of the believers church and Christendom paradigms. The founder of the movement, Uchimura Kanzo (1861-1930), left a vast paper trail, partly in English. And a considerable body of scholarly literature deals with both the founder and the movement.

The vision shaping the Mukyokai project arose from the experiences of founder Uchimura. As an emerging writer and journalist, by the beginning of the twentieth century he already appeared as a controversial national figure. A radical believer, his Christian practices and utterances collided with the "pagan" dimensions of Japanese life. Uchimura was reared in a samurai family. For centuries the samurai had been the aristocratic warrior class in Japanese society. With the ending of Japan's feudal period in 1868, as Uchimura was reaching adolescence, that class was dissolving. Thus his social position became uncertain.

Eventually (1878-1881) he enrolled in the Imperial Agricultural College in Sapporo, Japan (today Hokkaido University). Most courses offered there were taught in English. By age eleven, Uchimura had already begun the study of English. Through a tract left behind by William S. Clark (1825-1886), an influential guest professor at the college (1876-1877), Uchimura became a Christian. A bit later, along with several other young Japanese Christian converts, he ran into conflict with denominational missionary interests. As a result he became alienated from the institutionalizing of churches, though continuing in informal gatherings with fellow believers.

After graduation, then three years employment in the national agricultural ministry, Uchimura traveled to the United States as a student (1884-1888). Imagining America to be a Christian society, he came with high expectations. But beginning with the dock hands he met on landing in California, he quickly discovered otherwise. Disillusion mounted, and he almost lost his adopted faith. However, he was aided and influenced at the outset in the eastern United States by a Quaker couple, Mr. and Mrs. Wister Morris. Eventually he enrolled at Amherst College. There for the first and only time (and shortly before Clark's death in 1886), Uchimura met William S.. Clark, who had authored and left behind the tract that had led to Uchimura's conversion at Sapporo Agricultural College.

Soon after Clark's death, Uchimura was befriended by Julius H. Seelye, the president of Amherst College. Under the mentoring of Seelye, Uchimura's faith was renewed and more radically grounded. In a brief self-introduction in 1926, Uchimura wrote that "The great president [Seelye] opened my eyes to the evangelical truth in Christianity. He is my father in the faith. For forty years, since then, I preached the faith taught to me by that venerable teacher."

Repelled further by denominational confusion in American Christianity, he returned to Japan inspired by the notion that all creed, institution, and sacrament must be banned from the Christian response to the gospel, hence the term Mukyokai, that is, nonchurch or churchless Christianity.

Back in his native Japan, Uchimura took a radical stand, not only in contrast to organized Christianity but also against the divinization of the Japanese political ethos. Moreover, he became a Christian pacifist. Thereby on both scores he became a controversial national figure. He taught school and served in several public agencies. Though without a firm institutional base, he entered the field of journalism, writing in both Japanese and English. From 1900 until his death in 1930, he published a monthly biblical studies magazine in Japanese. All the while he led an unstructured Bible class (no membership listed or required). Since 1964 his voluminous writings have been archived in an Uchimura Memorial Collection at the International Christian University in Tokyo. His last will and testament ordered all his agencies dissolved at his death.

In relation to Uchimura's causes, his death seemed reason for despair. Effectively nothing would be left but memories and his paper trail. But then one by one some of those who had collaborated with him (several of whom I was privileged eventually to meet) sensed a call to act as he had. Each began to teach a noninstitutional Bible class and/or to write. What until then was merely the voice of a lonely prophet mutated into a movement, into Mukyokai, a churchless version of Christianity continuing to this day.

Here now are my limited Mukyokai experiences. In the summer of 1957, just before our departure to Japan, I had gone to Europe to attend several conferences. I was able to stop in Zurich briefly to visit a few acquaintances, including my former professor, Emil Brunner. He had returned a short while previously from a two-year stint as a guest professor in Japan, and I called on him for suggestions regarding my upcoming assignment there. During his time in Japan, he had befriended the Mukyokai movement and its leaders.

One of Brunner's own books, published shortly before he left for Japan, in some respects resonated with Mukyokai affirmations. Indeed that book, released in English as *The Misunderstanding of the Church* (Westminster Press, 1951), already contains a reference to Uchimura. Brunner suggested that I contact Yanaihara Tadao, professionally an economist and social scientist who had become president of Tokyo Imperial University, the top university in Japan. Yanaihara, the current senior figure in the Mukyokai movement, himself had been a member of the founder Uchimura's Bible class.

A month or two after our arrival in Tokyo, I scheduled a visit to Yanaihara in his office. On his desk—the desk of the university president—was a small stack of the current Bible study journals that he published periodically. What president of a public university in America would publish such a journal, let alone display it on the university president's desk? The visit was congenial and unhurried. Near the end, I asked, "Might I visit a Bible class of yours sometime?"

"Do you know Japanese?"

"No," I had to reply.

"Learn Japanese," he continued. "Then we'll see."

Shortly before, Yanaihara had received unfriendly treatment in the Western press. Was he putting me off for that reason, supposing that I was merely another journalistic critic? I'll never know. I didn't stay in Japan long enough to learn Japanese beyond a bit of daily jargon. But more than a year later I visited his class without his knowledge—and I hope justifiably without guilt! By then Ellen was teaching a women's conversational-English Bible class. A member of that group, herself formerly a professor at a women's college, had been in Yanaihara's Bible class. During the Christmas season, Yanaihara invited former students to a special session. She invited me to accompany her on that occasion.

We arrived early enough that I could count the seats in the large room, approximately 500. By the time the class began, all seats were filled, and several dozen people stood around the edges. Though this was a Christmas holiday season, there were no Christmas decorations, no singing, no liturgy. In succession, three Mukyokai men led a Bible study, each for nearly an hour. The youngest taught first, then a second from the middle generation, and finally the oldest, President Yanaihara. The participants sat with Bibles, some even in Greek and Hebrew. After the meeting ended, people went their separate ways. If people had gathered to chat with Yanaihara afterward, I might have waited in line for a turn. But he put on his overcoat and left without chatting with anyone.

I relived something of this seemingly stern session nearly two years later. During our stay in Japan, I had met another Mukyokai leader, Kurosaki Kochi, a generational peer of Yanaihara's, also Uchimura-taught. Soon after our return, I worked with some West Coast U.S. Japanese groups to arrange a visit of Kurosaki to the America. I was responsible, with the help of Mennonite Central Committee, for his itinerary in the eastern states, ending with a stop at the National Council of Churches center in New York.

We included a visit to Eastern Mennonite College. By that time Kurosaki had been surfeited with what appeared to him as the superficiality of worship in American churches. Comparing such worship to Bible class gatherings, he said to the astonishment of about twenty-five students to whom he spoke, "In Japan, when we finally decide to go to church, it's as if we were going to our death." In effect, the business of such a gathering is to deal with the boundary issues of life. It's not a time for frivolity. Was this an echo of the stern samurai ethos? Perhaps. Suddenly I better understood the character of President Yanaihara's Christmas gathering two years earlier.

What to Make of Mukyokai?

In my limited frame of reference, two features of Mukyokai are powerfully significant. The first is the force of particularity in the life of the individual, in this case, Uchimura Kanzo. On the one hand, in early childhood he was shaped by the heroic risk of personal life that was fundamental in the samurai ethos. But by the time of his adolescence that whole order was being dissolved. What now? That ethos was doubly rooted (radical): living by putting one's life on the line made life purposeful. And the samurai order provided both ends and means for doing so. Hence the comment of Kurosaki Kokichi to Eastern Mennonite College students in 1960: "In Japan, when we finally decide to go to church, it's as if we were going to our death." Is this not in some manner an echo of his mentor Uchimura Kanzo's native samurai legacy?

The second feature is more complex and far-reaching. How does one assess Uchimura's radical nonchurch reading and promulgation of the gospel story? On the surface this can easily be dismissed as outright heresy. After all, from the call to Abram, through the biblical story to the post-Pentecost era (Acts 1:8), it is through God's new people that "all the nations of the earth" will be blessed. But the Mukyokai venture and the action of its founder merit a more careful second look. First, as just noted, we need to compare Uchimura's entry into God's new people with a manner of entry that had prevailed over many centuries—a merely sacramental process without the subject's awareness. Compare that with both the circumstances and the agony whereby he was joined to that new people.

Then compare that experience further with the kinds of institutional disarray among the churches he found in his own "pagan" homeland and even confusingly in his ostensibly Christian host country, the United States. Which is worse, churches (and church membership) without believers, or believers without (institutional) churches? Moreover, was Mukyokai totally or fundamentally "church" less? Was not the Mukyokai Bible class at least seminally churchly (ecclesial)?

The Church as Institution

I am not an expert in ecclesiology, the doctrine of the church, but throughout my life I have had to wrestle with the diversity of institutions and their respective claims. I find it useful to think of Mukyokai and the papal Roman Catholic Church as polar opposite church archetypes. The former moves, as it were, from the individual rebirth to wider aggregations; the latter moves from a reification (a "thingifying") of such aggregation to the individual.

In both instances one can find New Testament proof texts. The Mukyokai, for example, look at the familiar words of Jesus in John 3:3: "Very truly, I tell you, no one can see the kingdom of God without being born from above." Papal Rome, on the other hand, recalls the apostle Paul's letter to the Ephesians where he sketches "the plan of the mystery hidden for ages . . . that through the church the wisdom of God . . . might now be made known" (3:9-10). What if Mukyokai and Roman Catholic believers each, while fully committed to their respective archetype, sought to turn their either/or polarity into a perpetual both/and symbiosis? And what would this entail for each of us? Such questions will engage us in and after chapter 13 below

Zen Buddhism: An Unexpected Encounter

On a night train between Tokyo and Hiroshima—it may have been my first trip—I encountered Heinrich Dumoulin, a German Jesuit scholar from Jochi Diagaku, the Jesuit university in Tokyo. Observing him reading a German book as I sat across from him in the dining car, I addressed him in German. It turned out that he was a specialist in the history of Zen Buddhism, having lived and worked in Japan for many years. He had written a one-volume history of Zen which was published in German.

By the time our meal and visit ended, he had invited me to translate that volume into English, and I had agreed to do so. This became my "free time" project during the remainder of our stay in Japan and for a few months after our return to the United States. I seized this opportunity because it provided a broader exposure to Japanese culture than my church-related assignment entailed. While Japanese cultural history was and remains polytheistic, Zen Buddhism played an elevating role in Japanese culture.

In an early visit to Tokyo Biblical Seminary, I interviewed a young professor of Old Testament study. Elsewhere I had also met the literary scholar who was translating Karl Barth's multi-volume *Kirchliche Dogmatik* from German to Japanese. So I asked this professor of Old Testament what in Barth's work attracted the Japanese. He offered two reasons. First, he noted, Barth was an important resource for Japanese Christians in dealing with the polytheism in their culture. But second, "Barth is pessimistic; we like that!"

Later during our stay, Paul Tillich (1886-1965), a birth-year twin of Barth, an Americanized German theologian far more philosophical than Barth, came to Japan on a lecture tour. Some of his followers hoped that Tillich's philosophical bent would resonate more readily with Japan's syncretistic climate, but this did not materialize. Apparently it was Barth's emphasis on the radical otherness of God as revealed in the Bible that gained attention.

Zen Buddhism is a far more important and substantive movement than the superficial faddist versions popularized in some circles in the United States in the late twentieth century. Buddhism itself emerged from Hinduism in North India in the fifth century BCE. Eventually it spread northward into China, and from there into Japan, primarily in its Zen form. *Dhyana*, the Sanskrit (Indian) term for meditation, rendered *ch'an* in Chinese, became *Zen* in Japanese. As a form of mysticism, meditation is a key feature of Zen Buddhism. In this development from India through China into Japan, it was influenced by other traditions along the way, especially Taoism in China.

Part of the popular appeal of Zen in our own American setting is that it appears as spirituality without the baffling concept of God. While formally that is true, it is nonetheless a superficial reading of the challenge that Zen itself entails. "The basic metaphysics of this Buddhology," Dumoulin writes, "is pantheistic or, as the Buddhists prefer to say, cosmotheistic." Meanwhile, trying to discern the relation of the biblical story to other religions and traditions is at best a mere work in progress. Nonetheless, I resonate with two sentences in which Dumoulin, concluding his volume *A History of Zen Buddhism* (Pantheon Books, 1963), says that

> as a mystical phenomenon, the satori [Enlightenment] experience is imperfect. No human effort to attain enlightenment, no

matter how honest and self-sacrificing, can ever lead to the perfect truth, but only the eternal Logos "who coming into the world enlightens every man." (John 1:9; p. 290)

A final observation in this regard. Translating does not guarantee comprehension. Over the years, in many international gatherings, I encountered professional interpreters who engaged in simultaneous translation—through a sound system they rendered a speech in another language as the speaker spoke. At the end of the day, they couldn't recall information they had processed. I myself experienced this in a few conference sessions where I served as simultaneous translator, German into English. This activity I found to be a kind of intellectual high, exhilarating but exhausting. It demands concentration at the expense of impacting memory. Somewhat similarly, the fact that I translated Fr. Dumoulin's erudite book doesn't mean that I now really understand Zen!

OTHER ASIAN COUNTRIES
AND RETURN VISITS TO JAPAN

Space does not permit detailing my weeklong visit to the Mennonite Central Committee program in Korea and to various Korean church and other activities as well. More substantial was a five-week visit to India, with contacts in Calcutta, Central and South India, and New Delhi in the north. Several Mennonite missions and associations of churches that are active there were included in my visit. Also on my agenda were visits to the Church of South India and with followers of the late Mahatma Gandhi. He himself had been assassinated a dozen years earlier.

Nor can the experience of two passing return visits to Japan meanwhile be fully included here. The first occurred in 1977, occasioned by a conference scheduled there by the Christian Peace Conference (see especially chapter 11) that was abruptly transferred back to Moscow. Because visits to Japanese churches with which I was in touch nearly twenty years previously had already been scheduled simultaneously for me, the Soviet CPC flew me by Aeroflot from Moscow to Tokyo for those appointments.

The second visit came another two decades later (1996) in a stopover visit, with Ellen along, enroute to conferences in China cosponsored by a Chinese agency and the Council for Research and Values at the Catholic University in America. The later developments

I thus experienced in Japan, though fleetingly indeed, tempered my earlier memories.

Awed and Humbled

Early in this chapter I indicated that our sally into Japan was for my family and me a happy and enriching experience. Without negating that statement, I must add that the Japan years nonetheless were awesome and humbling—because the reach of the realities confronting us were overwhelming.

How little were we prepared for what we met, and how inadequate were our responses! But then, given our human finitude, how limited is our grasp at most! Perhaps we can only implore the paraphrased axiom of Jesus in Luke 17:10: We are unworthy servants; we have only done (or tried to do) what was our duty. The clusters of experience here outlined—our encounter with Gensuikyo; the Hayama conference; the engagement with the Mukyokai Christians; and finally the exposure to Zen Buddhism—opened perspectives and left unanswered questions that will feed into chapter 7 and then more fully into part 4 of this book.

But Now Dismayed

Adding this note on August 15, 2005, I was dismayed by a report in the previous day's Sunday *Washington Post Outlook* by Ayako Doi and Kim Willenson, editor and publisher, respectively of the *Daily Japan Digest*, 1990 to 2004. They noted that the Bush administration, in preparing for the invasion of Iraq, "reassuringly insisted that once the combat was over, they would repeat America's post-World War II occupation success story—the reformation of Japan. . . . But these days the success of the postwar remaking of Japan seems to be partly unraveling."

They approvingly noted "that the U.S. occupation of Japan was remarkably successful in establishing a vibrant democracy in Japan." But they observed that "the pacifist fervor that characterized postwar is now starting to fade, partly at Washington's behest, and partly as a result of a surprising and unrelenting rise of animosity between Japan and its neighbors in China and North and South Korea."

They continued, "Since 9/11 Japan has shifted further away from pacifism. Starting in late 2001, it deployed a task force of destroyers and [tankers] to the Indian Ocean to help the allied fleet support operations in Afghanistan. And a few months after the United States toppled Saddam Hussein's government, Tokyo sent about 1,000 troops to [support] southern Iraq that so far have avoided conflict." Though it is too early to predict ultimate outcomes, this is a sobering turn of events.

Chapter 7

Jousting with the Legacy of Christendom

With Constantine the empire became holy.
The church was regarded as the empire at prayer.
—Dale W. Brown

Theology: Simply the attempt to get around the Sermon on the Mount without repudiating Jesus.
—Walter Kaufmann

. . . Serving the world by being other than the world.
—Gerard Loughlin

The term *Christendom*, in loose dictionary definition, refers to "the portion of the world in which Christianity prevails." Like the biblical story itself, Christendom is an ironic phenomenon. It emerged by what can only be described as self-contradiction. This is supremely evident even in the Passion, the founding moment of the faith. Jesus' violent death is the doorway into the nonviolence that Jesus himself launched.

Irony is bound up as well in the spread of that faith from its beginnings. It is evident already with the Judaic history from which Christendom descended. Christianity was outwardly perpetuated after the early centuries by the earthly power of the Roman Empire and lesser rulers inspired thereby. It is to that ironic historical embodiment that the term Christendom points.

Anabaptism, the "sectarian" believers church alternative to Christendom, is also ironically achieved. For while standing in radical opposition to Christendom, Anabaptism, the believers or free church movement in its diverse forms, hails from its Christendom parentage. Possibly the archetype of this irony is contained in the biblical account itself. The Abrahamic call, amplified in the covenant with the people of Israel at Mt. Sinai, is politically transcendent. Yet when Israel is historically imperiled, monarchy is temporarily grafted in (1 Sam. 8)—although with stark forewarning. Indeed, the Davidic royal theme is incorporated into the covenant legacy—as is the exilic Diaspora that emerged after the forewarning materialized.

The parallel to the fourth century CE Christian story is striking indeed. It has been suggested that just as the monarchy saved ancient Israel from extinction by its surrounding enemies, so too imperial Constantine rescued Christianity by incorporating it into the empire. Less evident perhaps are the parallels to the Jewish precedent of the resulting stages—corruption, implosion, exile, and reconstitution as diaspora in Christian history. Yet parallels there are—corruption in medieval Christendom, revival, Reformation, disestablishment (exile), incomplete even to this day.

Diaspora, the scattering of Christians among polities otherwise grounded, is increasingly emergent in our day, at least in our Western world. Even so, the fantasy of Christendom as politically incorporate Christianity still lingers. Today when traveling between Harrisonburg, Virginia, and Washington, D.C., on Interstate 66, one passes a sign pointing to Christendom College at nearby Front Royal, Virginia. This Roman Catholic college was formed in 1977 to renew the Catholic presence in higher education, a presence seen by some Catholics to have been weakened by the Vatican II Council of the previous decade. I will return to these several ironies in part 4 of this volume below.

Our Premature Return from Japan

My original two-year assignment in Japan had been extended to five years. While that decision did not imply that we would remain in Japan indefinitely, it did put in question my future at Eastern Mennonite College. After all, I had taken only a two-year leave of absence from EMC. Meanwhile, a different question was beginning to churn in my spirit. Might the Anabaptist project require some wider perspectives for me, such as those that my earlier experiences in Europe, then in Asia, had begun to provide? And might those earlier experiences be at once a preparation and a calling for me to enter that wider task?

When rather abruptly we had to return to the United States before the end of our third year in Japan, such longer-range planning was put completely on hold. I was offered, again unforeseen, a one-year research and writing fellowship by the Institute of Mennonite Studies (IMS) at Elkhart, Indiana. While this might entail taking up residence at Elkhart, that was not mandatory. Place of residence depended on the outcome of the medical or psychiatric diagnosis of our daughter.

It now appeared sensible to return temporarily to our Harrisonburg home. From there we had access to medical consultancies in Washington, D.C. It soon became clear that we needed to move to D.C. for our daughter's treatment. By summer's end in 1960, some two months after our return from Japan, we made that move, initially to a Virginia suburb. The following summer (1961), we bought and moved into a house in northwest Washington proper. As it turned out, we remained at that address for more than twenty-five years.

A Transitional Assignment

From the Institute of Mennonite Studies, I received two study and writing assignments. The first, on urban church extension, carried a seven-month deadline. The second, on challenges in our welfare society, was to be completed in five months. Either might well have filled the whole year or indeed a lifetime! But the two topics overlapped and for me were mutually enriching. Both included visiting, interviewing, and reading. Occasionally I needed to touch base at Elkhart. Relations to the institute through its director, Cornelius J. Dyck, were cordial and supportive. We lived about a mile from Wesley Theological Seminary (Methodist) in northwest Washington, where I had ready access to the library, librarians, and faculty. To them I am deeply indebted.

In connection with the social work and welfare assignment, I had occasion to contact the Catholic University of America (CUA), located across town in the northeast sector of the city. That university maintains an important School of Social Work, where I consulted the director and the library. This was shortly before the famed Vatican II Council that updated the Catholic Church during the mid-1960s. Since the Counter-Reformation of the sixteenth century, the Vatican had maintained an Index of Forbidden Books—forbidden, that is, to the Catholic reader. This list was updated several times over the centuries, most notably in 1864. Books on that list arriving in Mullen Library at CUA were kept in a locked iron cage on the third floor. By special permission I was able to obtain several volumes from that Index for my use in their library.

I mention this as a reminder of the legacy of a history less remote in time than we might think. This anecdote also has special meaning for me personally. As I made these few gingerly contacts at Catholic University, it would have been inconceivable to me that I would be employed there five years later. But thanks to the Vatican II Council, that cage of forbidden books soon disappeared from the library, as did the structures of the university that would have prohibited my employment in the social sciences—"sectarian" that I was and am!

Meanwhile, early in my IMS year came a real diversion, an invitation for a Church Peace Mission (CPM) assignment. Eventually an agreement emerged that I would combine the two assignments, IMS and CPM, each on a half-time basis, until the IMS commitment was completed. Though complicated, that arrangement yielded a cross-fertilizing bonus for me. By 1963 the institute published my 113-page report on my city assignment as a paperback, *The Church in the City* (number 2 in a new IMS booklet series). A shorter essay on social welfare, *Who Is My Neighbor? Christian Compassion in the Welfare Society*, was released as number 4 in the series.

Today these publications serve chiefly as period documents. Both studies struggled with the tension between the particularities of our centuries-old Anabaptist faith tradition and the gospel in modern urban settings. Here two brief quotes from the respective final chapters must suffice. From the urban study, under the subhead, "The Tension of Redemption":

> The vigor of Anabaptism lay, not as its enemies or its adherents in later quiescent periods supposed, in the withdrawal from the world, but in a radical acceptance of the thrust of redemption as reordering the total existence in the world. (p. 98)

And from the social work study, the final lines:

> Dietrich Bonhoeffer eloquently stated the task of every Christian and of every Christian social worker when he wrote, "The task of preparing the way . . . is . . . a charge of immense responsibility. . . . [If] a hungry man does not attain to faith, then the guilt falls on those who refused him bread. To provide the hungry man with bread is to prepare the way for the coming of grace." (p. 44)

The IMS interlude immersed me once more, in specialized ways, in the grandeur and the misery of my own Anabaptist believers church tradition. And by virtue of this I was about to be plunged into an intense engagement with the grandeur and the misery of Christendom, against which my own tradition defines itself.

JOUSTING WITH THE SPELL OF CHRISTENDOM

For more than a millennium in European history, Christianity as religion had been joined tumultuously to political rule. No such merger is foreseen in the New Testament gospel. But neither was monarchy intrinsic in the Mosaic covenant. In the Christ event, full realization will come only in the end (the *eschaton*). Instead, following the adoption of Christianity as imperial religion in the fourth century, justification for politically established Christianity was theologically brokered. And just as in the precedent of the royal period in ancient Israel, spiritual implosion within Christendom resulted. Nonetheless, the fact that "all things work together for good for those who love God" (Rom. 8:28) hardly authorizes such counterfeits!

Eventually in the fifteenth and sixteenth centuries came the Renaissance and the Reformation. But efforts at reform, however effective, resulted instead in a double schism—one with the Roman hierarchy whose domain was to have been reformed and the other ironically, as unrest loomed, by invoking political power to enforce reform. Thus political power was employed to suppress the believers church vision to which the reform had given rise in the first place. By this reversal, the Reformation effectively leaped from the boiling pot into the fire. Whereas linkage to empire faintly echoed the universality of the gospel, linkage to the warring nation states that emerged along with the Reformation became wholly contradictory. How can people who claim to follow Jesus the Christ kill each other by virtue of opposing political claims?

Eventually, by our twentieth century, a softening on both fronts was underway—state church versus believers church—especially in the United States. Retrospectively, one might say, history was moving toward the separation of church and state that in the Reformation era was violated anew.

This softening was exemplified in the mid-century Puidoux conference series in Europe and in the just-noted Church Peace Mission in the United States. Indeed, whereas in Europe external traces of state churchdom linger even today, in the United States church and state were constitutionally separate almost from the outset. On the one hand, the Puidoux and the CPM conversations exemplified the softening of the line between politically established and "free" churches. But on the other hand, they revealed that the establishment consciousness of the Christendom legacy remains too deeply ingrained in our consciousness to yield to mere academic or theological argument. Coming to terms with that legacy remains a challenge in this new millennium.

CPM, as noted above in chapter 4, sprang from a postwar national conference of representatives from Protestant denominational peace societies and the historic peace churches held in Detroit in the fall of 1950. Sensing the possible timeliness of a peacemaking mission to the churches, the conference appointed A. J. Muste, the executive of the Fellowship of Reconciliation (FOR), as missioner. Quickly, over the next year, regional conferences were held in a dozen cities. While peace church representatives participated actively, the brunt of the effort was carried by clergy, scholars, and activists from the mainline denominations whose constituencies were being addressed.

After the initial campaign, a decision was reached to continue two more years. An office was opened in New York City with Martin England as director. From 1953 to 1961, J. Harold Sherk, an official at the National Service Board for Religious Objectors, in Washington, D.C., served as secretary. A. J. Muste remained for a time as missioner. Various activities—conferences, educational initiatives, literature production, and distribution—continued.

Three major national and/or international troubles churned during the 1960s: the Cold War/nuclear arms race, the war in Vietnam, and the civil rights struggle in the United States. Beyond these, the aftermaths of World War II and the Korean War of the early 1950s still ricocheted. Numerous academic and public debates grappled with these complex issues intersecting with the CPM agenda. Particularly heated was a rising convergence between public criticism of United States enmeshment in the Vietnam War and the civil rights ferment. While these were separate problems, and in the early stages Martin Luther King Jr., the symbolic leader of the latter movement, kept his distance from the former, the prevalence of nonviolent protest eventually became mutually reinforcing for both movements.

Initially in early 1961, I had been asked by CPM to take a six-month assignment as organizing secretary for another in the series of national conferences begun during the previous decade (see above, chapter 4). Presumably my peace church legacy, my previous CPM participation, and my education and international experiences in both Europe and Asia provided the necessary qualification. But lack of direct acquaintance with the American church and seminary scenes, both historical and contemporary, was a handicap.

Despite this limitation, I accepted the invitation. But after working at the assignment for some months, I reported to the executive body of CPM that I did not find sufficient grounds in preexisting activity for convening such a conference. Whether that conclusion reflected actual conditions or just my inadequacy may never be clear. In any case, the CPM executive committee accepted my recommendation. They then redefined my task and invited me to accept a new three-year assignment as executive secretary of the CPM program.

The Church Peace Mission met annually. It consisted of a national board appointed by Protestant peace groups and by peace churches. A small executive committee met quarterly or as needed. I was directly dependent upon and accountable to the executive officers. Professor John Oliver Nelson of Yale University Divinity School served as president. Herman Will, a legal scholar on the Methodist Board of Christian Social Concern in Washington, was secretary. Regarding both program and logistics, I was in constant contact with both. Wilson Ames, a member of the Episcopal Peace Fellowship, served as treasurer from his Rhode Island location.

The task now was a focused conversation in the ecumenical scholarly community between pacifist and just war polarities in Christian thought and practice. An additional catalyst was the parallel series of Puidoux conferences (named after the Swiss village where the first conference in the series was held) in Europe during the 1950s and 1960s, to which I had indirectly related. The files for the entire CPM history (1950-1967) are archived in the Swarthmore (Pennsylvania) College Peace Collection. A summary introduction to this collection cites my formulation of my new assignment as being

> to probe at the frontiers of the churches' concerns with international questions. The technique [used] is conferences or seminars involving social scientists and theologians in dialogue, the former to elucidate social realities, the latter to speak to them in terms of their own disciplines.

A Focus on Biblical Theology?

But now the problem for me personally was, Where were we (CPM) heading? What were we trying to accomplish? And how could we, how could I, begin? We had as resource the decade-long experience of CPM to the churches generally. Now, however, we were to focus more narrowly on theological professionals—on the theological rationale that undergirded the support of wars waged by the regimes under whom Christians lived, in contrast to the gospel of peace. We were painfully conscious that World War II, though global in scope, originated among the nations comprising Christendom!

A suggestion came from an Old Testament scholar that the emerging specialty of biblical theology might well provide an opening for a new conversation about peace among scholars. That suggestion resonated with my experience, though I had no special skills in that regard. I decided to begin accordingly.

But at first blush, why "biblical" theology? Isn't all Christian theology biblical? Well, yes and no! The remarkable advances in science, technology, and social Darwinism in the nineteenth century heavily impacted religious thought and practice. A strong tendency emerged to equate Christian idealism and social progress. Christianity in many respects had been reduced increasingly to civilization. Second thoughts regarding such optimism followed the catastrophes of World War I. The biblical story, though calling for social change, is something radically other than humanly engineered civilized progress.

Thus (as briefly noted in chapter 4), a current of thought emerged that was widely known and espoused as neoorthodoxy. The publication of Swiss German theologian Karl Barth's book on the epistle to the Romans in 1918 (English translation, 1922) is widely viewed as the beginning of this renewal. By mid-century this resulted in a reorientation to the Bible known as "biblical theology" or "biblical realism." According to *The Oxford Companion to the Bible* (1993), in medieval and scholastic theology the "task of biblical theology [was] to provide the proof texts for the support of the dogmas of the church." The alternative (presumably "biblical theology) it says is to "try to let the Bible set the issues and determine the method." Effectively this means that God's action in history is the primary medium in revelation, as *The Oxford Dictionary of the Christian Church* (1997) understands it. Hence God's unique saving action, culminating in the Christ event, is communicated in the biblical story. This is seen as transcending appeals to mere human nature or reason that had long replaced the radical otherness of the "God who acts" (Wright) "vertically from above" (Barth).

So How Do We Begin?

In spring 1961, I drove from Washington, D.C., to Boston to begin exploratory conversations at a string of East Coast mainline Protestant seminaries. I had begun a list of scholars who were conversant in the biblical realism movement. Starting at Harvard, I then moved south through Brown, Yale, Union in New York, Princeton, and Eastern Baptist. Having mostly worked and studied abroad and in any case not being a full-fledged theologian, I was not only "sectarian" but a naïve outsider as well. One of my ploys was to ask, "After theologian/churchman Reinhold Niebuhr's defense of World War II, now what?" To this a professor at Yale Divinity School replied, "After Niebuhr, where do you want to go?"

Nonetheless, that humbling trip became a milestone in my life. Building on the contacts begun on that tour, by the following spring (1962) CPM sponsored a gathering of about two dozen scholars at a small rural center in Washington's Virginia suburbs. A number of papers were distributed among the participants in advance. A year later these edited papers were published as *Biblical Realism Confronts the Nation: Ten Christian Scholars Summon the Church to the Discipleship of Peace* (Fellowship Publications in association with CPM). Writers included scholars such as Norman Gottwald (then from Andover Newton); Otto Piper (Princeton); Krister Stendahl (Harvard), some at the peak of their careers, others younger.

The introduction to that volume asserts that in the churches of America the Christian ethical imperative has been so fully assimilated to the national ethos that the majority of church people can scarcely distinguish between the two. The concluding summary, drawing on citations from the contributors, observed that Christians cannot expect non-Christians to see the same reality that Christians see in the work of God unless they "become part of the redemptive center, the church" (Gottwald). To move directly into the political arena with the ethical demands of the gospel is to pay too little tribute to God's sustaining work in the world apart from the church, just as it is also to depreciate his high redemptive activity. One must distinguish between Christ's lordship and his victory. The locus of the victory, contrary to the lordship, is not "the cosmos in general," thus also the political powers, but rather the church. "The powers, sin, and death are defeated in relation to those who believe in what was manifest by God's act in Christ" (Morrison).

This book brought little response. It was published outside regular academic circles yet not addressed to the lay public. Nonetheless, it became the frame of reference for the five years of CPM work that followed.

In April 1963, we held a conference at Oberlin College, Ohio, on "Church and Nation-State in the East-West Conflict." In August came a two-day gathering of evangelical scholars at Winona Lake, Indiana, on "The Evangelical Christian and War." Incidentally, during a break in that conference, we watched and heard Martin Luther King Jr.'s "I Have a Dream" speech live from the Lincoln Memorial on TV. In October, two months later, Wesley Theological Seminary (Washington, D.C.) and CPM cosponsored a one-day conference featuring Krister Stendahl from Harvard Divinity School. This event, focusing on the use of the Bible in world affairs, was attended by about twenty-five Protestant and Catholic theologians.

From December 9 to 12, 1963, CPM convened some thirty churchmen and civil rights leaders at In-the-Oaks Episcopal Center, Black Mountain, North Carolina. This "Revolution, Nonviolence, and the Church" meeting was chaired jointly by CPM President John Oliver Nelson from Yale Divinity School and Andrew Young, program director of the Southern Christian Leadership Conference in Atlanta, Georgia. Major addresses were given by Charles Lawrence, a Brooklyn College sociologist; C. T. Vivian, a minister and staff member of the Christian Leadership Conference; and Everett Tilson, biblical scholar at the Methodist Theological School in Ohio. They dealt with issues arising at the interface between the churches and the civil rights movement. The purpose was to cross-fertilize the nonviolent experience in international relations and the civil rights movement domestically. Several months later I reported on this conference in an article published in *The Christian Century* (April 8, 1964), "Christian Obedience in a World We Don't Control."

From May 1963 to September-October 1966, we published a one-sheet newsletter, *War-Nation-Church-Paragraphs from the Church Peace Mission,* mailed from our Washington office. This provided a communication channel for reports on CPM or related events, brief discussion of appropriate topics, announcements, and comments. A total of thirty-three issues appeared.

Increasingly, after prolonged organizing work, I sensed the need for more guidance than the scattered executive committee could provide. Eventually they approved and financed a Committee on Issues and Direction to meet with me twice yearly for two days or a weekend. Their task was to help me identify the issues we would address and then determine the direction our CPM program should take. To form that committee, we drew on the informal pool of scholars and/or church leaders, pacifist and nonpacifist, Protestant and Catholic, touched by our previous work. This committee quickly became an invaluable resource to me as organizing secretary. By late 1966 the way was clearing at last for my return to academia, this time to a graduate research institution. The Church Peace Mission, informed of this well in advance, was facing uncertainty of its own. These conjoint developments led to a final issue of the newsletter which included the following update:

> At its annual meeting, the CPM looked at its role amid new movements and set up an eight-man committee to recommend a changed future shaped by (1) its growing concentration on theological exploration and change as the main CPM vocation in the churches; (2) the National Council of Churches' high-priority commission on peace and world affairs starting out under Robert S. Bilheimer's leadership; (3) a theological committee of the [Prague-based] Christian Peace Conference set up last spring; (4) continuing life in the Inter-Religious Conference on Peace following its Protestant-Catholic-Jewish event last spring; and (5) questioning by our sponsor groups of CPM structure and importance for any work beyond that of CPM's lively and rather historic Committee on Issues and Direction, which goes on with steady strength.

Three announcements also appeared in this issue—first, that a Committee on the Future of CPM was being formed (as noted above), scheduled to meet in early October 1966; second, that the Committee on Issues and Direction was to meet December 9-11; and, third, the chairman, John Oliver Nelson, reported that I (the executive) hoped "in the foreseeable future, to return to an academic post, and continue to serve as secretary of the CPM's Issues and Direction Group."

By year's end, Church Peace Mission decided to discontinue, while the Committee on Issues and Direction would continue independently. That committee renamed itself the War-Nation-Church Study Group (title taken over from the now-defunct CPM newsletter), and moved to recruit additional members. With a membership of about fifteen, that group met annually for the next twenty years (1967-1987). Membership was a commitment to an ongoing and mutually respectful conversation between academic and other professionals from the two traditions in the American churches, the just war majority and the pacifist minority.

Included among members were a number of highly visible figures in the academic and/or faith communities. The discussions were off the record, with benefits flowing into the life and career of the participants. The meetings usually ran from a Friday evening through Sunday noon, often with an outside guest speaker on a designated topic on Saturday morning. In the course of the weekend, each colleague present was given the opportunity to report on theme-related activities during the previous year. In a notable instance, a staff adviser to the U.S. Conference of Catholic Bishops was asked by the bishops to prepare a working draft of a paper they would eventually publish as a church policy statement. In a regular meeting of our study group, he floated ideas that eventually appeared in the document the bishops issued.

PEACEMAKING: A PERSONAL DILEMMA

As organizing secretary of the War-Nation-Church Study Group, I took and preserved extensive notes of all these meetings. Since the Church Peace Mission no longer existed, these records are not included in the CPM collection at Swarthmore. Instead I retained them among my personal papers, now deposited in the archives of the Menno Simons Historical Library at Eastern Mennonite University. To conclude this Church Peace Mission chapter, I can do no better than to reproduce here my concluding words to that agency in the final number of the *War-Nation-Church Letter:*

> A "peace church" heritage, more than seven years of work and study in immediate postwar Europe, a professional concern with societal issues—these were the principal factors that aroused in me a strong interest in the recovery of the church's long lost peace witness. One involvement led to another, including eventually a three-year peace assignment with the Mennonite Central Committee in Japan. Eventually a chain of circumstances brought me to Washington—and into the orbit of the Church Peace Mission.
>
> The CPM task has been far greater than its slender resources. As an informal and ecumenical grouping of views and societies, it embraced fruitful polarities in flexible tension. But if thus it is spared many common bureaucratic ills, the CPM has scarcely the strength of initiative that today's situation demands. The impact of contemporary events rapidly brings any vestigial wall of Christendom tumbling down. But what of

building anew? How will the lines of affirmative witness be traced anew in a pluralistic world where all "churches" are "sects?" Will this take place imperceptibly on dispersed fronts—like scattered monasteries in early medieval Europe? Could an energetic ecumenical forum or institute—perhaps a greatly enhanced CPM—help? No doubt both will be needed. Yet the plight of the churches is such that the "breakthrough," if any, will have to come from below, from "non-professional" levels of life and work. It is these tasks which now beckon. Yet I leave CPM reluctantly, and hope to participate further in its work, though less directly. I here salute my colleagues, notably the chairman, John Oliver Nelson, who have helped to make this work a rewarding experience.

A Concluding Note

The Church Peace Mission chapter in my life ended as it began—totally unexpectedly, a gift. Any attempt here to assess those years at this stage would be presumptuous. The CPM as such was but a phase of remarkable ecumenical changes under way in twentieth-century Christendom. While the legacy of Christendom—Christianity viewed as civilization—still lingers, the mood in that order shifted fundamentally during the past century. Christianity is now viewed more than before as peacemaking, as healing among the nations. And while this does not yet mean the triumph of pacifism, the authenticity of such a witness is being acknowledged, however vaguely, to unprecedented degrees by both churches and states.

As I will spell out more fully in part 4 below, these CPM years confirmed my eventual conclusion that the roots of the just war versus pacifist disagreement lay deeper than these contradictory reasonings.

Meanwhile, I conclude this chapter with another anecdote. During the war and the early postwar years I had a few brief contacts with General Lewis B. Hershey, the director of the federal Selective Service draft agency in Washington, D.C. I was privileged to escort him for part of two days on his visit of the first CO team permitted to perform alternative service abroad (in Germany!), a few years after war's end. Did the need for Selective Service to provide an alternate option for conscientious objectors seem bothersome to him? While I did not pose that question to him directly, the reply emerged indirectly. The answer between the lines seemed to be that sooner or later war will be eliminated. Today's COs may well be paving the way for that still remote outcome. Hence, accommodating the few who were prepared already to move in that direction appeared appropriate ultimately rather than merely disruptive today.

Chapter 8

A Midlife Fork in My Road

You'll probably die feeling defeated, but the trail is going to live. . . . Your experience, your background, is more important than your education.
—M. R. Zigler

Two roads diverged in a wood, and I—
I took the road less traveled by.
And that has made all the difference.
—Robert Frost

There is also the temptation to react to our fractured community by an inward trip to isolated individualism.
—Ralph Klein

On December 8, 1971, I attended the famous Amish education proceedings at the United States Supreme Court. With the hearing ended, I left. As I turned in the ticket for my topcoat at the cloakroom, M. R. Zigler, director of the Brethren Service Commission in Europe during the late 1940s and early 1950s, suddenly appeared at my elbow. While in Europe he had also been the contact person between the historic peace churches and the newly formed (1948) World Council of Churches. During my brief involvement in that dialogue (chapters 4 and 5), though Zigler was from an older generation, he and I became friends. In later years, while residing in Washington, D.C., I dropped in occasionally on events at the Brethren Service headquarters in New Windsor, Maryland, including the meeting in which he was welcomed back.

Meanwhile much had happened, and I was already several years into my career at Catholic University of America. Meeting at the Supreme Court for the first time since my 1967 appointment at CUA,

Zigler kidded me for taking that job. ("Peachey, what are you doing at Catholic University?") But quickly he affirmed my being there. ("I follow you—I know what you're doing.") Then he offered the encouraging epigraph following the chapter title above. Though I was heartened by his comments, I was also amazed. How did he arrive at such a reading of my situation, and such prescience, if indeed it was that?

Now more than thirty years later, I am even more intrigued by Zigler's comment. By the time of our D.C. encounter, Ziegler was retired. But back in the late 1940s and early 1950s he was an activist pastor administering a denomination-sponsored material aid program in postwar Europe. His denomination (Church of the Brethren) joined the newly formed (1948) World Council of Churches (WCC), based in Geneva, Switzerland. The WCC, though an organizational endeavor, was a creedal and scholarly effort. Zigler was an activist who left scholarly tasks to others.

A major concern in that global gathering of mainline Protestant and Eastern Orthodox representatives when the WCC began was the scandal of those church bodies being divided at the Lord's table. Though not involved in those proceedings myself, I recall vividly the stories of Zigler needling these ecumenists during those beginning years. "Don't worry so much about being divided at the Lord's table," he told them. "First you just have to stop shooting each other!" After all, both world wars began between "Christian" nations!

THE SCHOOL OF HARD KNOCKS

Why was I no longer at Eastern Mennonite College, for which I had trained and where expected to invest my life? How did I, while remaining a committed Anabaptist, come to work instead at the Catholic University of America in Washington, D.C.? What was the process whereby this costly and painful midlife shift emerged for me during the 1957-1967 decade? And what was the nature and outcome of that shift? The above anecdote at the Supreme Court suggests the nature and implications of that change. Zigler was not directly involved in that process, though his comments grew out of a worldview and experience similar to mine.

I mentioned early in this book that my autobiographical reflections are informed by Gerard Loughlin's realistic narrative imagery. By that term, Loughlin describes a manner of storytelling in which character and circumstance are so related that one's story cannot be known or portrayed otherwise.

So now came this spur-of-the-moment reencounter with Zigler at the Supreme Court in 1971 twenty years after our brief collaboration in Europe. Zigler was retired. I was in the prime of life, now working as a sociologist in a seemingly incongruous setting. Off the cuff, he remarked, "Your experience, your background, is more important than your education!" And he saw this as exemplified by my having become a professor at the Catholic University of America.

Did he mean this as a put-down? No. He recognized this development as realistic narrative, though this term is my borrowed term, not his! In commenting thus on my improbable employment at Catholic University, Zigler put hands and feet on Loughlin's abstract formula. He observed that the school of hard knocks more than academic wisdom had put me there.

My Unfolding Life

From my first-ever bus trip to the Young Peoples' Institute at Eastern Mennonite School outside Harrisonburg, Virginia, in August 1940, until I set sail for Japan with my family in September 1957, my life had unfolded coherently step-by-step. Oh, there were times of uncertainty and difficulties to surmount, but resolution followed in orderly sequence. My doctoral studies emerged from previous experiences and education at home in the United States, then more directly from my years of work and study in postwar Europe (1946-1953). By the time I began work on my dissertation, my appointment to the Eastern Mennonite College faculty was already in prospect.

But rather abruptly, four years later, by the time of our departure to Japan in late summer 1957 under the Peace Section of the Mennonite Central Committee, clouds of doubt were gathering around the track I was on. The detour to Japan as such was neither the problem nor the solution. Considering the peace questions that had arisen (chapter 4), a two-year leave of absence for a special assignment in Japan was fitting. The sally into the Orient (chapter 6) was a useful interlude.

But doubt had arisen regarding my *Concern*-related initiatives at both EMC and in its church constituency. They were working on one level. As was becoming increasingly evident, my Concern colleagues and I were working on another. Given what I had learned in the course of the previous decade, 1946-1956, might I not contribute more by further and deeper explorations elsewhere in wider contexts? A comparison of these two levels appeared to be called for.

The Two Differing Levels

Mennonites, along with Amish and Hutterites, appear among the many Christian splinter groups that found haven in the New World. As descendants of the sixteenth-century Anabaptists, however, they bore the classic sectarian onus placed upon them by the dominant Christendom that they had challenged. Politically, (adult) believer's (re)baptism was considered a criminal violation of law, and religiously a violation of churchly sacrament, hence blasphemous. For guards carrying out court sentences on sixteenth-century Anabaptists, I learned incidentally during my dissertation research, escorting such "subhuman" specimens to their sites of execution at times became sporting events.

The acculturation of European immigrants into the United States has been described as a three-generation process. Marcus Hansen, an early twentieth-century Scandinavian immigration historian, coined what came to be known as "Hansen's Law." He observed that what the second generation wants to forget, the third generation seeks to remember. Only after immigrants have been fully Americanized are their descendants likely to develop curiosity about the cultural past that their second-generation ancestors tried hard to shake off to become fully American.

In some cases, Mennonites among them, the assimilation process was further drawn out because their ancestors had left Europe to escape religious persecution. Under such circumstances, loosening the tie between faith and culture sufficiently to permit acculturation while retaining the faith frequently took additional time. For the Amish and the Hutterites, the process stretched out indefinitely. By the mid-twentieth century, the cultural assimilation of Mennonites into the American life was reaching full stream.

Lifestyles, as aspects of human demeanor, are always more or less time-and-place specific. Modes of dress are an important feature. Costumes may differentiate status or roles within cultures, such as uniforms worn by police or clergy. And modes of dress also serve more broadly in class and other social distinctions. Both extravagance and immodesty in dress have often been criticized in the course of Christian history, illustrating the tensions implicit in the "in but not of the world" conundrum in the Christian story.

It is hardly surprising, then, that as older cultural markers of Mennonite identity dissolved, attention would turn to dress as possible replacement. Uniformity of dress, however, was not part of Anabaptist belief and practice originally. In fact, the notion of uniformity adopted by some Mennonites is said to have been "imported" from a Holiness movement around the dawn of the twentieth century. In any case, the adoption and enforcement of that solution was linked to another more basic modification underway. This involved the incremental development of denominational organization and authority, along with professionalization of the ministry.

Church leaders during the 1950s at EMC and its sponsoring churches had to walk a tightrope. As the older external markers evaporated, how was this faith tradition to be perpetuated?

Founding church-sponsored schools, high schools, and even colleges, offered a bulwark in the minds of some. Others saw higher education itself as encouraging the assimilative influences they meant to evade. In effect, there were inconsistent contradictions. How can some forms of acculturation be invoked to avoid others? How can inconsistency be avoided?

One "absolute" that set Anabaptists apart clearly stood out—refusal to bear arms, or nonresistance as it came to be called, along with avoidance of legal and political action. After all, justification of war ranked high among the errors of Christendom against which Anabaptism had arisen in the first place. But Anabaptists withdrew as well from other "worldly" practices that flourished in such a society. Avoidances of the many immoralities in society gave rise to the concept of nonconformity. In some circles nonconformity and nonresistance were now put forward as markers between the church and the world, with the former serving to maintain the latter! Only if nurtured by a separate lifestyle, some thought, would the young have the inner strength needed to resist the call to arms, an argument with a degree of validity.

The Beginning of My Life-Course Change

At this juncture of the "realistic narrative" of my life, three circumstances converged: Mennonite acculturation to American society, the generational crisis of the 1950s evident in the Concern story (see chapter 3). and my personal dilemmas. My task here is to describe, not to defend. In any event, the Concern episode exemplifies Loughlin's formulation that personal character can be viewed interactively as cause and effect. Circumstance is the condition without which character could not be formed, yet only in that conditioning does it become fully circumstantial. But before tracing my interactive character-change, further comment on my circumstance is needed.

Paul Mininger, president of Goshen College in the 1950s, seemingly the most responsive of the leaders of his generation to the Concern initiative, saw it as a generational phenomenon. No doubt generational difference was a more important dimension than we realized. At the same time, our group did not agree on a particular formula or course of action. As our varied lives demonstrate, we each continued on our separate ways. Yet together we had shifted to a different level of praxis. While the prevailing understanding of our peoplehood focused on the externals of our Anabaptist identity, the Concern group probed the deeper roots and dynamics of our faith tradition.

As sketched in chapter 4, in summer 1957, institutional leaders from EMC, Goshen College, and the Mennonite publishing establishment at Scottdale, Pennsylvania, met with several members of the 1952 Amsterdam Concern group in a day-long conference at Cumberland, Maryland. They hoped to temper the malaise arising from our initiatives. The encounter itself was cordial, but the Concern agenda went beyond the reach of such a meeting. Though some matters were clarified, the deeper issues remained. Yet even that disappointing outcome became for me a step forward. It increased my awareness that the leaders were working sincerely within the frames of reference that confronted them. These could not easily be changed, nor were we in the Concern group able to offer immediate alternatives.

Instead of resolution, the Cumberland meeting became for me a major impetus to step outside the denominational structures, to take "a road less traveled." I hoped thereby to gain deeper understandings, even as I remained rooted in and was propelled by our Anabaptist tradition. I saw that the cultural packaging of boundary definitions of our Anabaptist-Mennonite faith communities was leading to wheel-spinning and fragmentation. Only later would I come to see this attempt at cultural packaging of the faith as an instance of the idolatry so relentlessly exposed in the biblical story. In this respect, between the Cumberland meeting in summer 1957 and our departure to Japan at summer's end, an even more traumatic problem emerged.

My Earlier Stint as a "Lay Minister"

As detailed in chapter 3, partly at my initiative Mennonite Central Committee (MCC), under whom I was serving in postwar Germany, established a small center in Frankfurt/Main in the American Zone to help with social and spiritual renewal. This required assisting or sponsoring voluntary reconstruction efforts, student exchanges, fraternal meetings among churches leaders and the like, along with continuing limited relief services.

MCC executive Orie Miller recommended that, considering these responsibilities, I should be ordained as a minister. He felt that this would enhance my ability to function effectively in the many important interchurch dimensions of this project. At that stage I understood my ordination in lay ministry terms, definitely not as an occupational profession. I assumed that I would continue my lay occupation in earning a living. What I did not yet sense was the degree to which the proposed ordination differed from the congregational emergence of the lay ministry in our Anabaptist tradition. Ellen and I were members in a congregation in the Virginia Mennonite Conference, under which church jurisdiction this ordination would occur. (See chapter 3 for details of the ordination service in Frankfurt.)

At only thirty years of age, I was inclined to follow church leaders' directives. Thus I accepted ordination, although I still thought of ministry in lay terms. After our Concern group initiatives, some discomfort developed among church leaders around that venture. In 1957, five years after our original Amsterdam Concern gathering, when I accepted the MCC Peace Section appointment to Japan, I experienced that discomfort firsthand from the conference official I contacted about our transition to Japan. I reported to him that Ellen and I would take our congregational membership along to the Mennonite congregation in Tokyo. When I asked what to do about my ministerial status, he immediately advised me to take my ordination certificate along as well. Was he perhaps happy for me to exit the scene in light of the just-noted ferment? I will never know.

When nearly three years later we returned unexpectedly to Virginia, we brought our congregational membership along back from Tokyo but left the ministerial certificate behind. That document had been formally useless, since the Tokyo congregation had not yet become independent from its missionary initiation. My ordination certificate may still lie somewhere in a musty missionary file in Tokyo! As it turned out, soon after our return we moved to Washington, D.C., for our daughter's therapy. Thereupon we transferred our membership from the Tokyo to the Hyattsville Mennonite congregation. Thereby we moved out of the Virginia district.

Meanwhile, however, during the 1950s, the Mennonite ministry was moving rapidly toward professionalization. I was not prepared to make this transition myself. My direct study of the Anabaptist movement's original sixteenth-century documents, beginning about two years after my ordination in Karlsruhe, Germany, confirmed my own sense of ministry as a lay vocation, not as a marketable profession. Since in any case differing districts were involved, I decided that the best procedure for me after several years in Japan was simply to bow out of the ministry, no ritual being available for doing so. To this day, I live with the awkwardness and pain of that solution.

Remaining Inside, Stepping Outside

In the course of my transitional decade, 1957-1967, in important respects this ministerial episode was my most traumatic experience. In the fall of 1957, as noted earlier, I left my position at Eastern Mennonite College. Then in 1967, a decade later, I received an appointment at the Catholic University of America (CUA) in Washington, D.C, despite my Anabaptist identity. I am indebted to Vatican II for creating the space that inadvertently made my appointment possible!

For several years early in the decade I had served under MCC in Japan (chapter 6), then for the equivalent of another year under the Institute of Mennonite Studies at Elkhart, Indiana (chapter 7). My assignment during the remainder of that decade, chiefly with the Church Peace Mission (also chapter 7), became my first real exposure to mainline American Protestantism.

As one might expect, there were upsides and downsides to the two decades I was privileged to spend at Catholic University until my retirement in 1987. Though as a Mennonite I remained a "resident alien," the years I served as a professor at CUA were happy and fulfilling. To be sure, there were limitations in my abilities and training as well as disadvantages in being an alien. Salaries were comparatively low as the university was moving from clerical to lay status, but my wife (third and fourth undergraduate years) and children received free college tuition.

Meanwhile, given my involvement with Christians Associated for Relations with Eastern Europe, an ecumenical agency of which I was a charter member, the international orientation of Catholic University was congenial. And as I was able eventually to collaborate with the Council for Research in Philosophy and Values, independently located at CUA, my horizons were further widened. With Ellen completing her undergraduate education there and participating in a short-lived faculty wives club, and with several children in graduate and undergraduate studies, Washington, D.C., and the Catholic University of America became our home for more than twenty-five years.

"WE WALK BY FAITH, NOT BY SIGHT"

The transitional decade between our 1957 departure for Japan under MCC—from our presumably permanent new home in Harrisonburg, Virginia, and at last in 1967 the beginning of a settled career at CUA—was at once agonizing and mystifying. The university is located a mile north and slightly to the east of the nation's capital. We lived some six or seven miles to the west, off Wisconsin Avenue, from 1961 to 1987. There, already before my employment by CUA, we had purchased an older two-story frame house with a basement and attic. Though begun as a suburb early in the twentieth century, by then that area was well incorporated into the city. Bus commuting between our home and the university was possible after a brisk ten-minute walk, and later by subway on a longer route through downtown. For personal reasons, I often commuted by car.

The turning point on the journey that took me to CUA happened already in 1964. This is explained in chapter 9, where I describe a church-persons' traveling seminar to Europe. Ripples of the 1957-1967 decade continued to baffle and enrich me during the years that followed. Though I could neither foresee nor predetermine the outcome, the uncertainty about where to look that shaped the previous decade had been surmounted. In times of overwhelming uncertainty, we wistfully long for resolution. But would we humans be happier if we foreknew every outcome? Would not such foreknowledge fundamentally alter our humanity—for the worse?

THE HIPPOCRATIC OATH

It is important to be forthright about the circumstances of my midlife crisis and course change. Because I sensed the issues to be fundamental rather than merely personal, accommodation to the lifestyle regimen of the denomination enforced at the Eastern Mennonite College, though surely possible, to me appeared inappropriate. Yet to choose another course, under the circumstances, meant to act by faith rather than by sight (2 Cor. 5:7).

Somehow I had become aware of the Hippocratic Oath, important to the medical profession. Before physically engaging a patient, the physician is to be certain the intervention will do no harm. My decision to step outside the Mennonite denominational enterprise was not a response to a more attractive offer elsewhere. Rather I chose this change of direction on the premise that first of all I should do no harm.

If something constructive resulted, this would become evident in due time. That decision came before any awareness of the events that would follow (as described in chapter 9). In spring 1964, I accepted the invitation to colead a church-persons' tour to Europe, primarily the Soviet bloc, with the approval of the Church Peace Mission, under which I was serving at the time. In doing so, I had no inkling that the seeds of my future employment at the Catholic University of America, and useful ongoing involvements in bridge-building efforts between the United States and the Soviet world, would unfold in the course of the next three decades.

Lessons of the 1957-1967 Decade

We exist humanly as molecules in a compound. Neither molecule nor compound exists without the other. Remarkably, in humans this situation transcends generations. It was implicit in Robert Zigler's comment to me at the Supreme Court cloakroom on December 8, 1971. My job decision was a mere echo of the dramatic archetype in the biblical accounts of Abraham and Moses. Both were called indelibly to begin a venture that in the end could not be realized in their own lifetime. This conundrum is captured dramatically in the previous subheading, "We walk by faith, not by sight."

As humans we are at once fully free and independent, yet totally interdependent. This mystery is well-captured by Paul in his letter to the small band of Christians in Corinth that emerged from his brief time with them: "What do you have that you did not receive? And if you received it, why do you boast as if were not a gift" (1 Cor. 4:7)? Abraham and Moses themselves did not get to enter the Promised Land their ministry proclaimed. (Nor, perhaps, do we.) Ponder what is said in Hebrews 11 regarding the celebrated cloud of witnesses:

> Yet all these, though they were commended for their faith, did not receive what was promised, since God had provided something better so that they would not, apart from us, be made perfect. (vv. 39-40)

What would happen if Christians today, individually and as church groups, understood and appropriated the penetrating message in these passages?

"The Road Not Taken"

Robert Frost (1874-1963) in late midlife wrote the four-stanza poem with the above title. I don't know when I was first alerted to his poetry, but certainly by early midlife. A phrase in the last stanza is widely quoted: "I took the one [road] less traveled by, and that has made all the difference." Why? May it be that "the road not taken" is more harsh than the one that is simply "less traveled"? Perhaps most of our choices have to do with *more/less* rather than with *either/or*? What if I had chosen *an* or *the* alternative that indeed would have been possible—simply conforming to the EMC context that inevitably would and did change—while abandoning further explorations otherwise?

Invoking the Hippocratic maxim, first to do no harm by stepping outside the institutionalizing of the Anabaptist Vision underway in the mid-twentieth century, I left open the question of what might be learned as a result of that decision.

I had no inkling, of course, that half a century later—there were occasional visits meanwhile—I would return to Harrisonburg. The Virginia Mennonite Retirement Community (VMRC), to which Ellen and I were privileged to be admitted in November 2001, is located next door to the EMS of the 1940s that has meanwhile become Eastern Mennonite University (EMU) and Eastern Mennonite Seminary (EMS). VMRC is a community of more than seven hundred residents, ranging from cottage living through condo's, assisted living to intensive care, most of whom are not Mennonites. The city meanwhile has grown rapidly, as has its largest "industry," James Madison University, a state institution located across town.

The Harrisonburg/Rockingham County "metropolis" is large enough to afford the globalizing complexity of modernity yet small enough to offer more personal intimacy than New York or Chicago. When we arrived here, an Anabaptist Center for Religion and Society (ACRS) was already in the making, independently formed by academic retirees from a variety of disciplines. EMU maintains a historical library and archives, to which ACRS is linked informally. Did I do no harm by stepping outside the midcentury Mennonite anachronisms? In doing so, did I learn something relevant, now worth reporting? Present-day Harrisonburg turns out to be an enriching context in which to address these questions.

Part Three

Chapter 9

A Churchman's European Journey

God moves in a mysterious way.
—A Hymn

Then the Lord said to [Moses], "What is that in your hand?"
—Exodus 4:2

Being human is being uncertain,
being on the way to an unknown place.
—Bruce Feiler

There is only one way to peace,
one way out of existing tensions:
 peaceful coexistence.
—Nikita S. Khrushchev

In 1964, while I was executive secretary of the Church Peace Mission, John Heidbrink of the Fellowship of Reconciliation in Nyack, New York, invited me to colead a six-week churchperson's traveling seminar to Europe, mostly to the east. The pivotal occasion was the six-day Second All-Christian Peace Assembly in Prague, Czechoslovakia, sponsored by the Christian Peace Conference headquartered there. The tour included visits to Paris and Rome before the conference. Afterward we stopped at Budapest and Debrecen in Hungary. Then we interacted with contacts at Kiev, Moscow, and Leningrad in the Soviet Union. With a slight sigh of relief, we exited from there to Helsinki, Finland, then traveled on to Oslo in Scandinavia. We ended eventually on the historic island of Iona off the coast of Scotland.

We were a full dozen in number, four Catholic priests and monks, the remainder Protestant clergy and lay leaders. This group was large enough for stimulating diversity yet small enough to manage. My designation as coleader would permit Heidbrink to bow out of the tour for part of the time after the Prague conference. He rejoined us in Leningrad. Because of a previous engagement, I joined the group only a day before their departure from Rome for Prague. On that part of the journey, we made an overnight stop in Zurich. There we had an engaging evening visit with Emil Brunner, my former professor. Like his contemporary Reinhold Niebuhr in the United States, Brunner regarded Christian pacifism as parasitic.

Our tour was entirely ad hoc. It came into existence only as we embarked on the journey, and it dissolved upon our return when our plane landed in New York. This did not rule out some interpersonal contacts that followed. We became personal friends during that six-week period even though we reflected the broad spectrum of American Christianity—Catholic, Protestant, and free church. We shared the awareness that the global political alignments of World War II had been reconstituted as the potentially even more perilous Cold War. We understood full well that the forthcoming Prague event originated in the "enemy" camp (as viewed by the triumphal United States). Participating in that event, then traveling however briefly to the Soviet world, would enrich our understanding, and hence our contribution to peacekeeping in the Cold War then at its peak. To experience all this as a cross-denominational American Christian promised to be an extraordinarily enriching and challenging privilege.

The Christian Peace Conference

The second All-Christian Peace Assembly held in Prague from June 28 through July 3, 1964, was the organizing pivot of our tour. The sponsoring organization, the Christian Peace Conference (CPC), had begun in 1958. The creation of the CPC was triggered by the complexities of the Cold War among Protestant church leaders in central Europe, beginning in Czechoslovakia. Discussions began there following the second meeting of the World Council of Churches (WCC), held in Evanston, Illinois, in summer 1954. After several smaller regional gatherings, the first All-Christian Assembly convened in Prague in 1961.

From the outset when the WCC was founded (Amsterdam, 1948), relations of the churches of the Soviet Union and the Soviet bloc to that global venture were precarious. A dramatic debate emerged on that founding occasion between John Foster Dulles, later to become U.S. Secretary of State, and Prague churchman/theologian Josef L. Hromadka (1889-1969). The Russian Orthodox Church did not join the WCC until the early 1960s. However, Protestants within the Soviet bloc, principally from central Europe, had joined from the outset. Central Europe functioned as an informal buffer zone between East and West in Europe with their very different histories. In that zone, Prague as the former seat of the Bohemian monarchy played an important role. Protestant history there was preceded and influenced by the legacy of John Huss (1369?-1415), the pre-Reformation martyred reformer.

The second WCC Assembly had met in Evanston, Illinois, in summer 1954. Along with visa problems to get there, the few delegates from central Europe felt snubbed at that assembly. Church leaders there were struggling to come to terms with the Soviet Communist control of the region and sensed as well the global jeopardy of the brewing nuclear arms race. Returning from the 1954 Evanston event, they began discussions about their dual plight: the global threat and the isolation of their churches from the global ecumenical community. In that discussion they concluded that the churches' backing of the Khruschev-embraced policy of peaceful coexistence might gain a bit of leverage internationally. The outcome of their explorations was the movement eventually formalized as the Christian Peace Conference (CPC).

Their leading spokesperson was Hromadka who during the World War II years, while the Nazis occupied Czechoslovakia, lived and taught at Princeton Theological Seminary. In 1961, years after his return to Prague, he traveled to the Puidoux Conference, a gathering of pacifist and nonpacifist theologians then at a formative stage, meeting near Paris. There Hrodmadka sought to establish contact with peace-minded persons from the United States and Western Europe. He was able to engage a dozen or more participants in North American and West European peace groups at CPC's first All-Christian Assembly in Prague later that year.

Returning Now to the 1964 Assembly

By 1964 the CPC had established contacts worldwide. About a thousand people attended the 1964 event. Though mostly European, participants came from some fifty countries. The meeting began with a Sunday worship service and keynote address on June 28. It ended with appropriate proceedings on the following Saturday, July 3. The opening message came from Martin Niemoeller, preaching on the text chosen as conference theme: "My covenant with him was a covenant of life and [peace]" (Mal. 2:5). This was followed by the keynote address on that theme in the afternoon, delivered by Hromadka, then dean of the Comenius (Theological) Faculty in Prague.

Hromadka had been the chief Eastern Europe spokesman from the Soviet world during the first decade of the World Council of Churches. Already at the founding event of that project at Amsterdam in 1948, as noted, Hromadka had tangled with John Foster Dulles. Dulles was an influential lay churchman who later became the American Secretary of State. I am not familiar with the detail of their debate but will risk the following interpretation.

The historical irony of that confrontation has largely escaped attention. Dulles worked out of the legacy of St. Augustine (354-430 CE) who theologically established the rationale for the fusion of church and state that has been foundational for Western Christendom. In effect, Professor Hromadka was undertaking a similar task in relation to the Marxist-Leninist enterprise that was the Soviet empire. Retaining a strong theological rooting, contrary to Marxist atheism, Hromadka sought a practical way of living with the existing polity. Was either of these protagonists aware of the irony of their situation? Was not Augustine's position, and hence that of Dulles, theologically more dubious than that of Hromadka, which he challenged? Augustine's position rested on the false assumption that the emperors, and hence the empire, had accepted Christ and thus been "Christianized." Hromadka, on the other hand, was reaching for a pragmatic accommodation with an empire that remained atheistic!

In the week that followed the Sunday opening of the 1964 Prague Assembly activities, five reports from younger theologians were presented. The conference participants were meanwhile divided into ten working groups. Reports from these working groups were officially endorsed by the whole assembly, with no attempt to reconcile the differences they contained. While lay participation was heralded in the reporting, the conference largely carried weight by virtue of the highly visible presence of patriarchs, metropolitans, bishops, and clergy from the various traditions.

A Footnote

Initially the Prague organizers, formalized as the Christian Peace Conference (CPC), had sought contact with peace groups in the American churches as a gateway into the churches generally and thereby into American society. Some seventy Americans showed up at this 1964 All-Christian Assembly, a miscellaneous assortment of people. Many were already in Europe for other reasons—tourists, students, professors on leave, and yes, a few "fellow travelers." One afternoon the Americans caucused for a discussion of the American response to the CPC. The CPC project, while church-initiated, nonetheless was tightly controlled by the Soviet regime. For that reason, response from churches in the United States would be dicey at best.

Meanwhile, during the assembly, John Heidbrink had been appointed to the international governing body of the CPC. As staff person at the American, loosely Christian, chapter of the Fellowship of Reconciliation (FOR), which had been formed in Europe at the outbreak of World War I, Heidbrink had already visited the CPC on earlier occasions. An informal consensus in this American caucus quickly emerged—we needed an organized channeling of the response in the United States to the CPC. With John Heidbrink now appointed to the governing body, we quickly agreed that he, an ordained Presbyterian minister and church secretary of FOR, should be the organizer. The implication was that an American chapter of the CPC might soon be formed.

Back to Our Churchpersons' 1964 Tour

The Prague Assembly was pivotal for our tour, not merely as the event around which the logistics of our trip were organized but as an encounter that enriched our agenda in the countries already mentioned. In Hungary we were invited and hosted by the Hungarian Reformed Church. In the three Soviet cities, Kiev, Moscow, and Leningrad (St. Petersburg), we were largely in the hands of the Intourist guide assigned to us, and Michael Zhidkov, a second-generation young Baptist minister.

Our visit to a summer camp in Kiev was unforgettable. While an official Party project, it obviously drew on both secular and religious sources of inspiration. Soon after entering this park, we came across of a life-size seated image of Lenin surrounded by an informal group of half-grown children. It appeared deliberately to mimic Jesus when he said, "Let the little children come to me, and do not stop them" (Matt. 19:14).

Later we entered the summer meeting hall of the camp, a roofed shelter with open sides and pillars all around. At the front, above a stage, were depictions of light and shade, designed to symbolize the spiritual powers of Communist party ideals. Near the top, the pillars featured photo-portraits of political figures. This all appeared to be the party's answer to the Christian cathedrals they were hoping to supplant. The historic sites, ancient and contemporary, of the three Ukrainian or Russian cities on the rest of this tour absorbed our energies and attention, embellished by incidental human contacts. To all this, the Prague Assembly provided an enriching backdrop.

Scandinavia provided a zone of transition back into our Western orbit. For our group, the Iona pause was a fitting finale. This ancient shrine on a bleak island off the west coast of Scotland has its own aura of mystery. A Celtic monastery founded there in the sixth century CE became an important missionary base for regions to its east. Passing through varied historical turbulences, this sanctuary was renewed in a Protestant context in 1938 by George MacLeod, a Church of Scotland (Presbyterian) pastor. The ruins of the Benedictine monastery were rebuilt by participating groups. This endeavor was oriented to the needs of industrial workers in Scotland, in part for those with summer residence on the island.

Our several-day visit included an evening in the home of Pastor and Mrs. MacLeod. Before leaving Iona, the Catholic members of our group asked to use the chapel for a mass in which we would all participate, marking the end of our tour. To our surprise, we discovered that conducting a Catholic mass on Scottish soil is illegal. So instead we found a niche in these ancient monastery ruins and there observed a simple, informal, bread-and-wine communion service. This served as a symbolically appropriate ending to our extraordinary tour, especially for me with my free church background. Heading home, we traveled briefly by boat but principally by train to London for our flight back to New York. I returned happily to home, family, and my Church Peace Mission job, blissfully unaware of what was about to spring from that European interlude.

The Outcome

A Catholic member of our tour was Daniel Berrigan, a Jesuit. I had met him briefly during a monastery retreat in New York some months before the tour. During this six-week fellowship, we became friends. I confided to him the critical turning point I had reached in my life journey. I still had a year or two ahead in my assignment with the Church Peace Mission, but then what? The route I would take after stepping outside the Mennonite superstructure was not yet in view.

I was hoping for a secular university opening. I had already made several university contacts about job possibilities in Washington, D.C., where I lived with my family, but nothing yet had crystallized. Then, several weeks after we returned from the tour, I received a telephone invitation from the chairperson of the sociology faculty at the Catholic University of America (CUA) inviting me to come for a job interview. Previously it had not occurred to me to inquire about employment there. I simply assumed that just as I would not want that university, they would not want me, "sectarian" that I was. I realized at once that only Daniel Berrigan could have triggered that call.

In 1964, the Second Vatican Council (Vatican II, 1962-1965) was still underway. Until then, CUA had the status of a pontifical institution, operating directly under papal control. In the wake of Vatican II, the relationship with Rome was modified. While theology and several related schools or faculties were retained pontifically, the rest of the university now was accountable only to the usual board of trustees. Non-Catholic faculty had taught in the secular disciplines of the university already before Vatican II. But because sociology had included the social teachings of the church, sociologists at CUA had to be Catholic as well as Catholic-educated.

Since the transition had barely begun, my courtship with the department was a somewhat tenuous and drawn out. Although I was invited to teach a summer school course already in 1965, my formal appointment to the sociology faculty at CUA did not take place until the fall of 1967. Those pending changes in the university both delayed and helped my appointment as the first non-Catholic at CUA with a full-time position on the sociology faculty. At last—the sociological yearning that first welled up within me more than twenty years earlier was about to be realized.

A Surprising Phone Call

In late fall of 1964, some weeks after the call from the sociology chair at CUA, came another outcropping from that summer's traveling seminar. John Heidbrink, the organizer of the tour, had fallen into a prolonged illness. He phoned, inviting me to take over his assignment to organize a church committee in the United States for the Christian Peace Conference. I was aware of the difficulties that plagued the relations between the churches in the Soviet world and ecumenical relations otherwise. Those issues would have to be addressed directly in the assignment given to Heidbrink.

How should I reply to Heidbrink's request? As with all my previous assignments, I was inadequately prepared for what this one entailed. While my earlier experience in Europe, in the Orient, and in the United States under the ecumenical Church Peace Mission (CPM) served importantly as applied sociology, those activities were not directly related to that discipline. Yielding to Heidbrink's request would simply perpetuate such mixing of science and practice. Besides, now that I was headed at last toward a graduate university faculty appointment, I already faced an overload of work ahead.

During these years of transition, however, I increasingly realized that in any career shift I needed to build on, not drop, the resources of my earlier experiences. Karl Marx had been an important figure in the development of sociology and of the history that followed. Bridge-building between the United States and the Soviet Marxist world could serve informally as a laboratory for my growing sociological understandings. In any event, Heidbrink's assignment was to be carried out on marginal time. I accepted his invitation.

The U.S. Committee for the Christian Peace Conference

There was no job description for that task and, as yet, no accountability structure. Yes, I understood the Christian commitment as pacifist, as nonviolent. I was a member of a peace church and had spent a decade in peace-related professional action. But CPC was not a pacifist endeavor. While seeking peace in the nuclear age, the CPC constituency was rooted in the Christendom tradition. Thus it was clear to me that the real dialogue partner in the United States with CPC was the mainline churches, not their socialist, pacifist, or peace-church fringes. It was evident likewise that the varied denominations would not formally participate in the politically regulated CPC.

However constituted, a chapter *of* CPC in the United States could not hope to gain a hearing in the mainline Protestant communities. Indeed, even an independent committee or group *for* the Christian Peace Conference would encounter suspicion. Much would depend on whether trusted people in the denominations could be won for membership in an independent committee *for* rather than *of* the CPC. In the end, forming an independent committee for the CPC by mainline churchpersons was the route I pursued. Drawing partly on my earlier Church Peace Mission circle of acquaintances for advice and candidates, over a number of months a group emerged. In spring 1965, I drove to Boston. Beginning with the Divinity School of Harvard University, I visited a thin string of seminary faculties from there through New York and Princeton back to Washington, D.C.

A year later, in spring 1966, the U.S. Committee for the Christian Peace Conference held its charter meeting in a Maryland suburb of Washington, D.C. But the CPC was disrupted in the fall of 1968, when Soviet troops marched into Prague to suppress the liberalizing regime that had emerged there. When at last a year and a half later the CPC was reconstituted, the U.S. Committee was reestablished as well, now as Christians Associated for Relations with Eastern Europe (CAREE). By the late 1970s, CAREE also formed and incorporated an Institute for Peace and Understanding (IPU), designed to help conversations of our American constituency with Marxist scholars and scientists in Soviet and Soviet bloc academies of science and universities.

My die was now cast. I became an eventually tenured associate professor of sociology at CUA, continuing there until my retirement twenty years later in 1987. Quite early in my tenure I served a three-year term as department chairperson. During the 1980s I also coordinated a newly established interdisciplinary program of peace studies at the university.

Meanwhile, during that entire period and a decade beyond, I was involved as well in the bridge-building efforts of CAREE and the IPU between our country and the Soviet bloc. For me those efforts eventually converged with another program, the Council for Research in Values and Philosophy, independently based at CUA. These activities are detailed in chapter 11. From my departure to Europe under MCC in early 1946 to the end of the century, I had traveled to Europe in various capacities more than fifty times.

The Rerouting I Had Long Awaited

Our goals and expectations for the 1964 churchpersons' traveling seminar had been richly realized. Touring in hitherto foreign countries is at best a superficial introduction. Processing our experiences through the ecumenical refractor of our group was an important enhancement. However, my dual encounter with the Christian traditions of Eastern Europe and our country's Cold War rival took on a profoundly different meaning for me as the above two outcomes emerged. I would now work in secular sociological terms, but in a Christendom setting, while directly engaging the multiple versions of Christendom against which Anabaptism arose. To all this the 1964 European tour served as prelude. Truly, God moves in a mysterious way.

This, of course, is a retrospective reading of the 1964 tour. Three more years were to pass before the external configuration of the second half of my life journey would be in place. And the configuration itself was in part surprising, indeed ironic. How could I engage the secular in a classic Christendom setting? In a sense, I could more effectively work from a Catholic university setting than if I were still in the institution of my own faith tradition, where I briefly served a decade earlier, 1953-1957. I was now in a position where neither criticism nor advocacy of the Roman Catholic institutionalization of the faith was appropriate. And this helped my secular empirical focus on the human social process.

Chapter 10

The Wealth and Poverty of Sociology

Place occupies a central role as we attempt to define who we are.
—Anthony M. Orum

Order is not pressure which is imposed on society from without, but an equilibrium that is set up from within.
—José Ortega y Gasset

For theology to build on sociology, understood as dispassionate analysis, is to betray its own task.
—Arne Rasmusson

My interest in sociology was first awakened by the introductory course taught by Guy F. Hershberger the summer of 1944 at Goshen (Ind.) College. The textbook was R. M. MacIver's *Society: Its Structures and Changes* (1931). MacIver, professor of sociology at Columbia University, was a prominent figure in the emerging field of sociology in the American academe. Hershberger himself, trained in history, could be described as a sociological historian.

By the 1940s, rural life in American society, compared to its earlier dominance, was on the defensive. Rural sociology, however, served as a specialty in sociology, linked partly to a rural life minority movement in the society. At that stage, Mennonites in the United States were primarily rural. Their communities, while reinforced by both ethnicity and Christian faith, attracted the attention of rural life specialists. Some Mennonite scholars, including Hershberger, drew on the resources of rural life advocates in efforts to perpetuate rural life as the preferred Mennonite way.

Somewhat ironically, Hershberger's work at Goshen College was closely linked to that of Harold S. Bender, then dean but primarily the pioneer, on the American side, in publishing the sixteenth-century primary sources of Anabaptist history. Anabaptism, however, had emerged in urban contexts, and indeed could not have developed otherwise. But persecution drove these radicals into rural hideouts, cut off from urban discourse. As a result, they became embodied as rural ethnic enclaves, in many ways cut off from their wider host societies. If in fact their faith had come to be thus defined, perpetuation of rural life might have been their only salvation.

As already indicated, when I returned to EMC for my final year in the college Bible course, I had reached the conclusion that while theology may reach heaven, it doesn't fully reach earth. Therefore I must study sociology as well. I was totally unaware of the irony of the rural interpretation of Anabaptism that I had espoused, along with the discovery of the sociological challenge. Hence the episode described in chapter 3 that led to publication of my article, "A Way of Life That Has Stood the Test," in the March 1949 issue of *Mennonite Community* magazine. That article celebrated a Mennonite family farm in southwest Germany, then it its eighth generation. Whatever the merits of that achievement in its own right, only in the course of the next few years did I become aware of the incongruity of such idealization.

Retrospectively, in these two episodes—my initial attraction to sociology and the subsequent historical downgrading of my rural utopianism—I sense hints of what became the organizing themes in the sociology component in my career—the interface between sociology and theology, more specifically the Christian story and the relation between community and society. The latter topic was front and center in my appointment to the sociology faculty at Catholic University of America (1967-1987), discussed in this chapter. The former, the theology/sociology dialectic, though diffused, is more evident in the bridge-building project into the Soviet world that I treat in the next chapter.

Sociology at Catholic University

The Catholic University of America was founded in 1889, the year of my father's birth. Its first rector, John Joseph Keane (1839-1918), who died the year I was born, had a high interest in "the social studies." He maintained that both clergy and laity, if they were to be scholars of the future, needed broad, deep, and careful study of the great social transformation which the march of events was bringing more and more to the surface and rendering of greater and greater importance. This budding graduate university began with two programs: a School of Philosophy and a School of the Social Sciences. Eventually several of the social sciences, notably anthropology, economics, politics, and sociology, came to be included in Arts and Sciences, and others, notably law, became separate schools within the university.

Though a pontifical university until Vatican Council II in the 1960s, and retaining its clear Catholic identity, CUA was a late entry among the emerging graduate universities in the United States. Until Vatican II, the sociology department in Arts and Science at CUA included also a program of the Social Teachings of the Church. Only practicing Catholics with Catholic training could be appointed to that faculty. Along with the laicism of the university (except for several theological disciplines), that latter program was dropped from sociology. That laicism both delayed and, in the end, helped my appointment as the first non-Catholic in that department.

The Community/Society Dialectic

The Catholic University of America, founded as a graduate institution, later added an undergraduate college. For the sociology department this translated into three-part assignments for the professors. We taught one undergraduate course per semester, one graduate course, and a research seminar or course in the professor's field of specialization. Given my background and resume, I was offered the sociology of religion as my field of research. And initially I taught that 500-level course. However, by then I was focused primarily on the processes and problems of community and urbanization to which the department agreed.

While by the 1960s sociology was a firmly established academic discipline, as a discipline it was still unfolding. The processes of modernization, and the accompanying problems, had triggered the rise of sociology in the first place. Among the founding fathers, a useful conceptualization was put forward in 1887 by Ferdinand Toennies, a German scholar, in a book translated as *Community and Society*. In community, he proposed, people "remain essentially united despite all separating factors, whereas in society they are essentially separated despite all uniting factors." Family, neighborhood, and even village exemplified community, while society referred to the nature of large-scale associations and interdependencies that emerge in the processes of modernization. My life experience and engagement with the sociological literature after my 1944 introduction to the sociological perspective steered me toward the above focus in my own work.

The national and international ferment of the 1960s had its corollaries in urban affairs. Civic and political initiatives emerged in the United States regarding urban racial and ethnic problems and related economic and political issues. A Washington Center for Metropolitan Studies (WCMS) was active in downtown Washington, operating in relation to a variety of political and other agencies. The half-dozen universities in the region collaborated by each appointing a professor semester-by-semester, to serve part-time on WCMS projects. Given my focus on community and urbanization, C. J. Nuesse, then chairman of the sociology department at CUA, graciously offered the CUA-WCMS slot to me, an assignment that subsequently was extended to two full academic years. This opportunity served as the research third in my schedule and thereby contributed importantly to the retooling I needed at that stage.

New Towns, Old Habits

Already in 1967 at WCMS I wrote an unpublished paper on "The Social Impact of Physical Change." University fellows there were drawn continuously into varied projects. The most important one for me became the planning and early stages of the Fort Lincoln New Town project in southeast Washington, D.C. Urban renewal and citizen participation projects figured importantly during the Kennedy and Johnson administrations in the 1960s.

A tract of several hundred acres, formerly occupied by the National Training School for Boys at the juncture of Bladensburg Road and South Dakota Avenue and bordering on Prince George's County (Maryland), became free for urban development. President Johnson had succeeded in obtaining congressional enactment, in November 1965, of the Federal Housing and Urban Development (HUD) program to help with the revitalization of decadent areas in American cities. This proposal had been initiated but not yet successfully launched, by President Kennedy. With HUD already underway, on August 30, 1967, President Johnson seized on the Fort Lincoln project as a kind of bellwether for that entire program.

The tract was large enough for a "new town in town" venture, an ideal opportunity to model the various features idealized in urban renewal efforts, including citizen participation in the design. Implementing citizen participation in such ventures, difficult at best, was particularly so in this instance. No one resided on the site as yet. Not only were citizens from surrounding districts unable to speak for future residents, but their own interests did not fully coincide with the logic of the project. Nonetheless, citizen participation was promoted. After three differing and conflicting citizen groups emerged—details cannot be traced here—the mayor announced the formation of the Citizens' Planning Council for the Fort Lincoln Project, Inc., on May 25, 1968. Through my involvement at WCMS, I became one of eight public members on that council.

Meanwhile there were problems among the federal and municipal agencies, not always readily resolved, given particularly the unique position of the District of Columbia without representation in the United States Congress. Just as the injection of citizen issues entailed problems for the federal and municipal agencies, so their problems aggravated difficulties emerging among citizen interests. By September 1969, the above Citizen's Planning Council was caught up in the internal conflict it was intended to surmount, and once more was replaced by the mayor. With that my direct contact with the Fort Lincoln New Town Project ended. WCMS published my fifty-two-page report of the citizen side of this early stage of the project as *New Town, Old Habits: Citizen Participation at Fort Lincoln*, WCMS (Aug. 1970). Martha Derthick published an outsider account of the same period in *The Public Interest* (No. 20, Summer 1970). Neither account was available to the other author at the time of writing, nor have the authors ever met.

My assignment at WCMS greatly enriched my beginning work at CUA on community and urbanization issues. This rather superficial dip into political activism resonated in later opportunities to participate in civic affairs, first in the neighborhood association in my residential community in northwest Washington, then later in Jefferson County and the Eastern Panhandle of West Virginia while I resided there. Soon after the Fort Lincoln episode, I was drawn into an urban ethnic study project initiated by Msgr. Geno Baroni, initially under the umbrellas of the U.S. Conference of Catholic Bishops. I served as an advisor for this project for several years.

With regard to the Fort Lincoln New Town project today, several hundred entries are listed by the Google Search on the Internet. According to a documentary published there on May 6, 2002, citing current Fort Lincoln Civic Association reporting, none of the managers of the project ever met many of the projected obligations to residents and the Redevelopment Land Agency. Nor have they developed Fort Lincoln Town in the form originally agreed to as a full-blown "town within a town" with its own schools, full-service town center, and man-made lake. Even the residential portion of Fort Lincoln stands only about half built.

Teaching and Research at CUA

My undergraduate teaching at CUA was limited to a few basic courses such as marriage and the family, social problems, and urban society. Given my own research and extracurricular activity (see especially the next chapter) I ranged more widely on the graduate level. As indicated, in keeping with the departmental interest, I taught religion and society in the early years. The research-related graduate program, with the granting of master and doctoral degrees, was the preoccupation of the department. While I served frequently on normally three-person supervisory teams for doctoral study, occasionally I was the primary director. My own research was still at an early stage.

In the graduate teaching program, I regularly taught two basic courses: development of sociological theory and social organization. I offered additional courses sporadically such as community; urban society; modern societies; community action and public policy; sociology of urban planning, law, and society; and Soviet society. During my beginning years at WCMS, with the help of faculty colleagues and graduate students, I began local community surveys in adjacent areas in Washington.

In the early 1970s I was asked to serve a three-year term (1971-1974) as department chair. During that time efforts were underway to promote communication among sociology faculties in the consortium of Washington, D.C. universities. As chairperson I benefited from these inter-university contacts, as I did also from membership in the D.C. Sociological Society. And finally, in the early 1980s, I was asked to coordinate the formation of an interdepartmental peace studies program among the appropriate departments at CUA.

All of these secondary activities provided belated academic orientation for me, given the fact that before my Catholic University appointment, my exposure to American universities had been limited. (I had had only a summer at the University of Pennsylvania at the beginning of graduate school and a part-time post-doctoral summer at the University of Chicago.)

The laicizing of CUA after Vatican II entailed major institutional adjustments, especially financial. Until then both faculty and students had been largely members of orders and other church-related professions that supported them. But now CUA financing increasingly entered the secular market for both faculty and students. Salaries were below average, although the free tuition for family members in my case served as important compensation. My wife Ellen, who had completed junior college in her youth, as our children grew older finished her liberal arts degree, graduating at Catholic University along with our second son in 1981. As the number of married faculty at CUA increased in the late 1960s and early 1970s, a faculty wives club began to play an active role on campus. In this, Ellen readily participated. But then as female appointments to the faculty increased, after a few years the wives club evaporated.

A Sabbatical Leave

Despite financial limitations in its new status, CUA maintained their sabbatical (seventh year) leave practice for faculty. This provided full pay for a semester's leave, or half-time pay for a full-year leave. Arriving at CUA in late midlife, I took the sabbatical project seriously. At most, I would receive only two such opportunities before retirement. Even so, because of scheduling constraints, my first sabbatical came in 1974-1975, a year late. Meanwhile, with my focus on the interface between communal and societal processes in the modernizing era, I was impressed increasingly with the vulnerability of the communal fabric in urbanizing and modernizing societies. Addressing that vulnerability in some specific manner seemed like an appropriate focus for my upcoming sabbatical year in the mid-1970s.

The concepts related to community are too varied and complex for research uses without further definition. Traditionally, in sociology community has been territorial and hence ecological. Ecology refers to the branch of biology dealing with the relations of organisms and their environment. Moving toward a more operational definition, locality (place) has been defined as the datum apart from which a group is not a community. But modernizing technologies and public policies increasingly extend the scale of social organization, reducing the likelihood that place results in communal attachment.

Considering my previous international experiences in Europe and Asia, the possibility of a comparative cross-national study as a sabbatical-year project appealed to me. Comparing samples from countries at differing stages of urbanizing and/or modernizing could shed light on both the nature and the fate of local attachments in that process. Alas, I had not yet developed the tools of measurement that such comparison required. On the other hand, my earlier decade of international experience, plus my bridge-building assignment that emerged from the "churchmen's European journey" (chapter 9), and my continuing frequent travel to Eastern Europe (chapter 11), seemed to justify such a study for me. Would a three-region comparison—Eastern Europe, Western Europe, and United States (or North America) be feasible, on the assumption that, proceeding from east to west would reveal increasing "delocalizing" of human togetherness?

Then at a meeting in New York in 1973 I learned that UNESCO had established a center in Vienna, Austria, to help communication and cooperative research by social scientists from Eastern and Western Europe. The European Coordination Center for Research and Documentation in Social Sciences was dubbed "the Vienna Center." A favorable response to my exploratory letter addressed to that center tipped the scales in favor of the three-region possibility just sketched. Circumstances appeared to warrant proceeding with my plan in spite of incomplete preparation for the tasks, which, as we shall see, we did not fully surmount.

Ten Months in Vienna

My wife and I with three of our five children flew from New York to Luxemburg on August 20, 1974, and from there traveled to Vienna by train. With the help of American acquaintances already in Vienna, we had made preliminary arrangements for an apartment on Gumpendorfer Strasse in the western district of the city proper. Our oldest daughter, whose difficulties were noted earlier, was partly self-supporting and a part-time student at Catholic University. Our oldest son, who had just completed high school, had enrolled as a freshman there as well. With us was our second daughter, who having graduated from college at CUA with a music major, gained access in Vienna to a conservatory, the *Hochschule fuer Musik und darstellende Kunst*. Our two younger sons attended Austrian public schools, one in middle and the other in elementary school.

My request to the Vienna Center was mostly for sponsorship and consultation. Initially I had been in contact by mail with Adam Schaff, a well-known Polish Marxist scholar, then director of the Vienna Center. I first chanced to meet him personally on a plane flight from

Frankfurt to Warsaw and later audited a course he taught at the University of Vienna during our time there. My proposal, "The Residential Areal Bond" (RAB), was formally submitted and approved by the Vienna Center in April, 1975. The Center was not involved in the RAB project either financially or administratively. The center's sponsorship, information, and scholarly connections were invaluable, however, especially throughout Eastern Europe.

More direct help was forthcoming from the sociology faculty at the University of Vienna. There Professor Erich Bodzenta joined the effort directly, and through his help and that of colleagues, the project got underway. I made personal visits to scholars in Russia, Hungary, Czechoslovakia, and Poland. There were Cold War barriers to deal with. Only in Poland did my east European contact succeed. Vlodzimierz Morowski, a researcher in the Community Section of the Institute of Philosophy and Sociology of the Polish Academy of Sciences in Warsaw, actively joined the project and with Bodzenta and me coedited the one published volume the project produced: *The Residential Areal Bond: Local Attachments in Delocalized Societies* (New York: Irvington Press, 1984).

With these two colleagues on board by the end of our sabbatical in Vienna, the project was underway. As a meeting point between east and west, Vienna remained the base of operation. The most intensive research was conducted by a young colleague of Bodzenta, Karl Thum, who had been trained by Professor Bodzenta. Other European participants came from West Germany, Belgium, Switzerland, Sweden, and Spain. Contributions from a total of eight countries were included in the volume. Donald Warren, a Michigan sociologist, joined me from the American side, and after the publication of the book, a Canadian scholar came on board.

What Did We Find?

"The Residential Areal Bond" was the title of the project proposal submitted to the Vienna Center in April 1975. The first meeting of the country participants was held there two years later. Thereafter we met annually till our final meeting in Bilbao, Spain, in 1981. The 1975 meeting outlined the goals of this inquiry as follows:

(1) To identify and to conceptualize the locality-generated social psychological "zone" that emerges between the dwelling unit and the wider community;

(2) To identify and conceptualize the "bonding" significance of this zone for household members of both personality and household/family;

(3) To measure the effects of the "delocalization" of the wider areas within which the dwelling is located, and thus the effect of spatial organization and locational relations on the RAB; and

(4) To identify macro-societal variables associated with RAB variations (strength, intensity, forms, etc.) which can be used in comparative, cross-societal analysis.

Backdrop and Focus

According to archeology and other inferences, early humans were largely nomadic, living from hunting and food gathering. Such mobility, however, occurred mostly within limited territories. Settled living, linked to the emergence of agriculture, developed later. Some analysts note parallels between prehistoric nomadic living and the "delocalizing" of existence in our modern and postmodern era—despite the radical differences between these two modes. Others note parallels to the dynamics between movement (motility) and attachment or rest (sessility). The more intense or extended our movements, the more important the possibility of repose.

The above four-point goal of the RAB project had, nonetheless, a clear focus: the communal link or cushion between the family/household unit and the surrounding societal fluidity. Until the scientific and industrial revolutions, taking off in the eighteenth century, the household unit tended to be nested in adjacent local neighboring and kinship networks. Today these increasingly evaporate. Families, and even individuals, deprived of such support, become less and less stable. Some observers are ready to write off the family as obsolete, as passé. The fate of that communal matrix and its consequences were the focus of the RAB inquiry. Are viable alternatives or adaptations arising, or was such communality merely a transitional phenomenon in the first place?

After reaching this broad basis of agreement, we decided to assemble and publish a current state-of-the art report from each country, with an appropriate introduction and summarizing conclusion. We hoped that we could assemble either primary or secondary data from each country that would permit some comparative generalizations in a second volume. On that basis, I hoped vaguely that a further monograph might follow. The second step, however, never materialized. Participants forwarded to me one or more volumes of related in-country studies in their respective languages. In two instances, surveys underway were modified to accommodate RAB questions.

Only in Austria was a full-blown RAB study undertaken and subsequently published in Austria (German language). The survey questionnaire employed there is included in our published volume. Karl Thum (now deceased), who directed that study, experimented further with measuring instruments for what we termed the "residential areal bond" and concluded that he did not succeed. Though several secondary items were published in the countries included in our project, I did not compile them.

A Passing Note on Peace Studies

Peace studies, briefly mentioned above, began at CUA with the birth of the 1980s, roughly midpoint between my initial engagement in 1952 in the ecumenical peace/war discourse and 2005. It soon became evident, however, that the experience that I brought into this newly emerging arena was outdated. The student initiative that triggered this venture was action-motivated.

Moreover, though accommodated in interdisciplinary adjustments, the program remained limited in both scope and resources. And while I continued to participate until my retirement in 1987, my 1982-1983 sabbatical-year leave at that juncture conveniently permitted a shift of coordinating tasks to another faculty person.

My Sociological Saga

Sociology has been viewed broadly as the science of society, thus of human social relations at all levels. Though a broadly inclusive discipline, any investigation is directed at particular social modes, instances, or problems. Sociology is but one of half a dozen social sciences such as economics and politics. These, however, can be described as more specialized regarding particular aspects of society. For my part, I simply drew on some sociological tools to address life issues that had emerged for me.

In some respects, sociology has proved indispensable for coping with modernization and what is now called postmodernity. How do we come to terms in human relations with the radical changes brought by the continuing scientific and industrial revolutions and globalization? Yet the sociology that as such is indispensable, also by its very nature is part of the problem, since it is rooted, as are the sciences generally, in the determinisms of our material universe. While as humans, along with the countless other living species, we are embedded biologically in that material universe, at the same time as humans we are uniquely endowed with a dimension of indeterminacy, of spirit, of the power of choice between good and evil.

In respect to the dimension of indeterminacy in human affairs, sociology as the science of society cannot account for the intrusions of human freedom, whether for good of for ill. Religions have appeared universally in the wake of that indeterminacy, whether understood as the human in search God or God in search of the human (Heschel). Christianity, within which I stand, falls into this latter category. Sociology, however, has shown an indirect awareness of the indeterminacy enigma in its wrestling with the psychological dimensions of the human relations challenge. Since the perspectives of metaphysics are beyond its boundaries, however, sociology arrived at no solution.

All this lay buried in my naïve formulation in summer 1944, "Theology may reach heaven, but I'm not sure it reaches the earth." This meant presumably that I would have to study sociology as well as theology, though at that moment it meant little more than a mere insight. There was little inkling of the decades-long wandering in the desert that this would entail for me, and even less the deeper meanings and complexities that lay within. Only recently did I come across the following comment in the writing of theologian Oscar Cullman, the Swiss German whose lectures I had attended at the University of Basel (1948) and at the Sorbonne in Paris (1952): "Paradoxical as it may seem, the concentration upon redemptive history signifies the very opposite of indifference toward the world process."

Cullmann's statement goes to heart of the Mennonite anomaly that only surfaced for me years later. Our rural—and ethnically kinship-encased Mennonite faith communities—tended to result in distancing from the world process. "Do not love the world or the things in the world (*cosmos* in Greek)" (1 John 2:15). "World" in this setting is all too readily read indiscriminately as referring to the Creation. Contextually, however, it is clear that the writer of that text refers to the human realm as corrupted. Given the prolonged persecution that our ancestors in the Anabaptist movement had undergone, their withdrawal from the public domain is readily understandable. On the contrary, the ease with which we are reabsorbed into that world once persecution ceases is equally plausible.

Chapter 11

Cold War Bridge-Building

First keep peace within yourself, then you can also bring peace to others
—Thomas à Kempis

I cease not to advocate peace; even though unjust it is better than the most just war.
—Cicero

We shall not survive war, but shall,
as well as our adversaries, be destroyed by war.
—Agatha Christie

President Wilson fostered the illusion that World War I would be a war to end wars. When Ellen and I began our second term with MCC in Frankfurt, Germany, in the fall of 1948, we began with Wilsonian optimism. That surfaced for me the morning I began to dismantle the bomb shelter in the basement of the slightly war-damaged upscale house MCC rented near a small park for our center in Frankfurt. The war was past, definitively. Dismantling this shelter was a tiny celebrative act. Bomb shelters now were out-of-date!

Realistically, however, the lineaments of a new conflict were already emerging, a conflict eventually named the Cold War. Cynics might well argue that the Cold War merely brought a reversal of friend and foe. The Soviet Union, a former ally, now became the enemy, while Germany, the former enemy, was now gently coaxed into the alliance against the USSR. I say gently because World War II ended with the defeat and a total disarmament of Nazi Germany. This was followed by the Nuremberg Trials of wartime German leaders, a dozen of whom received death sentences. But with the emergence of the Federal Republic of Germany (1949), consisting of the three former occupied zones of West Germany—American, British, and French—Germans, though disarmed, were rather blatantly steered into the Western alliance as a staging area against the Soviet empire.

From the new MCC center in Frankfurt, I addressed a letter to the United States High Commissioner in Germany expressing concern about the irony, indeed contradiction, in United States policy there. The United States, while judging the defeated German leaders in a war just past, was now somehow drawing this defeated nation into a new military constellation. His office sent a lengthy and thoughtful reply.

The inherent political ambiguity of this change from ally to enemy is an instructive case study. In an earlier chapter I referred to the disarray in Iraq as I write. We have been constantly inundated for the last few years with charges of the demonic nature of Saddam Hussein, the former ruler of Iraq. Yet in the previous Iran-Iraq War (1980s), though officially neutral, the United States provided nonmilitary assistance to the Hussein regime. If national self-interest is basic in foreign policy, adaptation of this sort goes with the territory—national self-interest justifies teaming up with any ally willing to join us in battle. But how can one square this with the salvific healing that Jesus initiates and sustains? That question looms large in the concluding chapters of this book.

Encountering the Soviet World

In postwar MCC work in Western Europe during the 1940s and 1950s, the Soviet world lay mostly beyond the eastern margin of our sphere of activity. The exception was the direct MCC aid to Mennonite refugees from Russia, originally of Dutch-German descent, seeking entry into Western Europe. Already adversely affected by the 1917 Leninist revolution, many Russian Mennonites followed the German troops as they withdrew westward in 1943 after their defeat at Stalingrad, deep inside the USSR. MCC assisted that movement where possible, first in emergency terms, then in their eventual migration to South America. Apart from passing contacts with refugee projects, however, my MCC assignments lay elsewhere.

On several occasions during the late 1940s and early 1950s, I traveled by air from Frankfurt to Berlin, crossing the Soviet-occupied zone of east Germany, then also visiting the Soviet-controlled district of East Berlin. Once the trip to Berlin was by overnight rail, with the windows draped to block views of East Germany! On another occasion, several members of our MCC team in Frankfurt traveled to Vienna, Austria, a city quartered by the four wartime allies, similarly to Berlin. The two women in the group, my wife and our secretary, then returned to Frankfurt. An MCC colleague and a German Mennonite minister-businessman and I proceeded south on a camping trip through Yugoslavia, Greece, and Turkey.

That tour had several objectives, one of which was to gain some firsthand experience in a communist-controlled society. By then, Tito's Yugoslavia had become independent from Moscow but retained its communist character. Though not a fully open society, it was more accessible than the Soviet Union. Visiting the archeological traces of the Bogomils, a medieval sect in southern Yugoslavia, was included on our itinerary to make our visit nonpolitical. As it turned out, however, the roads south of Belgrade were so rugged that we never reached the Bogomil ruins. Nonetheless our inquiry about them in the government ministry in Belgrade responsible for historic monuments was worth the effort. Overall, the Yugoslav camping journey was an adventurous one (more in chapter 16), but not directly part of the present story.

By the mid-1950s the deadlock between the United States and the USSR appeared bleak, both governmentally and non-governmentally. By then, while at EMC, I served also as secretary of the Mennonite Church Peace Problems Committee (PPC). Given the impossibility of contact between the American and Soviet societies, I circulated a naïve proposal to members of our PPC that we dispatch a team to work their way into the Soviet world by knocking on doors, as it were, instead of seeking visas. One need that reached the committee was the fact that in the wartime population displacements in the USSR about a hundred Mennonite married couples had become separated and needed help to find each other. A discussion of these needs was held in Chicago in a meeting of several church committees. From these discussions emerged a visit of a three-man team to Moscow, the first such contact in four decades.

A year or so later, the five-person executive committee of the Russian Baptist association was brought on a visit to the United States by American Baptists. A brief meeting with Mennonites was included in their itinerary here. Along with informal contacts, a meeting, including a meal, with about a dozen of American Mennonite representatives was held in Chicago. As secretary of the Mennonite Peace Problems Committee, I attended that gathering. I was seated next to the secretary of the Russian team, who happened to know German.

This permitted some direct communication with him. Years later we met again in Moscow in connection with Christian Peace Conference (CPC) activity. From him I learned who the government plant was in the Russian Baptist CPC contingent and how he got there.

Ecumenical and Cold War Polarities

Retrospectively, a venture such as the CPC in the context of the Cold War appears inevitable. Broadly, the earth's peoples in that era fell into three major groupings: the United States and the Soviet (Marxist) spheres, mostly in the northern hemisphere, and the less-industrial Third World, mostly in the southern hemisphere. But these spheres were disrupted by various fissures, notably between China and the USSR among the Marxist regimes. Meanwhile globalizing impulses and trends were mounting, transcending, and permeating these differences.

Along with the Cold War, the second half of the twentieth century brought also a quickening of ecumenical impulses and awareness among the diversity of Christian groupings around the world. The two World Wars of the first half of the century at once had hindered and stimulated those dynamics. During that period, several important international ecumenical conferences were held. By 1948 a World Council of Churches (WCC) was formed in Amsterdam, consisting mostly of major Protestant denominations. Not until 1961 did Eastern Orthodox bodies become full participants. Even today, WCC ties to Roman Catholics, though improved, remain informal. At stake, of course, is the much older division between East and West that dates from the eleventh century CE.

Retrospectively, it is not surprising that this ostensibly worldwide coming together of church leaders was energized and dominated by the West. For it was in the context of Western Christendom hat the revolutions of modernity had originated. Eastern Christendom, however, though comparable in scope and older than its Western counterpart, was barely represented in the new WCC. And the Cold War lineaments roughly reflected the 1054 schism between the eastern and western wings of Christendom. Ironically, as we shall have occasion to note, the ideological moorings of Cold War rivals, eventually the NATO and the Soviet blocs, emerged in the process of Western Enlightenment itself, in the revolutions of modernity.

That irony is at once intellectual and historical. The commingling of the Greek, Latin, and Hebrew cultural legacies in Western history resulted in the increasing individualizing of the human person. In the course of eighteenth-century Enlightenment, individuality and communality became progressively polarized, with the latter emerging in reaction to the advance of the former.

Thus the perpetual riddle: Does society form (and hence precede) the individual, or do individuals create (and hence precede) society? The discovery of the ostensibly empty New World permitted an unprecedented experiment with the latter claim—self-sufficient individuals, coming first, construct society. Formal, member-based organizations exemplify this claim. Preindustrial peasant Russia meanwhile became an equally unprecedented experiment with the former claim, namely that preexisting collectivities form (hence precede) individuals.

To illustrate, here follows a nineteenth-century quotation from each of these two opposing views: John Stuart Mill wrote in *A System of Logic* (1872): "Men are not, when brought together, converted into another kind of substance, with different properties.... Human beings in society have no properties but those derived from, and may be resolved into, the laws of the nature of individual man." In the opposite direction Karl Marx had already written in his *Theses of Feuerbach* (1845): "The human essence is no abstraction inherent in each single individual. In its reality it is the ensemble of social relations."

THE PRAGUE-BASED CHRISTIAN PEACE CONFERENCE

The Christian Peace Conference, though pivotal to chapter 9, received only marginal treatment there. More must be said at this juncture about that venture. Already by the late 1940s, as historians note, world affairs were increasingly dominated by the contest between the Soviet and American blocs. They likewise observe that most of the social and political ideas shaping the World Council of Churches came from the West.

This was not yet fully evident in the founding session in Amsterdam. Journalist Willmar Thorkelson, press officer for that occasion, also covered the seven Assembly gatherings that followed. He noted in celebrating the fiftieth anniversary, in 1998, that the 1948 occasion pitted John Foster Dulles (later to become U. S. secretary of state) against Czech theology professor Joseph Hromadka, who believed communism was a force embodying much of the concern for social justice. At this assembly, the WCC gave socialism an implied boost through criticism of both laissez-faire capitalism and communism.

By the second WCC Assembly, however, held at Evanston, Illinois, in 1954, the small delegation, including Hromadka from the Soviet bloc, had trouble traveling and at the assembly itself. The impact on those few delegates was great. Between 1948 and 1954, lines between the blocs had hardened, with no softening in sight. Now what?

Reflection and informal conversations began among church leaders and scholars in central Europe that now found itself in the Soviet bloc. By the mid-1950s travel to and from the Soviet bloc was limited and tightly controlled, while sympathies for the communist cause in the West declined. Churches and churchmen were increasingly cut off from the international ecumenical community. By 1958 nearly forty leaders from seven central European countries met in Prague, the capital of Czechoslovakia, and formed what they called a Christian Peace Conference. A year later, April 16-19, 1959, they met again in a larger gathering. They then issued a call:

> We think the time has come when the churches should meet, in a way transcending the present form of their cooperation, for an All-Christian Assembly for the Peace of the World. It will be its task to help in the establishment of a lasting peace and the conclusion of treaties to this end, to work for general disarmament, especially the nuclear disarmament, and through all this to serve understanding between the nations. . . .

By 1961 this call brought together in Prague more than 600 churchmen and theologians from forty-two different countries in the first All-Christian Peace Assembly. This gathering also included some Roman Catholics, both priests and laity, as well as three delegates from Communist China. Issues surrounding the Cold War and the dangers of nuclear armaments dominated the agenda.

By late June into early July 1964, the second All-Christian Assembly was convened, again in Prague, with the theme, "My Covenant Is Life and Peace." Martin Niemoeller, president of one of the West German Protestant regional synods, presented the opening address. He cited Malachi 2:5, from which the above theme was taken.

The CPC convened six more assemblies over the next twenty years, the last one in 1985. I was privileged to attend the second (as described in chapter 9 above), third, fifth, and sixth of these conferences. If the second was something of a high point, the third (spring 1968) became a low point, partly but not entirely due to the Soviet suppression of the Dubcek reform in August that year. In the ensuing turmoil, J. N. Ondra as General Secretary was removed from office and Professor Hromadka withdrew from the Communist Party. Before matters were resolved, in 1969 Hromadka died a natural death.

After much internal ferment, a fourth assembly met September 29 through October 3, 1971, again in Prague, under interim leadership of the Russian Orthodox Metropolitan Nikodim (of Leningrad and Novgorod).This assembly's theme was "Our Common Responsibility for a Better World," and the biblical text was, "Mercy and truth are met together; righteousness and peace have kissed each other" (Ps. 85 10, KJV).The Metropolitan brought due theological gravitas to the meeting. Though far more tempered than the third assembly in its political judgments, as could be expected, conference perspectives were largely East European and solicitous of the Third World.

The disruption of the CPC led to inactive waiting by the U.S. Committee for the CPC. Since our U.S. Committee was not attending the 1971 assembly, in the end MCC supported my going as an observer. I quickly obtained a tourist visa to the USSR, uncertain whether I would actually gain admission to the country. Changing planes enroute at the Frankfurt airport, I spotted some assembly participants from other countries, including two invited Americans, connecting to the flight from Frankfurt to Prague. I lined up with them at the Prague airport, hoping that this might help my entry, but to no avail. I was denied entry. With no more flights heading to the West that day, I was put the next flight to Vienna. Meanwhile the assembly colleagues I met were to report my plight to the CPC leadership, and I might still be admitted. I waited in Vienna until Monday (this was Friday evening), hoping that by then a solution might be worked out. But when Monday came, the phone system between Vienna and Prague had broken down.

All I could do was to return home. Two flights were available. I chose Air France, which included an overnight stop at a new town on the eastern outskirts of Paris. Observing new town developments was then on my sociology agenda at Catholic University. The flight to New York would leave late enough the following day to permit a quick new town tour. Thus I could salvage something from this disappointing trip!

Christians Associated for
Relations with Eastern Europe (CAREE)

With the CPC reconstituted in that 1971 assembly, by 1972 our inactive U.S. Committee for the CPC called a meeting early the next year to reconstitute itself. By then our former membership had grown. From the beginning, other men with appropriate professional or institutional identities assumed leadership. I mention two examples: Paul Mojzes, a Yugoslav-born American scholar, was teaching at Rosemont College. Charles West was an ecumenically experienced and recognized Presbyterian ethics professor at Princeton. Lacking such qualifications, once the committee had been fully constituted, I dropped to membership without administrative responsibility.

Meanwhile the committee had also attracted persons with strong socialist interests, able thus to resonate with the socialist hopes still common among some east European Christians. Others in our membership, though dedicated to the bridge-building task during the Cold War, were more skeptical regarding the socialist ideal. As I recall, our 1972 meeting to reconstitute our committee drew some forty to fifty participants.

Consensus readily emerged that in the future our tie to CPC should lessen, while we pursued other bridge-building agendas as well. We adopted the name Christians Associated for Relations with Eastern Europe (CAREE), and reorganized accordingly. Eventually we incorporated this new association in Pennsylvania.

When it came to actual definition and election of leadership, the above-noted difference in attitudes toward socialism surfaced in the course of the meeting. Reluctantly, to help the process along, I allowed my name to be included on the slate for president, on the assumption that my election was improbable. I do not recall the slate that was presented. I offer merely my reading of the election result—friendliness versus unfriendliness toward the CPC agenda became the deciding factor. As a Mennonite pacifist I didn't fit into either camp and thus was not distasteful to either side. I was elected and served a two-year term (1972-1974) as the first president/chairman of CAREE. Beginning a year's sabbatical from the Catholic University of America in late summer of 1974, I terminated my CAREE term of service. Meanwhile temporary residence in Vienna permitted continuing contacts with CPC-related developments.

An Institute of Peace and Understanding

Awareness of the possibility of a Christian/Marxist dialogue grew during our CAREE years, but our label as Christian limited our contact with thought leaders in the State Academies of Sciences in the Soviet bloc states. By the late 1970s, the idea surfaced of forming a secular association to help our CAREE constituency interface with the Soviet academic world. I was invited to join a committee to organize what came to be called the Institute for Peace and Understanding (IPU), eventually legally incorporated in the State of New York. While at one level this was merely another hat for CAREE members to wear, the IPU constituency and agenda eventually differed somewhat.

During the 1980s, under IPU sponsorship, I organized and led three academic tours to the Soviet Union (1984, 1987, and 1988), in each case with the help of others. We worked out an itinerary, a theme, and an agenda, and made initial contacts with Soviet institutes and universities. We then sent out announcements to professors in a variety of colleges and universities, inviting interested scholars and scientists to join the tour. Before announcing the first tour, we were denied admission by Intourist, the Soviet travel agency, because the term *human rights* was mistakenly introduced as our theme. Eventually we obtained in invitation from the Soviet Peace Society, which meant that that agency would host our first event on arrival in Moscow.

After being turned down initially, I went to the Kennan Institute in Washington, D.C., an agency specializing in Russian studies and affairs, for literature and advice. In a directory of Soviet academic institutions I discovered that the Institute of Philosophy of the Georgian Academy of Sciences in the capital city of Tbilisi specialized in personality studies. I wrote to that agency and, though receiving no reply, put that city on our itinerary. Our four destinations on that tour became Leningrad (today once more St. Petersburg), Moscow, Novosibirsk (the gateway to Siberia), and Tbilisi. Arriving in Tbilisi, our interpreter, a native Russian who is now an American citizen, phoned the institute, eventually reaching the director, (now the late) Nikko Chavchavadze.

He had just returned from vacation and agreed to meet us in our hotel (as I learned later, contrary to party instructions, who had listened in on that telephone invitation). The meeting for the first half hour was strained. Preconceptions troubled both sides. But then we began to connect. Our conversation, far removed from Moscow, became productive. In a country with its own ancient culture, Chachavadze had successfully continued what he considered the classic tradition of Western philosophy. As we later discovered, this did not mean that he was a committed Christian, or that his personal life was entirely exemplary. Yet by the deft use of labels, such as Marxism and the classic names and categories in philosophy, he and his associates kept the classic traditions alive.

After the meeting, Paul Mojzes, the tour coleader, and I explored with Chavchavadze the possibility of a visit by him to the United States. Eventually he came, along with a young English-speaking colleague. This was followed by several visits by his colleagues. Eventually a team of five Georgians, including Chavchavadze, came for a conference at Catholic University. By then, my wife and I were residents at the Rolling Ridge Study Retreat Community, a project to be introduced in the next chapter. They were brought there for a visit as well. Papers from those two conferences appeared in the series of books published in Washington, D.C., by the Council for Research in Philosophy and Values. I contributed a chapter and was listed as coeditor.

The Cold War Ends

As noted, the last All-Christian Peace Assembly was held in 1985. When the Berlin wall came down four years later, the Cold War and former barriers between churches in East and West began to dissolve, hence the original reason for the CPC and CAREE lessened. However, shadow versions of both continued into the early years of the new millennium, and for good reason. Whatever the eventual verdict of the activities of these efforts—the latter was little more than an echo of the former—they leave legacies that must be taken seriously.

There is ample ground for criticism of both the Christian Peace Conference and our American response. I shall not comment on the former, except to note that initially the CPC was suspected by some to have emerged as a competing alternative to the World Council of Churches. CAREE and its antecedent, the U.S. Committee for the CPC, were often criticized, at best for being naïve or at worst for being pink, if not outright red (in any case, for simply being used).

And not without reason! For example, on one occasion before 1968, I attended a working committee meeting in Bucharest. An evening session was blatantly positive regarding Soviet foreign-policy interest in Third World unrest. Whether I walked out of that session—I was the only American present—I can't recall. I do remember a late night stroll through the streets of Bucharest conversing about this impasse with two delegates, an Englishman and a Dutch lady.

But that was merely one side of the story. Later while on sabbatical in Vienna, I became casually acquainted with an Austrian scholar who was outspokenly critical of efforts by those of us who seemingly appeared to collaborate with Soviet initiatives. He refused to travel to

Moscow during that era. After the Soviet Union dissolved in 1991, he made his first trip there and returned to Vienna with a different reading. Soviet colleagues who had contact with Western churchmen on such occasions told him that, without such outside contacts, they would have despaired. My experience, over twenty-five years and dozens of visits in CPC-related encounters in the Soviet bloc, corroborated the observation of this Austrian scholar.

One summer (1974?), late in my short term as CAREE chairman, we had been asked to convene an unofficial and off-the-record meeting of East European and American church leaders in the Czech resort town of Karlovy Vary. On Sunday, the day after the conference, the participants fanned out to preach in churches in or around Prague.

Appropriately enough, as a Mennonite, I was assigned to an evangelical free church congregation. A young man with a half-grown son came to my Prague hotel to pick me up. It was a relatively large and seemingly vigorous gathering. Given all the ambiguities of the situation, my task was clearly to speak from the heart of the gospel. The lay leader of the congregation, who as scientist had spent a term in Canada, stood with me in the pulpit to interpret. Everything went smoothly, and I sensed a warm response.

The same man who brought me from the hotel was scheduled to take me back. When the service and the following chats ended, suddenly the interpreter intervened and invited me to his house for dinner, assuring me that he would return me to the hotel afterward. Another guest or two were present, along with his family. After a cordial meal and visit, we headed back to the hotel. In the privacy of his automobile, he told me that he was employed by a state agency. "Tomorrow morning," he said, "I'll have to report promptly to my head office that I interpreted for you and had you as a guest at my house. This will be costly for me, but less so than if the spies planted in the congregation are the only ones to report."

In my sermon and our subsequent visit, we shared as believing Christians across the gulf of the Cold War divide. Underground exchanges of this sort occurred on every trip through the Iron Curtain. A further footnote regarding the Cold War climate in the Soviet bloc involved my Residential Areal Bond (RAB) project, based in Vienna, getting underway (chapter 10). When I asked my host about local ties in Marxist societies, he indicated that, at least in his city, neighboring in the traditional sense was nonexistent. Everything was spy-ridden. One couldn't be sure who could be trusted, even of people living next door. A high-ranking official in the Orthodox Church in Moscow later made the same point. These observations factored in my failure to achieve East European (other than Poland) participation in that project.

THE COUNCIL FOR RESEARCH IN VALUES AND PHILOSOPHY

By the early 1980s I had become acquainted with, and befriended by, a professor in the CUA School of Philosophy, a priest and a member of a priestly order, named George F. McLean (see the Foreword above). He participated in hosting international students at the university. McLean served also as secretary of the International Society of Metaphysics, thereby becoming acquainted with philosophers around the world. Out of these experiences emerged the vision of deeper cross-national probing than existing contacts afforded. Eventually, with the help of philosophers around the world, he established the Council for Research in Values and Philosophy (CRVP), located independently at CUA. He began to convene international symposia, initially across Cold War barriers in Eastern Europe and elsewhere. Eventually he was able to enlist foundation funding for his work.

As a first step, he invited me to participate in one of his symposia. Soon those occasions and our work in the above ventures, both CAREE and IPU, became reciprocally helpful. That process developed most fully in the instance of our IPU entry into Soviet Georgia. As the exchanges with the Institute of Philosophy there unfolded, McLean's Council (CRVP) in its university niche was far better suited to serve as host on the American side than was IPU, since the IPU had no real institutional base. The following episode exemplifies this line of development and summarizes in dramatic form the conundrum that I faced.

In 1988, on a high feast day of the Georgian Orthodox Church, I found myself at the cathedral in Georgia's capital city of Tbilisi. Georgia, a small country on the east coast of the Black Sea, with a population of some five million, is bordered by the Caucasian Mountains and Russia to the north and Armenia to the south. For nearly seventy years, since 1921, Georgia had been incorporated into the Soviet Union.

Historically, there are unconfirmed claims that the apostle Andrew had traveled to this region. More definite is the tale that a Christian slave named Nina aided the wife of the Georgian king, and won the sovereign to the faith. Historians disagree on the date of that conversion, though some place it as early as mid-fourth century CE. While Georgia as a territorial state includes other minorities, as a nation it has been identified as Christian ever since. With varied affinities to the other traditions of Eastern Orthodoxy, the Georgian church retains its own autonomy and headship (*catholikos*).

Together with a colleague and his wife from the Catholic University of America, I briefly was a guest of the Institute of Philosophy of the Georgian Academy of Sciences in Tbilisi. The clerical ritual on this occasion was long and elaborate. As in Eastern Orthodoxy, the cathedral had no pews. Instead, worshippers stood. The sanctuary was well-filled. Those who attended the entire service clustered front and center. At the periphery there was more movement, as others came and went. Around the edges, other activities appeared to be underway. In one spot a priest apparently was conducting a confessional.

As a mere visitor, knowing neither the language nor history of this ancient people, my comprehension of the cathedral service on this festive occasion remained superficial. Increasingly curious about the fluidity of this scene, I stepped outside to view the surrounding activity. As I looked about, I soon spotted a handsome middle-aged scholar whom I had met the previous week at our host institute. We greeted each other and then chatted briefly. Suddenly he offered this spontaneous comment, now etched in my memory: "Well, you see, here I am—a Marxist, an atheist, but I had my children baptized. Somehow it belongs to being Georgian."

Those words abruptly and unexpectedly dramatized the challenge that has increasingly shaped my own life, including this Tbilisi visit. Recounting the emergence of a focused calling in my early adult years, and more importantly the midlife course change triggered thereby, is the occasion and the content of this book. Doubtless one can find believing Christians among the peoples of Christendom. But what do we make of the reduction of the gospel to mere civic ritual—baptism, the symbol and seal of Christian commitment, being perpetuated "because it belongs to being Georgian" or any other national identity?

Conclusion

The Marxist scholar that day in Tbilisi captured the puzzling core of Christendom. Whether in its Eastern or its Western version, baptism has so profoundly shaped whole civilizations that its ritual survives even in a movement committed to its uprooting. Apparently I was too intrigued by his remarks to remember my reply to him. More troubling is the possibility that I was not up to the occasion! What would have been an appropriate witnessing response on my part?

Leaving that question unanswered, in the attempt here to understand backward what over the past few decades I had lived forwards (Kierkegaard, above in chapter 1), I am amazed.

The previous chapter included a passing reference to my involvement in the interdisciplinary peace studies program at Catholic University. That project was student-energized, and in the absence of faculty otherwise involved in that emerging field, I was asked to coordinate the project. As indicated, however, the earlier peace-war discussions between the peace churches (HPC) and the main-line traditions of Christendom on the surface were scarcely recognized as relevant to the activism that was now front and center.

My 1982-1983 sabbatical eased me out of the coordinating assignment in peace studies at CUA, even as that earlier experience was drawing me more deeply into the turbulence of the Cold War. Yet ironically, there too I found myself at the margins, not possessing the skills and experience essential for that dialogue. Insofar as the efforts of CAREE and the IPU and eventually CRVP bore fruit, this resulted from the participation and contribution of professionals in both the Western and the Soviet worlds.

The place of John the Baptist in the gospel story is instructive for all of us, whatever our particular calling. Jesus makes this unmistakably clear: "We are worthless slaves; we have done only what we ought to have done!" (Luke 17:10)—faithfully carrying out the calling given to us. And in doing so, the admonition of Paul in 2 Corinthians 10:12 appears pertinent: "We do not dare to classify or compare ourselves with some of those who commend themselves . . . . [T]hey do not show good sense." As he reminds us in 1 Corinthians 4:7, "What do you have that you did not receive?"

In any event, we recall historically the two modes of leadership among the Israelites and ancient peoples more generally: prophets and priests. Prophets, when authentic, spoke from and for God; priests spoke and acted on behalf of the people. Given our human condition, both modes all too readily are corruptible. If we think of a continuum between these two modes, my life calling was more prophetic than priestly. Since claiming to be a prophet to me appears presumptuous, I trust that I am simply a Christian witness.

Chapter 12

RETREAT IN A WILDERNESS

A voice cries out: "In the wilderness prepare the way of the Lord. . . ."
—Isaiah the Prophet

Good company and good discourse are the very sinews of virtue.
—Izaak Walton

Here each may say, and each may ask, whatever he/she wishes.
—Evangelical Academy at Loccum

At 7:00 a.m., Monday, July 5, 1976, Ellen and I with James, our youngest son, then ten, left our Washington, D.C., home on a five-day tenting excursion. We drove about sixty miles northwest to a wilderness spot on the lower west slope of the Blue Ridge Mountains, barely a mile above the Shenandoah River. We camped on a 1,400-acre nature preserve, perhaps seven miles south of Harpers Ferry, West Virginia, as the crow flies, where the Shenandoah joins the Potomac River. From there the enlarged Potomac flows south and east through Washington into the Chesapeake Bay.

A working week rather than vacation lay ahead. We were one of four couples each bringing a small overnight tent. The newly formed Rolling Ridge Foundation owned the nature preserve on which we camped. We four couples were beginning a project that eventually became the Rolling Ridge Study Retreat Community (RRSRC). We had reached a tentative agreement with the foundation that we would be awarded a hundred-plus-acre lease of land on which to develop facilities for an ecumenical Christian retreat. This was to become a center for contemplation and for an independent conversation concerning faith and the issues of our era. The task of our group during that week was to explore the land to find a site on that large tract that would be suitable for the project we were proposing.

The Stories Behind This Week

This retreat was the setting of the opening chapter of this book. Who or what is the Rolling Ridge Foundation? How did this nature preserve come into existence? Who were the four couples camping there together during that July week in 1976, to begin what became the Rolling Ridge Study Retreat Community? Why and how did all this come about? (Though slightly awkward, with the permission of the foundation, we later included the first two words "Rolling Ridge" of the foundation name in the title of our own retreat. Unless indicated otherwise, I will use that label in abbreviated reference to our study retreat and not to the foundation.)

First, much abbreviated, comes the Rolling Ridge Foundation story. Areas of the foothills on the western slope of the Blue Ridge south of Harpers Ferry had been sparsely settled already in colonial times. By the nineteenth century several forestry related industries emerged along the banks of the North Shenandoah River before it flowed into the Potomac. Once the land was cut over and those industries faded, suitable scraps of land were cleared for small-scale farming.

With the early twentieth-century mechanizing of farming, these farms were no longer economically viable and thus were abandoned. With little immediate economic value, this cut-over land now appeared on the market.

By the early 1950s, Henry and Mary Cushing Niles, a well-to-do professional Quaker couple from Baltimore, bought a small estate for a summer weekend cottage in this area. Along the way they had also served a term under the Ford Foundation in India. There as Quakers they explored spiritual kinship with the religious traditions of that vast country, including with the followers of the late Mohandas Gandhi. As land tracts adjacent to their cottage off the Shenandoah came on to that low-priced market, they bought additional holdings. Over the next decade or two, they acquired roughly 2,000 acres, stretching from the Appalachian Trail atop the Blue Ridge immediately to their east and at one point all the way down to the Shenandoah River.

But now they faced the question of what to do with all this land. With their own Quaker heritage further stimulated by their meditative enrichment in India, by the early 1970s they had responded readily to a suggestion to create a nature preserve from this vast holding. I will not trace here the complex financial, tax, and other legal proceedings this entailed. But after selling to the Appalachian Trail a strip of acreage immediately contiguous to theirs, they created the Rolling Ridge Foundation, ceding to it the remaining 1,400 acres. Later, while retaining the foundation's independent identity, this entire holding became coordinate with the National Park system. While now a nature preserve in perpetuity, the foundation could permit and control limited meditative and environmentally wholesome uses of its land holding.

THE FOUR-COUPLE COMPACT

During the ferment in American society in the 1960s and early 1970s, varied intentional communities emerged, mostly in urban settings, with a few moving into rural landscapes. Highly utopian in character, few of these survived the initial emotion of the era. Among the numerous faith-based communal conversations in the Washington area was that of a group composed of Church of the Savior members and scattered Mennonites. The former was a mid-twentieth century development, whereas the latter tradition hailed from the sixteenth century. However, their common accent on small-group, bottom-up faith commitments afforded some affinity among them. Already that circle had toyed with the possibility of a creating a group-based retreat in the mountains to the west of the city. But possessing neither land nor money, that discussion had gone nowhere.

Suddenly in early 1974 exciting news arrived at the Church of the Savior, headquartered at 2025 Massachusetts Avenue NW, in Washington, D.C. The FLOC Outdoor Learning Center, one of the cells nurtured by Church of the Savior, addressing the needs of inner city youth, was in search of land for summer camping activity. News of the foundation's new nature preserve turned up in the FLOC land search.

When the Church of the Savior and Mennonite group heard of this emerging nature preserve, their dormant dream quickly awakened. Two Church of the Savior couples (Verle and Vivian Headings and Dabney and Alta Miller) and two Mennonite couples (Nelson and Betty Good and Paul and Ellen Peachey) signed on. They declared their readiness to invest themselves in establishing a program for study and retreat on a cost-free land-lease grant from the Rolling Ridge Foundation.

But Ellen and I already had scheduled a yearlong (1974-1975) leave of absence from CUA for a research project in Vienna, Austria (chapter 11), and thus were physically absent from the early negotiations with the foundation. These in any case were drawn out, and we had returned from that leave well before the initial onsite event sketched above.

Why Another Religious Retreat Center?

Sacred shrines reach back into prehistoric times. In our Christian story, monasteries arose as the faith became widespread—and eventually watered down. Their renewal and commitment emphasis penetrated far beyond the monastery walls. In our own time, organized church bodies officially sponsor centers for enrichment and renewal. Other such projects are envisioned by individuals or groups around particular themes or problems. Both Roman Catholic and Protestant retreats and conference centers flourish here in the Mid-Atlantic region.

Why, then, the Rolling Ridge Study Retreat Community? As Mennonites and Church of the Savior people with a shared believers church commitment and a strong ethical and communal reach, we felt we had a contribution to make by establishing such a retreat.

In a larger sense, the promptings leading to our new Rolling Ridge venture echoed stirrings in both society and the churches of the past half century. At the same time, our yearnings were anchored anew in the fullness of the Christian story. What would we discover if we formed a semi-intentional, self-sustaining rural center, with believers church orientations, addressing anew the basic issues confronting church and society in our time, in contemplation, in study, and in exploration? And how would we proceed to bring such an endeavor into existence in the first place? Tom Donlon, who with his young family became an early participant in this venture, brought both building expertise and writing skills to our group. His published account explains the development of the project from the late 1980s when activity began in earnest. (See *Faith Road to Rolling Ridge,* Study Retreat Associates of Rolling Ridge, Inc., 1991, 2001.)

A Fragile Venture

Most rural conference or retreat centers are founded and funded by denominations or other institutions, or by individuals with resources sufficient to support the endeavor. An example of the latter is the Kirkridge Ridge Retreat in the Pocono Mountains of northeastern

Pennsylvania. The founder was the late John Oliver Nelson, a professor in Yale University Divinity School and an heir to the Pittsburgh Mellon fortune. That combination permitted an energetic beginning, even as additional funding had to be mobilized. Kirkridge drew on, and contributed to, the best in liberal Protestant ecumenism. I worked with Nelson in the 1960s, when he chaired the Church Peace Mission and in later years the War-Nation-Church Study Group that followed (see chapter 4 above).

The new RRSRC venture fell into neither of the two above classes of retreats. In our northwest Washington network, we arrived at a bottom-up, hands-on paradigm. Clearly this would be a Christian project, open to all denominations, yet administratively not tied directly to a particular church. This meant that both the vision and the energy of the venture would have to emerge from the common experience itself. Freed from the distractions of denomination-building, might we be able to work more directly at the interface of the biblical story and emerging contemporary issues? Later a management and planning professional who had been recruited to advise us described our venture as "faith-based planning."

None of the typical retreat-center paradigms applied to the manner in which RRSRC originated. This was not an engineered project, but as we experienced the process it developed providentially. During the years that Henry and Mary Cushing Niles were creating the Rolling Ridge Foundation and consolidating their various separate tracts into the foundation holding, our networking conversations were underway in Washington, with budding inklings of a possible retreat. Neither process—the Niles land acquisition nor our emerging group—was aware of the existence of the other. And the sudden availability of land crystallized those inklings, bringing together four couples prepared to risk a faith commitment to this venture.

A full history of RRSRC would involve the individual life stories of the eight charter members and a few interested parties. However, for the purposes of this book, I will merely note some important perspectives from my own pilgrimage. By the late 1960s, Ellen and I were musing that in later life we would enter some kind of retreat center. The seed of that thought lay in our experience with international voluntary service work camps under Mennonite Central Committee in Europe in the late 1940s and early 1950s, as well as our fleeting contact with the Evangelical Academies developing among postwar German Protestant churches. Leaders of the underground Confessing Church that emerged when Hitler co-opted the institutional church were often imprisoned. Among them, in prison, emerged the vision of possible postwar church centers where on neutral turf persons from differing sectors could meet to work at new solutions to social problems. In that context the term *Das Gespraech*—the conversation—became important, and has stayed with me in some form ever since.

Experiences during the two intervening decades, from early 1950s to early 1970s, reinforced those inner promptings that began in postwar Europe. Those years were not problem-free as the churches' peace probings diverted my sociological career. This also entailed considerable mobility pressure on my young family. But they were enriching years as well. Increasingly it became clear to me that the vitality of the Christian peace witness is tied closely to the vitalization of church life from below.

Returning now to our European experience, the Evangelische Akademie at Loccum, one of the first of those ventures, defined its mission as follows: "Here each may say, and each may ask, whatever he/she wishes, and each is to be prepared to change opinion/interpretation upon seeing that the one in opposition is right (my translation)."

Now in our own RRSRC setting, the founding 1976-1985 decade was particularly instructive. Two of the charter member couples and their children, the Headings and the Millers, moved at the outset from Washington, D.C., to a partnering two-house, three-household small estate outside Shepherdstown, West Virginia, about fifteen miles north of Rolling Ridge. Meanwhile, they continued their separate careers. At the time, both those couples were members of the Church of Savior. There Verle and Vivian Headings contacted the Niles and spread the word. As responses came in, they became the conveners of the group that emerged.

The two other couples, the Goods and the Peacheys with their families, remained in separate households in Washington. We, too, as those in Shepherdstown, continued our separate households and careers. Insofar as the study retreat was primarily Washington oriented, this arrangement with two families remaining in the city was appropriate. To share and continue envisioning and planning, along with organizing preliminary onsite activities, we four couples met monthly in a community supper rotating in our homes. We were bonded by a sense of common destiny in this new venture. Given our diverse careers and activity programs, the flow of volunteering as group tasks emerged was invigorating.

A New Threshold

After a decade of summer tenting events, and hauling tents, supplies, and equipment from and to Washington, signs of fatigue emerged in us all. Meanwhile Jay Good, a former Peace Corpsman with wife Marilyn and three children, had served four years onsite as interns in our venture, rendering important maintenance services. A small stream marked an informal line between the area designated for staff-community residence and for retreat buildings and activities. During this period Dabney Miller, with wife Alta, a nurse at the Veterans Hospital in Martinsburg, had enough career flexibility to engage in some onsite construction and forestry work. Construction included an outdoor privy, a storage shed, and finally a multi-purpose cabin. The cabin later was turned into the meditative arts cottage that emerged as part of the retreat program.

By summer 1985, two important new steps were taken. Ellen and I, the oldest charter-member couple in the group, children now grown, decided to move to Rolling Ridge and build a simple two-story cottage in which to live. With Jay Good as construction foreman, I forwent summer school teaching at Catholic University in summer 1985 to assist him in constructing our house.

By the end of August the shell of the simple 32' x 40' cottage was under roof, with further construction continuing during fall weekends. As much as possible we used onsite wood and stone in building. Meanwhile our group began negotiations with the appropriate West Virginia state agency to incorporate our association as a tax-free entity. Until then, we had worked formally under the umbrella of the Church of the Savior, incorporated in Washington, D.C.

Further work on the house continued through summer 1986, largely with the help of volunteers. Meanwhile, the Jay Goods followed their calling back to their native Pennsylvania by June 15 of that year. Ellen and I then moved from Washington to Rolling Ridge as scheduled in late August 1986. We spent three days weekly in Washington for my final year of teaching, while lodging at our Emery Place NW house in Washington, shared temporarily by our youngest son and several renters.

At Last, a Retreat House

Incorporation of our project as Study Retreat Associates of Rolling Ridge (SRARR), along with the onsite move of a charter member household, at last provided the impetus for constructing a tri-function year-round retreat facility. This included a meeting room, dining area and kitchen, and a few bedrooms. In the development of this project, charter member Nelson Good moved into the mobilizing niche. David Conrad, a young newly graduated professional architect, designed the structure under the guidance of a Rolling Ridge committee.

While we were able to obtain a few contributions to the building fund, Nelson Good (deceased in July 2005), was in a position to implement a shareholding program among Washington churches and church groups. Nelson and wife Betty Wenger Good had worked in Washington for more than twenty years, directing two volunteer projects there. A share in SRARR entitled a member group to use the retreat house two weeks annually per share, and to purchase one or more shares. A program and calendar resulted, totaling twenty shares, hence forty weeks, leaving twelve weeks open to others.

The three-year period, 1985-1988, brought the beginning of a resident staff (and staff house), the incorporation of the association, and above all the formation of a retreat facility and user constituency. This fleshed out both the identity and thrust of the Rolling Ridge venture for the years ahead. Environmental concerns, family and community, peace and justice all became program themes. Underlying these were the basic themes of Christian faith and life.

In the search for a unifying focal logo, we experienced some tension between programs aimed at personal spiritual enrichment and programs oriented more toward problems of a collective nature. We tried to bury that tension by adopting as our theme, "Nurturing persons and communities."

An Identity Crisis Transition

Until the mid-1980s the Rolling Ridge Study Retreat Community consisted only of the circle of the eight charter members, with Church of the Savior providing a legal face. We were united by the common vision of an eventual onsite community that would engage in sharing, learning, and reaching out to others. Our personal gifts found expression as we volunteered individually for emerging tasks as appropriate. Moving forward together toward an onsite venture served as communal bonding. All in all, 1976-1985 was an inspiring and unifying decade for our still unnamed group.

During the next three years, 1985-1988, the working dynamics changed in unforeseen ways. The time had come to begin actual program development. Our four couples were now dispersed in three locations. A board of directors, though including two or three charter members, now vied for control of our common endeavor. The net effect was a dispersal of decision and action. Mobilizing and coordinating partner groups and retreat house operations quickly added further complexity.

Suddenly we became more like an ordinary formal organization than a community. In fact, we now wore two faces. In everyday terms, we remained a study retreat community, even as formally and legally we became the Study Retreat Associates of Rolling Ridge. We now found ourselves functioning as a group of independent, bartering individuals, the problem we had set out somehow to surmount. Nonetheless, our effort moved forward.

By July 1988, following a rainy spring, *RIDGE-WAYS*, our quarterly newsletter, reported progress in building the retreat house:

> BUT THE DOUGHTY CREW PERSEVERED—Tom Donlon, the chief builder, Bob and Terry Edwards, Stephanie Johnston, and above all our own stalwart Nelson Good, who is honchoing the venture. Now, in early July, it's the heat. But the building is underway, headed toward a September finishing date. The first floor has already been framed in, with the second floor to be completed during the week beginning July 11.
>
> SIXTEEN AND ONE-HALF of the twenty shares have been contracted. Partners taking one or more shares include Community of Hope, Luther Place Memorial Church, Christian Family Community, Seekers Community of the Church of the Savior, Sojourners Fellowship, Hyattsville Mennonite Church, Community House Church and EMC's Washington Study Service Year, all from the Washington, D.C. area—truly an exciting circle and a great gift.

Meanwhile, our Study Retreat Community, drawing on a general audience, maintained its own schedule of events. Thus, for example, by April, 1992, *RIDGE-WAYS* listed this calendar:

> **May 15-16, 1992** A symposium on Nationalism and Democracy: Post-Communist Options, organized around the work of Ghia Nodia, a visiting scholar from Tbilisi, (past Soviet) Georgia, currently at Kennan Institute in Washington. A meeting of invited scholars.
>
> **May 30-June 1, 1992** A Meditative Arts retreat (Ikebana—Japanese flower arranging): nature appreciation and meditation. Organized by Ellen S. Peachey.

> **September 25-26, 1992** An Ecological Responsibility retreat organized by Verle Headings, with James Nash, Director of the Churches Center for Theology and Public Policy in Washington, author of a recently published book, *Loving Nature* (Abingdon Press). (Note the upcoming Earth Day, a UN-sponsored world event in Buenos Aires in June.)
>
> **October 2-4, 1992 Engaging the Bible** The Old Testament as spiritual resource, retreat led by Bruce Birch, Professor of Old Testament, Wesley Theological Seminary, Washington, D.C.
>
> **November 13-15, 1992** SRARR Annual Meeting. Getting to know the rhythm of life on our mountain. Intended especially for members and associates. Details later. (From the July number.)

Earlier, the July 1989 reverse page of *RIDGE-WAYS* had illustrated another dimension of RRSRC charter-member orientation:

> Wanderlust seems to have seized core members of the Retreat this spring and summer. In addition to attending a few state-side professional meetings, several headed overseas. Alta and Dabney Miller led off with a visit to their daughter Lynn on the Cape Verde Islands off the coast of Africa. Paul Peachey participated in two academic events in Poland. Verle Headings joined a service project in Haiti for ten days, sponsored by the Shepherdstown Presbyterian Church. No sooner [had he] returned than Vivian Headings headed off, with [their] daughter Caroline, to a peace convocation in Ireland, a trip likewise sponsored by the Church. Rolling Ridge—dedicated to local community? Well—yes, but also to peace and global issues. Rationalization? Readers decide.

AFTER TWO DECADES, "UNDERSTANDING BACKWARDS"

An evaluation of RRSRC for the past twenty years is beyond reach in these pages. Ellen and I left Rolling Ridge in November 2001 to move to the Virginia Mennonite Retirement Community at Harrisonburg, Virginia. Although we have not been a part of Rolling Ridge since then, I will offer a few personal reflections on our years there.

From the outset, Ellen and I were heartened and awed by the nature preserve and the four couples that became the Rolling Ridge Study Retreat Community. Both of these were gifts of God, not our own contrivances. For the first decade, we four couples had functioned as a community, not a formal organization. And following this, for Ellen and me the fifteen years of onsite resident participation was truly a crowning chapter in our lives. Our departure from Rolling Ridge came about cordially, at our initiative, not from pressures from our colleagues there. We keep in touch and return for occasional visits. The fact that Rolling Ridge has been a blessing to many people adds to our joy.

The motto we adopted early in the incorporation process, "Nurturing persons and community," without favoring one over the other, served interactively as our organizing theme. This duality was reflected as well by the slightly awkward name we had already chosen for this endeavor—"A study retreat community." While both categories benefit from study and retreat, *retreat* pertains more to personal inner life, while social issues are more likely to invoke *study*. And though our inclusive frame of reference helped this duality to some extent, it is my impression that it also deflected us from working at our unifying spiritual foundation.

The formalizing of our community as an association in 1985, while presupposing a unifying vision and mission, tended to detract from our fundamental communal discourse. Five of the original eight charter members remained influential as participants, but our seminal group conversation was now eclipsed. For the first half of our onsite residence, Ellen and I were the only full-time presence and staff of the association. Along the way came the proposal (not my own idea) that I be appointed as *study director*, an assignment I accepted.

Only now, in "understanding backwards," do I ask, What if I had been invited to be *retreat director*? The answer, of course, is that I was/am an academic, not a pastoral person. The result is evident in the above listing of the 1992 calendar of events sponsored by our (SRARR) association. Note again my reference there to the impact of the Evangelical Academy paradigm of the 1940s and thereafter in Germany. The academies, one in each province, served as centers for dialogue, affording possibilities for conversation that neither organizational nor academic settings provided otherwise. Linked to the unofficial underground confessional church that emerged during the Hitler era in Germany, the spiritual grounding for the conversational ambience (see again, the citation above from the Evangelical Academy at Loccum) could be taken for granted.

In our Rolling Ridge setting, we presupposed the bottom-up, core-Christian, ecumenical believers' reading of the biblical story. But practically this remained largely inarticulate, once our four-couple *community* became an *association*. Something more than a mere name change was underway. I recall vividly an informal conversation after an end-of-the century event at Rolling Ridge among a motley group of half-a-dozen participants that vividly demonstrated the absence of a common understanding of our spiritual presuppositions. The core group had apparently morphed into some of the problems we were formed to overcome. Yet at the emergence of a new millennium, history is crying out for precisely such an articulation.

THREE ROLLING RIDGE CASE STUDIES

To further illustrate the dilemma that emerged in the above development at Rolling Ridge, I take brief note of three examples that occurred on my watch as study director.

The first was the publication of my book, *Leaving and Clinging: The Human Significance of the Conjugal Union* (University Press of America, 2001). This was triggered in part by several retreats I led at Rolling Ridge in the mid-1990s.

The second example was a project, the Forum for the Common Good (in Jefferson County, West Virginia). Although born at Rolling Ridge, it reached into the surrounding community, where it continued for several years with my personal participation.

The third example was a cross-national event at Rolling Ridge led by Ghia Nodia, a visiting scholar from Soviet Georgia. This visit became a link in a larger process completed under other sponsorships (note the above announcement list from the April 1992 *RIDGEWAYS*). The proceedings of the several symposia that followed were eventually published in Washington, D.C., in an edited volume entitled *Knowledge and Morality: Georgian Philosophical Studies*.

ROLLING RIDGE: A SCHOOL OF HARD KNOCKS

The inclusion of this chapter about the Rolling Ridge Study Retreat Community does not pretend to offer a full review of that project. It serves merely as a culminating chapter in my autobiographical account. Kierkegaard's adage, adopted at the outset of this writing, has repeatedly been ratified throughout: "Life can only be understood backwards; but it must be lived forwards." Whether or not that sage was familiar with the biblical passage, his words echo Hebrews 11:39-40 regarding the cloud of witnesses: "Yet all these, though they were commended for their faith, did not receive what was promised, since God had provided something better so that they would not, apart from us, be made perfect."

Like the rest of my story, what we lived forwards at Rolling Ridge, I am here seeking to understand backwards. I note only two striking lessons that emerged. The first is the reinforced awareness that the origin of this venture was *graced* from the outset and not merely humanly *engineered*. This does not rule out the human flaws that lurk in all human endeavors. The cloud of witnesses in the biblical story anticipates a reality reaching beyond themselves. Nonetheless, what they have already experienced by faith enables them to act in faith regarding the not-yet aspects that in the end remain beyond reach. The rich blessings already bestowed, are faith-enabling, into the indefinite future. Rolling Ridge has yet fully to emerge.

Second, despite the fact that the Rolling Ridge Study Retreat Community was from the outset a graced venture, it was at the same time a school of hard knocks. The problems this retreat community was called to address quickly revealed their reasons for being experienced as problematic in the first place. How do we traverse the gulf between theory or doctrine and practice? How do we harmonize the bottom-up and top-down dynamics in human groupings, whether natural or religious? How are we to respond to God's action as Creator and as Redeemer/Savior? In sponsoring workshops on large public issues, as the three just listed, the concerns are often beyond the technical competencies of the staff. Should we first be working more intently at retreat, at our biblical and spiritual foundations? It is easier to frame the question than to determine their answer.

From the beginning, Rolling Ridge was described as a haven for contemplation and dialogue. Both dimensions were built into the three projects just described. There are reasons to believe that this haven ambience enhanced both individual and shared experiences for the participants. But there were problems as well. A retreat is intended to foster holistic experiences in an overly specialized era. Yet identity crisis emerged in the transition from the communal envisioning of the charter members into a formal organization. The project leading to the Forum for the Common Good raised additional questions. That a center for retreat should engage directly in public action is questionable. While approving my personal participation in the emergence of that forum, Rolling Ridge did not engage in that project beyond the original workshop retreat. But might even that indirect participation have been inappropriate?

Whatever our answers, this much remains. An attractive benefit of this retreat is its inspiring mountain location, with access to the entire land-holding on which it is situated. In my memory, gratitude for the natural ambience and quietude of this recluse was by far the most frequently expressed appreciation that I heard from persons on retreat there. Yet for those responsible for onsite projects, this must not serve as a cop-out. Without excluding interfaith encounters, as charter members we were united in the ecumenical challenge within our Christian tradition. And while in important respects this has been realized—the Christian map has been widely represented—a fundamental articulation in regard to our spiritual foundation is a far more difficult and time-consuming task.

Excursus

On rare occasions, a book author may insert an excursus to account for a serious change in direction or content that emerged while the writing was under way. To rewrite the portion already written might well be more disruptive than the momentary digression such an insertion entails. The time has come for me to connect the dots and conclude this story. The purpose of this excursus is to alert readers to the shift in focus and style in part 4, the concluding chapters 13-16. This was triggered by criticisms from a perceptive reader of the original draft, particularly of chapter 13, since revised.

The focus of this conclusion is my "Hippocratic" midlife course change as traced in chapters 8 and 9. Did I, by stepping outside the Mennonite occupational apparatus in the early 1960s, "first, do no harm"? And did something worthwhile emerge in the endeavors that followed? Answering these questions fully, of course, lies beyond my reach. Above all, there is "the Judge of all the earth" (Gen.s 18:25) who alone can and will assess my life fully. But meanwhile there are the persons and communities affected by what transpired in the process, including those who skim through these pages. All I can do here is to identify what I have learned in this long and unexpected process.

Until this point in the book, circumstances and events gave rise to perceptions and issues. Beginning with chapter 13 that order is reversed. Now the focus is on the conditioning consequences of those changes on circumstances and events. My own changing preconceptions condition my readings in ways I had not perceived.

This is but an example of the age-old gulf between theory and practice in human existence. Often when theorists begin to hold forth, the eyes of hands-on practitioners quickly glaze over. In turn, hands-on bickering may trigger eye-glazing responses from on-looking theorists. On this occasion, it is important to recognize the transition at which we have arrived and to hang in through the final chapters, wherever we may find ourselves on theory/praxis continuum. For a continuum it is, each incomplete without the other.

Relating the Phenomenal and Noumenal

This gap between theory and praxis is further compounded with the contrast between visible (phenomenal) and invisible (noumenal) dimensions of reality, particularly regarding religious reality. Synonyms of these terms, such as material and immaterial (or spiritual), may be more familiar. This distinction is discussed briefly in the next chapter. While these terms already may seem abstract and academic, the distinction is one that confronts us all. Who would hold that only what we can see and touch is real? Though we always deal with objects in time and space, we constantly engage intangible realities as well. But the reverse is also true. Indeed there is a sense in which phenomenal and noumenal perspectives tend to be reciprocally haunting. Each, as it were, lurks inseparably behind or within the other.

Theology, our God-talk, in the academic context all too readily reduces to mere secularity, to quasi-empirical reasoning. Yet talk we must. On the other hand, language itself is already richly metaphoric and figurative. It conveys meanings and messages that reach far beyond literal limits, as noted in the familiar proverb, "Actions speak louder than words." Jesus uses both devices, metaphoric and figurative, creatively. For example, in parables and figures of speech he often says, "The kingdom of God is like. . . ." In the Sermon on the Mount (Matt. 5-7), Jesus employs numerous figures of speech to announce the new reign he came to establish. His followers he describes as salt of the earth, as a light to the world, and as leaven in a lump of dough. Yet finally Jesus declares, "The kingdom of God is not coming with things that can be observed" (Luke 17:20). All this should be taken into account when reading the remaining chapters of this book.

God in Search of Humankind

In the early 1960s, I had the privilege of interviewing Abraham Joshua Herschel (1907-1972), the Polish-born Jewish rabbi then teaching at the Jewish Theological Seminary in New York. A quotation of his appears as an epigraph at the head of chapter 1 above. By 1951 Heschel had published a book titled, *Man Is Not Alone: A Philosophy of*

Religion; and in 1955, another titled, *God in Search of Man: A Philosophy of Judaism.* I do not recall when I first became aware of these books, nor am I familiar with their content today. Whether correctly or incorrectly, in contrast to the theme of the latter, "God in search of man," the reverse of that theme, "man in search of God," received attention in the former volume.

The contrast between the two phrases is pertinent here. For while the biblical story is devoted to God's initiative, to his redeeming search for humans, our God-talk all too readily reduces to becoming merely a human search for God. In summarizing our earlier chapters, this quandary must now be engaged.

These opposing searches appeared dramatically in the twentieth-century neoorthodox (Karl) Barthian confrontation with the conceits of nineteenth-century liberal Protestant theology. G. Ernest Wright's *God Who Acts: Biblical Theology as Recital* (SCM Press, 1952), coming in the wake of Barth, energized me a decade later, as I began my Church Peace Mission assignment (chapter 7 above). The Bible, he wrote, "is not primarily the Word of God, but the record of the acts of God, together with the human response" (107); not the triumph of human progress and achievement, but our submission to God who seeks us.

The focus of chapter 13 is set forth in the biblical story (Gen. 8: 21):

> "And when the LORD smelled the pleasing odor [of Noah's sacrifice], the LORD said in his heart, 'I will never again curse the ground because of humankind, for the inclination of the human heart is evil from youth; nor will I ever again destroy every living creature as I have done.'"

It continues with the next crisis, when the people of the earth were scattered at the Tower of Babel, then in the saving process initiated with the call to Abram. God kept responding to the evil inclinations of the human heart over many centuries, allowing history to continue until end-time fulfillment (1 Cor. 15:20-28).

PART FOUR

Chapter 13

The Creation/Salvation Symbiosis

Here [John 18:36-37] we must divide the children of Adam and all mankind into two classes, the first belonging to the kingdom of God, the second to the kingdom of the world. . . .
—Martin Luther

The question before the human race is whether the God of nature shall govern the world by his own laws, or whether priests and kings shall rule by fictitious miracles.
—John Adams to Thomas Jefferson, 1815

Paradoxical as it may seem, the concentration upon redemptive history signifies the very opposite of indifference toward the world process. Christian existence involves polarities that pull us in opposite directions and sometimes seem like contradictions, yet must be held in creative tension.
—Duane Friesen

In the several chapters comprising the final section of this story, we come now to engage the end result. What do we learn from the experiences here described? And if there are valid results, what are the implications as we continue our journeys? The preceding excursus provides a bit of context for the task before us. There are many shelves of books that relate to the issues we thus face. I am indebted to a few of them. Here, however, I continue (more or less) informally.

In these remaining chapters, we confront the perennial puzzle of how to reach across the gap between theory and practice. Theologians, other academics, and teachers of doctrine all too often seem far removed from the real life situations that confront us. Yet far more than we realize we are shaped by them, mostly by way of the culture and the institutions that surround us. Grappling with that dilemma is the challenge that we, from our varied backgrounds and life contexts, together face in these final chapters.

A full-blown autobiography might end with lessons to draw from my life. In these final chapters, the vocational focus that emerged for me in the debate between the just war and the pacifist traditions in the global ecumenical Christian community (see part 2), becomes the fitting focus. Particularly during 1957-1967, when that debate was central in my life, I sensed that the issue lies beyond resolution in those terms. With the opportunity to resume my sociological interest, the just war/pacifist deadlock was put on hold. The rubric that emerged from all of this as the underlying deeper problem is the title of this chapter, to be elaborated further in the rest of this book.

A Pause That Refreshed

During August 1967, in a break between assignments in Europe, I spent a week on personal retreat at Maria-Laach, the ancient Benedictine monastery in Germany's Westerwald region. Within several weeks, back home in Washington, D.C., I would finally begin my second career, as a sociology professor at Catholic University of America. After arriving at the monastery, I outlined a series of day-by-day themes for reflection during that week. According to that outline, the theme on the fourth day was to be my profession/career.

In preparation for the present chapter, I was somewhat surprised—and slightly embarrassed—to find the following introductory paragraphs from the journal I kept during this Maria-Laach pause, copied here in part from the notes I took that day:

> Somehow, however, something seems to hold together across the whole development—all the way from my passion for good farms to my current "return" to the world. Curiously it might be said: it is harder to take God the Creator seriously than God the Savior. For out of the latter it is easy enough to manufacture a special vocation—monastic, teacher, missionary or something else that dispenses one from the necessity of taking the world seriously. Thus now my life fronts as it were against two perversions: (a) the self-sufficient secularity of "Christian" and non-Christian alike; and (b) the interpretation of the faith as an

epiphenomenon—an additional institution superimposed upon life, a haven for professionals, and impoverishment and bondage to the "common people."

Professionally this means that I must earn my bread in the fulfillment of our destiny in the world, that I must labor at the same time as a "lay theologian," esp. at the one "theological" work I should produce in my life-time (the "church from within," sketches I've been making), that I must invest myself in the basic questions of *das menschliche Zusammenleben* [human togetherness] which have engaged me (often on the back burner), in clear continuity these 24 years. While for the moment, the CUA-WCMS [Catholic University of America, and the Washington Center for Metropolitan Studies] appointment where I was about to begin—ateliers [workshops] seemingly tailored precisely, I must now await the new content to be poured. (It is interesting to recall the question I asked of Samuel Zwemer, following a missionary lecture at Goshen [College], summer 1944—how to relate Gen[esis] 1 & the great commission. . . .)

"Harder to take God the Creator seriously than God the Savior"? . . . "Await the new content to be poured"? Above all: "how to relate Gen[esis] 1 & the great commission." (Matt. 28:19-20)

After wrestling for some years (particularly 1957-1967) with the dissonance on peace-and-war issues between the mainline church traditions of Christendom and the Anabaptist believers church alternative, by midlife I was concluding that the root of this disagreement lay deeper than the terms of the just war/pacifist debate itself. That growing awareness was reinforced by mounting malaise within my own professional life at Eastern Mennonite College. EMC and much of its constituency were culturally conservative. There surface debates obscured substantive issues.

Uncertain where that deeper problem lay, I had decided on a change in my life course, awaiting broader understanding as I labored at tasks at hand. Soon I was working in settings other than those in which I had found myself so far. While I could not foresee where this would lead, I realized at least to some degree that such a change would be costly, both professionally and for our family.

Only recently, as I tackled the writing of this book, did the creation/salvation symbiosis addressed in this chapter come sharply into focus for me. As the above anecdote indicates, however, the embryo of this awareness was taking shape already in my early adulthood. As the reference above to my question to Samuel Zwemer

(1867–1952, evangelist to the Muslim world) suggests, I had an inkling in this direction already by my senior year in college (1944–1945). Now by midlife, some twenty years later, as this slightly awkward Maria-Laach journal entry regarding "God the Creator" versus "God the Savior" indicates, this puzzle had already become an important point in my frame of reference.

Moreover, there was the apparent irony of the course on which I was embarking. If I found the denominational structuring of the Mennonite believers church problematic, was not my surprising appointment to the faculty of Catholic University of America, a United States embodiment of classic Christendom and the antithesis of the Radical Reformation out of which Mennonites had come, a leap from the frying pan into the fire? More on this conundrum later.

THE CREATION/SALVATION SYMBIOSIS

Jesus began his ministry with forceful simplicity and clarity. "The time is fulfilled, and the kingdom of God has come near; repent, and believe in the good news," he announced (Mark 1:15). Yet on another level, this good news remains veiled in mystery, indeed veiled to this day and in time to come. In the account of Jesus' farewell from his inner circle (Acts 1:6-8), at their excitement that this would suddenly be the grand finale, the end time, came a profound reply.

> "It is not for you to know the times or the periods that the Father has set by his own authority. But you will receive power when the Holy Spirit has come upon you; and you will be my witnesses in Jerusalem, in all Judea and Samaria, and to the ends of the earth."

Earlier in his ministry, in announcing the kingdom of God, Jesus celebrated

> "the lilies of the field, how they grow; they neither toil nor spin, yet I tell you, even Solomon in all his glory was not clothed like one of these. But if God so clothes the grass of the field . . . will he not much more clothe you—you of little faith?" (Matt. 6:28-29)

God is at once Creator and Savior. Two gods or the one true God wearing two hats, as it were? Which was it? Which is it? Indeed, soon a further complexity arose. God the Savior incarnate in Jesus of Nazareth, after Jesus' ascension implemented his saving intervention by way of the Holy Spirit. What does all that signify?

In the early centuries following the Christ event, in that polytheistic era, the believing followers of Jesus wrestled with precisely these mysteries. First, that of God as Creator and as Savior, as Father and Son. Then the Savior as Jesus and as Holy Spirit. And eventually God, though one, came to be understood as triune, as Trinity. Christians have widely come to live with these mysteries, but as matters of faith, hardly of reason. In instruction of the faith at all levels God the Father, God the Son (Jesus), and God the Holy Spirit receive appropriate attention.

But, in keeping with the title of this chapter, in some contexts the focus is on one or the other of the two modes of divine action in the world, *creation* and *salvation*. (*Grace, salvation,* and *redemption* are synonyms used variously in New Testament language. In our references to symbiosis we will mostly use the word *salvation*.)

Examples abound. The distinction (and separation) of church and state is a dramatic instance. For centuries, that distinction was badly blurred. It began to reemerge in the sixteenth-century Protestant Reformation but then was further delayed. Clear separation survived only marginally in the widely persecuted Anabaptist beginnings. Evident in previous chapters of this book was my own heritage in that duality.

On the surface, I was shaped by the sharp historical duality between the religious communities rooted in the tradition of medieval Christendom, by then both Catholic and Protestant, and the Anabaptist believers church communities, proposed as the fundamentally true alternative. While repudiation of violence by Christians was viewed by those communities as intrinsic in the life of Christians, these were not in the first instance mere antiwar movements.

The two world wars of the twentieth century, erupting largely among nations known as part of Christendom, heightened the importance of nonresistance or nonviolence in the identity of Mennonites. Though not all Mennonite draftees signed on as conscientious objectors (COs), a small majority did. These contributed importantly to the alternative service and postwar relief and reconstruction programs implemented by Mennonite Central Committee, and subsequent developments.

How then did I come to attribute the disagreement between the Anabaptist and Christendom traditions to the creation/salvation distinction? Surely both traditions sprang in some measure from God's saving grace. Why then the sharp difference between them? Among the various sources of disagreement was their reading of God's creation apart from his saving agency. Whatever other influences may have been at work as well, this one figured importantly in my experiences. So we turn now to the problem of Christendom in the symbiosis (interaction) of creation and salvation in Christian history.

Jesus came announcing the arrival of the reign of God. Describing the blessings of the coming kingdom, occasionally he attached the sobering qualifier, "with persecutions" (Mark 10:30). Indeed, in the early centuries persecution of Christians often occurred. And, at one place or another, persecution is underway even to this day. What quickly became clear was this: The radical life change acceptance of the new reign of God entailed might well be perceived as disrupting any public order not based on that change.

"In the beginning when God created. . . ." These are the familiar opening words of what became known as the biblical story. Today that beginning is often described as the Big Bang. However that beginning came about, creation as set forth in the two opening chapters of Genesis appears as an unfolding process. But once the human species is introduced, by design as collaborator with the Creator in the stewardship of the earthly part of reation, something quickly goes amiss. After or during undefined eons of time, catastrophes follow, first a flood and then a scattering of the peoples that emerged from a surviving minority from that flood. All this is compressed in the first eleven chapters of Genesis, the first of the sixty-six books comprising the biblical collection (as most widely accepted).

Then in chapter 12 a remedial new beginning is introduced:

> Now the Lord said to Abram, "Go from your country and your kindred and your father's house to the land that I will show you. I will make of you a great nation, and I will bless you, and make your name great, so that you will be a blessing. I will bless those who bless you, and the one who curses you I will curse; and in you all the families of the earth shall be blessed." (vv. 1-3)

Thus Abram, whose genealogy is listed in the previous chapter of Genesis and whose name will be changed, is told to pack up with his wife and household and leave his homeland for an unknown destination. That summons came from the Creator God, unknown beneath the polytheistically clouded sky of that time. Only by responding step by step did Abraham come to know that Supreme Being, eventually called Yahweh by his Hebrew descendants. Thereby a duality, a saving story within the original biblical story, is introduced and infused into the larger account.

That duality becomes the organizing focus of, and indeed the occasion for, what can be seen as Act I of the biblical story. The rest of the Old Testament, the history and vocation of the Israelites (ultimately the Jews) can be described as Act II. This eventually grows into Act III, the Christ event, today still in progress and ultimately to climax in Act IV, eschatologically beyond the present age.

God the Creator Is Savior as Well

We now arrive at the baffling heart of the biblical mystery, and the confusing human responses to that mystery for Jews and Christians. (References to other religions are not part of the agenda here.) Four distinct stages in the unfolding of the biblical story have just been outlined. The first and the last of these lie outside the time frame of Acts II and III, the Jewish and Christian eras. In the first act, God's supplementary saving action does not yet occur, while in Act IV, beyond the reach of our human comprehension, it is no longer in effect. As noted in 1 Corinthians 15:24, "Then comes the end, when he [Christ] hands over the kingdom to God the Father." Act II, beginning with the call to Abraham, covers the Old Testament Jewish phase of the biblical story. Act III begins with the coming of Christ, extending from New Testament times until the end.

During the entire sweep of Acts II and III, God's saving intervention operates within the realm of the Creation. Moreover, Act III passes through two stages: (1) the New Testament era of the incarnation; and (2) the post-incarnation era, the age of the Holy Spirit. Given this latter distinction, with reference to God we commonly think of the Trinity: God the Father, God the Son, and God the Holy Spirit.

All this, of course, elicits great complexity and confusion in our finite minds. To simplify for our present analytical purpose, I use this four-act scheme and the more common creation/salvation duality. The focus of our problem is the confusion that arises from this duality. According to the biblical story, God's creating and saving agencies are continuously interactive to the end of time.

The contrasting interactions between these two modes of divine presence in part restore and enhance the human presence and participation in God's Creation, on planes both individual and social. Both modes of God's sovereignty, creation and salvation, transcend our human finitude. Yet on another plane, the fulfillment of God's purpose depends on human responses. God respects the freedom with which he endowed us, a capacity mysteriously flawed in "the Fall"

(Gen. 3). In the story begun in the call to Abram and traced in the biblical narrative unfolding over many centuries, an emerging remedy is offered to those who respond to the salvation thus offered.

The term *symbiosis*, applied to the interaction of creation and salvation (or grace) in human affairs, is introduced here a bit uneasily. I borrow this word from biology, where it refers to the process of organisms living together, implying interdependence. Hints of symbiosis reside already in the call to Abram. Not only will the great nation arising from his action be beneficial in itself, but dispersed among others it will be a blessing to all the families of the earth.

I was steered to this symbiosis by the inconclusive just war/pacifist debates among Christian scholars in which I participated for a number of years. During that time I benefited greatly from a mid-twentieth century theological discussion concerning the "God who acts" in contrast to a supreme concern with the Word of God. (See for example G. Ernest Wright, *God Who Acts: Biblical Theology as Recital*, SCM Press, 1952.)

The context of that discussion was the rise of neoorthodox theological thought, overcoming the longtime triumph of theological liberalism in the modern era. God came to be seen anew in his acting and saving intervention in the world. This recognition bears directly not only on our understanding of God but also correspondingly on our believing and repenting responses.

Acutely missing, not only in our war/peace discussions but more broadly as well, is clarity regarding the redeeming activity of God at the core of the biblical story through the Old and New Testaments, with important milestones along the way culminating in the mission and ministry of Jesus the Christ and the launching of Pentecost, the coming of the Holy Spirit. This underscores the primal importance of the symbiosis of creation and salvation in the current discussion. What is needed first is not an intellectual creedal consensus but a shared existential recognition of God who acts. Certainly theologizing has its place, but it is merely a conceptual aid in our communication. Faith presupposes knowledge—information, if you wish. But faith means the staking of the self on God-awareness.

A forceful New Testament exclusion of any assimilation of the gospel into the fallen secular order appears in the final departure of Jesus the Christ from his apostles as recorded in Acts 1:6-9:

> So when they had come together, they asked him, "Lord, is this the time when you will restore the kingdom to Israel?" He

replied, "It is not for you to know the times or periods that the Father has set by his own authority. But you will receive power when the Holy Spirit has come upon you; and you will be my witnesses in Jerusalem, in all Judea and Samaria, and to the ends of the earth." When he had said this, as they were watching, he was lifted up, and a cloud took him out of their sight.

Note that Jesus' followers are to be witnesses, not external enforcers or rulers. This term reaches deep into Old Testament times, notably the prophecies of Isaiah. Building on Isaiah, Jesus' mystifyingly pronounced that "one who believes in me . . . will do greater works than these, because I am going to the Father" (John 14:12). How does this square with the earlier claim in the same chapter, "I am the way, and the truth, and the life. No one comes to the Father except through me" (v. 6)? Later, at the end of his earthly ministry, Jesus unmistakably told his inner circle to stay put in Jerusalem after his departure until the Holy Spirit came and empowered them to become his witnesses to the ends of the earth.

A number of days later, as recounted in Acts 2, the Holy Spirit came dramatically on believers gathered in Jerusalem awaiting that coming. Peter, addressing the Pentecost crowd, emerged as a clearly changed person. We can only conclude that this change is what Jesus meant in the announcement that something greater than his earthly presence would happen after his departure. The indwelling Holy Spirit, not achievable apart from or before Jesus' Passion, would effect a transformation that mere external proclamation and discipleship could not!

The Rise of Christendom

Initially, Christians broke radically with the prevailing religious and cultural practices that surrounded them. Turbulence followed. In the fourth century of the Christian era, the Roman Empire sought to accord priority to Christianity over the other religions that prevailed throughout the imperial domain. By early in the fifth century, Augustine (354–430), a bishop/theologian in North Africa, by then the leading Christian scholar in the Mediterranean world, provided a theological rationale for this abrupt change. The earlier aloofness of Christians in the empire, notably in their refusal to bear arms, was because the rulers still were pagan, Augustine argued. But now that rulers had become Christian, he reasoned, what Christian could deny their use of force to prevent the greater evils of unbelief? By further reasoning, it came to be argued that Jesus specially transmitted to Peter the keys of the kingdom. That endowment he was to pass on to his successors (Matt. 16:18–19), a process eventually understood as grounding for the Roman papacy.

To make his original case, Augustine cited what he interpreted as biblical precedents for the use of force in the cause of Christ. For example, he mentioned Jesus' parable of a man who gave a banquet. When the invitees failed to show up, the man sent his servants to the roads to compel people to come in to fill the vacant seats. And a second one: How did Saul become Paul? God smote him down. By interpreting, or twisting, such examples as these, Augustine justified sending "Christian" troops to root out the Donatist heretics in North Africa. War, the epitome of human fallenness in the sphere of creation, thereby was ritualized, ostensibly becoming part of the salvation that in reality it supplants!

FROM COVENANT TO MONARCHY: THE ISRAELITES

For more than a millennium directly (and indirectly), Augustine's reasoning came to prevail in the Mediterranean world, spreading northward into Europe. Outwardly, one might claim, Christianity had triumphed. In reality the symphony of creation and salvation was reformulated in the Constantinian/Augustinian epoch into an ostensible fusion of these two irreducible modes of divine initiative.

Increasingly, however (especially since the eighteenth-century Enlightenment), this conflation of church and state has proved to be impractical. This is true historically and politically quite apart from the basic contradiction of such a claim. Nonetheless, this legacy of Christendom remains embedded in our Western ethos, and in our psyches, particularly in the United States where, since the adoption of its constitution, church and state have been formally separated.

Confusedly, "God bless America" in myriad forms has become a mantra in our society. Retrospectively, it has been suggested that had Constantine not acted as he did in the early fourth century, Christianity might not have survived. A precedent for such a claim is taken from the crisis in ancient Israel in its premonarchy days as recorded in 1 Samuel 8–9. Though monarchy was not included in the Mosaic covenant, it was permitted as an emergency measure, albeit with qualifications and forewarnings, when the outward survival of the covenant people of Israel was endangered by surrounding regimes.

Indeed, royal imagery was assimilated to some degree into Israelite language and ritual!

Despite this, as forewarned, the royal stage of Israelite history ended disastrously. In that outcome, Jewish identity was reconstituted, with dispersion and synagogue replacing land and temple as the grounding of Semitic peoplehood. Diaspora as witness, not this-worldly political rule, thus emerged as the destiny and mission of the Abrahamic "great nation." The Constantinian mutation of the Christian movement, though resembling the Jewish story, is without the biblical sanction accorded to the crowning of Saul and the eventual Davidic monarchy. In any event, the era of Christendom has likewise long since ended. Christians, however, are still struggling to find their identity in this post-Christendom diaspora.

The Confusion of Christendom

A critical aspect of the reign of God announced by Jesus of Nazareth was this distinction between the *already* and the *not yet* phases of that reign (the threshold between Act III and Act IV). In the good news that is the gospel, the reign of God already has broken into the world, transforming those who repent and believe. Yet equally emphatic is the assertion that the completion and the consummation of that reign lies in the still indefinite and mysterious future. As noted above, Jesus in announcing the reign of God in equally forthright words, forewarns that the reign comes "with persecutions" (Mark 10:30). Though Jesus calls us to live in the world even as he lived in it, this commitment remains to some degree at odds with the world. Eventually, as response to the transforming process became more widespread, the human propensity all too readily took over. The story tended to become increasingly popularized and thereby watered down.

This happened classically in the emergence of Western Christendom. By the fourth century, Christianity had spread widely among the many diverse peoples of the Mediterranean world, but with local persecutions emerging sporadically. Meanwhile, occupation of the Roman Empire's seat of authority, which imposed a minimum of order on that region, still was contested. In 312, as Constantine, a regional ruler, prepared for his finally victorious battle over his rival for that seat, according to legend a vision of the cross appeared in the sky above him, along with the words in Latin: "In this sign [you will] conquer." Following this vision, he ordered the cross painted on the shields of his soldiers—and won the battle! Herewith we have the birth of Christendom: the blurring of the line between state and church, between the realm of creation (nature) and that of salvation (grace).

Thereby the ostensible assimilation of the processes of grace into those of nature was set in motion, *ostensibly* because in reality such a reduction is humanly impossible. Insofar as such change occurs outwardly, as the structures of grace are subsumed into those of nature, as in the state church, the outcome is neither nature nor grace. Often it becomes idolatry instead.

Remarkably, however, this confusion did not preclude authentic experiences of grace on their own merits. Such occurrences are reminiscent of times of such compromise in ancient Israel. When under the reign of King Ahab corruption flourished, God spoke to and through the Prophet Elijah at Horeb: "Yet I will leave seven thousand in Israel, all the knees that have not bowed to Baal, and every mouth that has not kissed him" (1 Kings 19:18).

THE PETER AND PAUL DUO

Returning now to the New Testament era, the distinction between Jesus' earthly ministry and the dramatic outpouring of the indwelling Spirit surfaced in the subsequent encounter of Peter and Paul in chapters 13–15 of the book of Acts. This engagement of these two preeminent apostles is poorly understood and sorely neglected in our churches today. I don't presume here to explain fully what transpired in that encounter. Instead, I simply urge reflection on the varied experiences these two pioneering disciples/apostles brought to their Jerusalem meeting. Note their different yet partly parallel "aha moment"—Paul's in chapter 9, Peter's in chapter 10.

Peter had followed Jesus around Palestine, possibly for as long as three years, yet he became an inwardly transformed person only at Pentecost. Paul, on the other hand, presumably had never seen, heard, or met Jesus in the flesh. Yet what happened to Paul on the road to Damascus a few years earlier resonated profoundly with Peter's inner experience at Pentecost. As becomes evident in the Acts accounts, both men needed "sorting-out time" after their particular coming-of-the-Spirit life experiences.

Are we inferring too much if we conclude that Paul was sent by God expressly so we don't misunderstand or misapply the paradigm that Peter rightly became? Neither Peter's nor Paul's story can be understood fully without the other. Without the Pauline chapter, Petrine discipleship can be reduced to mere external imitation. On the other hand, without the Petrine chapter, the Pauline story may evaporate in our perception into simple subjectivity, even hallucination. Might it be useful analytically to suggest that the rise of Christendom—the story of Constantine in the fourth century, a story theologically baptized a century later by church father Augustine—effectively dissolved the symbolic synergism of the lives of Peter and Paul?

Christianity as Christendom (Peter without Paul) reduces readily to the perpetuation of external ritual practice without the inner transformation by the Holy Spirit. Might it also be said that, in reverse, varied charismatic movements over the centuries have promoted conversion as emotion without communal life ethics (Paul without Peter)? And what about other readings of the gospel story, including the attempted Anabaptist both/and alternative? In Christian disputes and schisms generally, this question haunts us. At what point are we turning Petrine at the expense of the Pauline alternative? And when do Pauline challenges to the Petrine become little more than the reverse error?

THE PREMATURE PROTESTANT AND ANABAPTIST REFORMATIONS

Just as the monarchy was a temporary phase in Israelite history, so also was Christendom transitional in the Christian era. As the rise of Israelite kingship brought with it the challenge of a new era of prophecy, so too did the rise of imperially established Christendom. Here the prophetic challenge came in the form of monasticism that spread throughout Europe. Occasionally "heretical" movements emerged as well. But gradually monasticism became domesticated within Christendom at the expense of its prophetic vocation.

Eventually, in the context of the Renaissance (the invention of the printing press, the Peasants' War, and other socioeconomic changes) the Protestant Reformation arose. At an early stage came a reciprocal excommunication between the Lutheran reform movement and the Church of Rome (both by 1521). But meanwhile the question of alternative paradigms was becoming urgent. The complexity of the problems at the time stretches our imagination. Translations of Scripture, liturgy, and administration from Latin and the biblical languages into German was an enormous task. But perhaps the most dramatic problem was the Peasants' War (1524-1525). This provoked an emotional appeal from Martin Luther to political authorities to brutally suppress the peasant revolt, an appeal titled, "Against the Thieving and Murderous Hordes of Peasants" (1525). Effectively the reform was stalled, and the church thrown back into the arms of the state.

Of more importance here is Luther's essay of January 1526, "The German Mass and Order of Divine Service." Still reaffirming the medieval Latin mass as the basic Christian order, Luther authorized a German translation of the mass for uneducated commoners. After a passing reference to the Latin service and detailing the new German version, he outlined a third option. He suggested the possibility of a new church order in some indefinite future, implying his readiness to support it should it arise. In that instruction Luther wrote:

> Here there would not be need of much fine singing. Here we could have baptism and the sacrament in short and simple fashion: and direct everything toward the Word and prayer and love. Here we should have a good short Catechism about the Creed, the Ten Commandments, and the Lord's Prayer. In one word, if we only had people who longed to be Christians in earnest, Form and Order would soon shape itself. But I cannot and would not order or arrange such a community or congregation at present. I have not the requisite persons for it, nor do I see many who are urgent for it.

Striking here is Luther's awareness that a full disentanglement of church and state might well be appropriate, with the implication that it might come about eventually, but that the time did not yet seem right for so drastic a change

How fascinating that Luther released the above-mentioned treatise in January 1526, a year to the month after the first Anabaptist (re)baptisms had occurred in Zurich, Switzerland, in January 1525. Did Luther know that such an act had taken place? He wrote seemingly unaware of that development. Yet it is hard to imagine that, given his prominence in that turbulent time, the news of the Zurich event had not yet reached him!

In any case, Luther shared openly his inkling in 1526 that a free church, indeed a believers church, while perhaps appropriate was not yet timely. Meanwhile as earlier mentioned, Fritz Blanke, the twentieth-century Protestant historian of sixteenth-century Anabaptism, concluded that the only mistake of that movement was that historically it came too early. Whereas Luther urged the suppression of the budding Anabaptist movement, indeed brutally so, Professor Blanke shortly after mid-twentieth century wrote:

> In reality that [starting an independent believers church in the heart of Christendom] was no fault but a heroic deed. There will always be a need for men who, unconfused by the spirit of the age, set out for new goals and strive toward a new dawn. The Zollikon "Brothers in Christ" [the first such actual congregation] were such a vanguard. Their daring has not been in vain. In gratitude we bow before them today. (B*rothers in Christ: The History of the Oldest Anabaptist Congregation, Zollikon, Near Zurich, Switzerland*, Herald Press, 1961, p. 71)

Broadly speaking, both Luther and Blanke stood in what long since has become known as the Protestant Reformation, but with more than four centuries of modern history between them. When that sixteenth-century Reformation first began, the church had been incorporated into the public order for more than a millennium. The dissolution of the interdependence of church and state had long since become inconceivable.

THE SECULAR OUTMODING OF CHRISTENDOM

It is difficult to surmise how church/state relations might have been resolved in the Reformation had there not been the peasant uprising. Whatever the answer, the Protestant movement in both its Lutheran and Calvinist versions returned to state control. They differed from the Roman Catholic/imperial scheme because their scale was regionally national and royal rather than universal and imperial. Still some greater variation in church proceedings became possible.

But contrary to reintegration of the church into the political order in Protestantism, the flow of secular forces (society, economics, polity, and eventually the Enlightenment) was in the opposite direction. Over the next few centuries the North American continent, a haven for restless Europeans, offered promising opportunities and resources. Once the United States had been formed (1776), and its constitution adopted (1787), the First Amendment added (1791) this famed declaration:

> Congress shall make no law respecting an establishment of religion, or prohibiting the exercise thereof; or abridging the freedom of speech, or of the press; or the right of the people peaceably to assemble, and to petition the Government for a redress of grievances.

To describe and assess the achievement of this amendment I turn to words of noted historian, Perry Miller, who wrote almost two centuries later:

> The point is, to put it baldly, that both in education and in religion, we didn't aspire to freedom, we didn't march steadily toward it, we didn't unfold the inevitable propulsion of our hidden nature: we stumbled into it . . . denominations and sciences multiplied until there was nothing anybody could do about them. Wherefore we gave them freedom to exist, and called the result freedom of the mind. Then we found, to our vast delight, that by thus negatively surrendering we could congratulate ourselves on a positive and heroic victory. (*Nature's Nation*, Belknap Press, 1967, p. 155)

Politically and historically the separation of church and state was indeed a positive and heroic victory—but in reality merely stumbled into. To this day the underlying issues remain unaddressed in the American ethos. Despite the external separation of church and state, the Christendom legacy of church without believers lives on in the American psyche.

The Anabaptist Alternative

Since antiquity, institutional religion and forms of mysticism have appeared as opposites. That contrast appears within particular religions as well. Christianity has been no exception. Particularly during medieval times, as Christendom became more fully institutionalized, mysticism likewise flourished both within and contrary to Roman Catholicism. For comparative purposes, it may be helpful to think of Anabaptism as emerging midway between these two extremes yet partly participating in both. To do so need not include the claim that the Anabaptists fully succeeded.

Such an exercise is helpful in our reading of the Anabaptist consensus achieved at Schleitheim on February 27, 1527. The seven-article "Brotherly Union" drawn up on that occasion likely was triggered by the drowning of Felix Manz in the Limmat River in Zurich in early January 1527, nearly two months before. Manz, a cofounder of the Anabaptist movement (1525), was the first such leader to be executed by the Zurich regime. These besieged pioneers realized that the time had come to declare themselves, which they did in the "Brotherly Union."

Here we can only note in passing the enriching explosion of Anabaptist studies that grew in the decades that followed the mid-century Harold S. Bender era. Already by the 1980s some scholars were abandoning a monogenetic(one source) reading of Anabaptist origins in favor of a polygenetic (many sources) version. An example of this was the failed attempts in several cities in the early Reformation era simply to rebaptize the locally established churches, notably in Waldshut (South Germany) and St. Gall (Switzerland),

The fact that there were confusing efforts to redefine the church during those troubled sixteenth-century upheavals was inevitable. But far from relativizing the Anabaptist vision achieved in the Brotherly Union, both its emergence and its subsequent stabilizing impact become the more remarkable. To be sure, there is debatable detail in that document. But in the context of our chapter heading, "The Creation/Salvation Symbiosis," the key phrasing of that Schleitheim statement ("the sword is an ordering of God outside the perfection of Christ") remains fundamentally incisive.

Church historian Fritz Blanke (1900–1967) directed my cross-disciplinary dissertation at the University of Zurich in the early 1950s (see chapter 3 above). This was a sociological study of Swiss Anabaptist origins during the formative years from 1525 to 1540. Professor Blanke commented briefly in a German essay (*Aus der Welt der Reformation*, Zwingli Verlag, 1960, p. 80) on the state of European Christendom during that sixteenth-century era. He referred to the state-established church traditions as *corpus christianum* (the Christian body), and the dissenting Anabaptists (the Radical Reformation) as an apolitical alternative. He concluded that "one can no more approve *corpus christianum* than *apoliticism*. We must find a solution that supersedes both (*eine Loesung die ueber beides hinausfuehrt*)."

Blanke, while taking seriously the Protestant paradigm (the Reformed version of which had shaped him), clearly moved beyond both the Christendom and Anabaptist formulations. He recognized the fallacy of Christendom (*corpus christianum*) but likewise the insufficiency of the Anabaptist believers church alternative. The Anabaptists no longer found any relation to the state, Blanke argued, and naturally that was likewise false.

He challenged Christians to move beyond both alternatives, as well as to reject the sectarian label applied to the Anabaptists. "The defining trait of a 'sect' is the recognition of other authorities in addition to Christ," he maintained. But "the circles endorsing the Schleitheim Articles are consciously aware that in the core Christian teachings they agree with Luther and Zwingli." Therefore "the only 'mistake' of which we may accuse the men and women of Zollikon [the Zurich suburb where the first congregation was formed] would be that they went at their task too early. . . ." Appropriately, he concludes that superseding both the Christendom and the Anabaptist paradigms remains to this day our challenge. That is, we need to recognize and cope with the continuing mystery of God's symbiotic presence as Creator and Savior in our particular time and place.

In the remaining chapters of this book, I offer some reflections on the implications of all this for us today. By now it seems abundantly clear that the search for the true church (in an organizational or institutional form that is universally applicable) is futile, if not indeed idolatrous. The biblical story offers the criteria that guide us as we seek to respond to the gospel in every time and place. In that process, the sharing of experiences among gatherings of believers today, along with the cloud of witnesses that has gone before (Heb. 12:1) is fundamental.

It is clear that we have suffered over the centuries, and that we still suffer today, from institutional top-heaviness in church life at the expense of the primary cells of a shared living faith. Much of the muddled bewilderment among modern Christians derives from both past and current deficiencies in this regard. Nonetheless, in the words of Jesus, the primal challenge remains: "Do not be afraid, little flock, for it is your Father's good pleasure to give you the kingdom" (Luke 12:32).

Chapter 14

Ekklesia and Diaspora

The Holy One, blessed be he, gave Israel over into galuth [exile, dispersion] among nations only in order that they might attract to themselves proselytes.
—Rabbi Simon ben Eleazar (Second Century CE)

The [Anabaptists] recognized that the Theodosian way (380 CE) of bringing church and state together cannot be done without damaging both partners. Hence their renunciation of the corpus christianum.
—Fritz Blanke

The disengagement of the church from the state has allowed both to function more authentically.
—Robert G. Clouse, et al.

In recent years, religious leaders have been paying increasing attention to small groups. Bible studies, prayer fellowships, house churches and covenant groups are being touted as the wave of the future.
—Robert Wuthnow

The last chapter referred to controversies that disrupt Christian faith communities. This chapter addresses the most disruptive, the aggregating of Christian believers. Dormant in every commitment we make is the potential for hegemony and exclusion. Both are alien to Christian commitments. Jesus said, "I am among you as one who serves" (Luke 22:27). However, mutations of hegemony and exclusion within and among groups of Christians, as well as between Christian and other groupings, have plagued Christians from the outset. In key ways, in the gatherings of Christians as churches is where, in the symbiosis of creation and salvation, "the rubber hits the road."

Etched in My Memory

As earlier noted, in 1088 in Tbilisi, Goergia, a scholar told me that though he was Marxist and atheist, "I had my children baptized; somehow that belongs to being Georgian."Minutes later, I recorded his comment on a scrap of paper. That paper fell from a collection of folders, happily I must say, only recently as I prepared to write this chapter. Those words had become for me a key part of the puzzle that is the "grandeur and the misery" of Christendom, the puzzle that long since had become my life challenge. What do we make of the several Christendoms that for many centuries have ruled whole populations, without necessarily involving personal faith commitments, and at times even prosecuting believers who took that faith seriously? And what is to be made of my own readings of this puzzle?

As noted earlier, especially in chapters 2 and 3, I grew up in a relatively ossified Anabaptist enclave in Pennsylvania between the two world wars. Both these wars originated between nations within European Christendom, who likewise were ossified, but to a far greater degree than were the Anabaptists. In early adulthood, I graduated from an emerging college in the Anabaptist tradition. Then I plunged into postwar relief and rehabilitation among those war-ravaged nations (notably Germany), and finally into completion of graduate study. That study climaxed in a sociological dissertation on the origin of the sixteenth-century Anabaptist movement in Switzerland.

With my arrival in Europe in early 1946, ecumenical sensibility became part of my life, and, at times, my active agenda. My peace dialogue assignments from 1957 through 1967 were essentially ecumenical. Ecumenical discourse along with academic exchanges figured importantly in bridge-building responses in the Soviet bloc nearly two decades later. The Tbilisi encounter came just as the ferment had begun that would end that conflict several years later. Recalling the Tbilisi conversation captures for me, almost as an archetype, the mutation of the gospel that is Christendom, and against which the Anabaptist legacy that shaped me had arisen.

To be sure, the institutional church traditions engendered by these polar extremes—believers churches versus politically and sacramentally implemented regimens—still linger, perhaps indefinitely. Nonetheless, the era of both of these polarities has ended. For this ending, the dawn of the third millennium becomes a convenient benchmark. So now what? As Fritz Blanke so poignantly observed, today we must find a solution that supersedes both the original misconception (*corpus christianum*) and the incomplete alternative (*Ana-*

baptism) that arose in the sixteenth-century to the contrary. But what would be a superseding replacement?

CHURCH IN THE SYMBIOTIC PROCESS

Even more challenging than our comprehension of the symbiotic duality of creation and salvation is the realization of this symbiosis in the faith community we know as "church." At the outset of the biblical story comes the pronouncement, "It is not good that the man should be alone" (Gen. 2:18). Adam has appeared initially as a solitary creature. Then God says, "I will make him a helper as his partner."

Thereafter the human story develops communally. The bonding between Adam and his partner, Eve, is reproductive. Familial bonding is supplemented by equally familiar ties of time and space, and eventually by far more complex forms of the division of labor. Yet in that communality, the individual does not disappear. When a man and a woman leave father and mother (2:24) and become marriage partners, personal autonomy is affirmed.

As the saving process in the biblical story unfolds, individuals similarly must leave their past behind to enter a qualitatively unique bonding to others undergoing the same experience. Though very differently, this parallels the leaving of parental ties in the assumption of new commitments. Earlier ties are transcended rather than ended. At the same time, however, the qualitative bonding between faith and natural community differs uniquely. Neither displaces, nor is reducible to, the other. As noted in the previous chapter, natural ties are materially grounded, hence essentially *phenomenal*, while faith experiences are spiritually grounded, hence *noumenal*. But just as in the personal domain, even more visibly, the communal dimension of the Christian faith experience meets in time and space (place), hence the frustrating paradox of faith community. In the Tbilisi instance noted above, the faith experience has mutated into the natural order without noumenal grounding.

FROM TEMPLE TO SYNAGOGUE

Christianity sprang from the Christ event: the life, the teachings, the passion and ascension of Jesus of Nazareth, thereby disclosed as the Messiah, culminating in the coming of the Holy Spirit at Pentecost. All this emerged from the Jewish saga, recognized by us Christians as the beginning of our own story.

In Jerusalem, the hearth of that antecedent Jewish movement, this new stage came quickly to be seen as a threat to the existing order, and accordingly came to be outlawed. The persecution that began with martyring Stephen in that city led to a scattering of the followers of Jesus throughout the surrounding countryside and eventually far beyond. Those followers, those believers, became witnesses to the Christ event, consummated in the coming of the Holy Spirit. They were witnesses, not conquerors or controllers. This scattering echoed the Diaspora that pinnacled the preceding Jewish stage of the biblical story.

By the first century CE, the wider Mediterranean region had been brought under the control of Rome as empire. Over succeeding decades, as Christianity spread, Christians gradually became numerous enough in places to be viewed, rightly or wrongly, as a threat to the existing religions and regimes. Sporadic local persecutions began to occur. By the fourth century CE, Christians were scattered widely enough that Emperor Constantine, soon after coming to power, viewed them as a potential imperial asset. Thereupon he declared Christianity to be the imperial religion (313 CE), seeing identification with the faith more as an advantage than a liability. Near the end of that century (396 CE), Emperor Theodosius, a successor to Constantine, declared and enforced Christianity as the only legal religion in the empire. Thus in course of that fourth century, Christianity moved from being *persecuted* to being the *persecutor*!

Temples in ancient times were thought to serve as the dwelling-places of gods. In and around temples such gods were served by special castes of priests. Well before the time of Christ, Jews had been dispersed throughout the empire, eventually losing their own land and temple. For Jews in dispersion, local synagogues came instead to anchor their identity. These contrasted dramatically to the more rare and exalted temple ritual, above all the sacrificial system spelled out extensively in the book of Leviticus. Synagogues served as gathering places for the people, for worship in song, prayer, and instruction and, above all in those preliterate times, for public reading from scrolls of the Torah. From dwelling places for gods to gathering places for people, waiting and listening in worship—what a shift!

From Synagogue to Ekklesia

The early story of the two peoples, the Israelites and then the Christians, passed through somewhat parallel crises and stages. Both arose as covenantal movements, scattered among naturally configured populations. Eventually the Israelites, jeopardizing their covenant, demanded a king. Samuel, their covenantal seer (leader), refused to permit this. Earthly monarchy was not part of their divinely constituted covenantal package. But given the peril that surrounded them, God authorized Samuel to grant them a king after all.

However, a grave warning was appended: The monarchy might result in an inner implosion of the covenant community. Such an implosion, as it turned out, followed all too soon. Within generations came inner decay leading to outside invasion, the destruction of Jerusalem, and the gradual exile of the Jewish survivors to Babylonian captivity.

Humanly speaking, Christian churches emerged from the Jewish synagogue. The two terms, *ekklesia* and *synagogue,* are Greek synonyms for human gatherings. Jesus, of course, was himself a Jew, and synagogues were the settings of early Christian germination. Whereas in the Jewish story, the synagogues in dispersion historically succeeded the temple era, in the following Christian story that sequence was reversed. People-gatherings came first, and only later, under imperial rule, those gatherings morphed into forms of templehood.

Hints of that shift in Christian history appear in the above-noted etymology of the word *church*. In several European languages, including English, German, and Dutch, the term for Christian gatherings is derived, not from the Greek noun *ekklesia* (assembly) but from the adjective *kuriakos,* from *kurios*, Lord (the Lord's house).

THE JEWISH ANTECEDENT

Despite the fundamental differences between the earlier Jewish and later Christian stages of the biblical story, there is an instructive parallel between the crisis giving rise to the Jewish monarchy and the later crisis giving rise to Christendom, the absorption of Christianity into Roman imperial rule. Instructive also is the simultaneous emergence of Jewish prophecy in the former instance and of monasticism and outright dissenting groups in the latter. In both cases, once God's saving initiative morphs into earthly political rule (contrary to mere temporary crisis management), God's transcendent voice sounds forth anew, prophetically or monastically.

That temporary adaptation in the Jewish crisis is detailed in the Old Testament account. If the prophetic response is fully contextualized, it becomes clear that the royal stream of the story is supplanted by the prophetic stream, rather than the other way around. The great prophetic voices of the royal era spell out the fundamental unfolding of God's aving intervention across the blighted human saga.

The canonical New Testament writings do not extend down to the fourth century, but the parallels to the royal Israelite (Jewish) precedent are striking. Some hold without direct canonical support that without the imperial adoption of Christianity in the fourth century, Christianity might not have survived. Given our confusions and disagreements about "church," we nonetheless look in vain for a New Testament normative church blueprint. Indeed, such an expectation reflects a deeper misunderstanding of the Christ event. For the spiritual process that is the New Testament, the ekklesia becomes explicit in the book of the Acts and the epistles that follow.

We have just identified the external contexts of the beginnings of New Testament ekklesias—Jewish synagogues and gatherings in believers' homes. But at times there are also gatherings in other larger public spaces. And there is communication and sharing between ekklesias as well. All this appears in keeping with Jesus' familiar words in Matthew 18:20, "For where two or three are gathered in my name, I am there among them," by way of the Holy Spirit. Such gatherings are spiritually emergent rather than externally engineered.

The Church (Ekklesia) as Reified Mystery

Two lessons may be drawn from the intertwined Jewish and Christian stories. First, the substance of both stories is fundamentally spiritual, though both were/are materially embedded. Neither can be fully realized without such embedding, including even the possibility that in emerging the latter, seemingly and momentarily, may overshadow the former. Second, while the role of the spiritual within the material is redemptive, it achieves that purpose only by remaining redemptively distinct from that which it redeems and thus tempers.

We now confront the fundamental paradox of the New Testament faith community. Only by visible gathering and interacting can it be realized. Yet the larger and more regular a grouping is, the greater the danger that it will mutate into mere sociocultural configuration. Elsewhere, as an analytical tool, I once suggested the distinction between primary, secondary, and tertiary levels of ecclesial gathering. The primary level exemplifies Jesus' pronouncement regarding his presence where two or three people meet with him in their midst. The secondary level begins when institutional linkages are formed between such gatherings. A tertiary level emerges when linking organizations form joint task groups beyond and apart from the secondary level. (Additional, more specialized or extended levels are conceivable.)

A church college exemplifies the third level. A college is not and cannot be both a church and a college. If Christian groups (congregations) find it appropriate to construct and maintain a college, they must recognize that it is not and cannot be made into a church. Colleges seeking to become both in the end will not be fully either college or church. Meanwhile the larger, the more organized, the more structured and real-estate-based the ecclesially grounded gathering, the higher the probability that the secular dynamics of culture and society will take over.

If these dynamics were better understood and respected, radical changes in our faith communities would emerge. Indeed, while spiritual vitality would be well advanced by such changes, initial numerical shrinkage might well result. Here we may well note the changes that overcame "Christianity" in its historical process, exemplified in the above episode in Tbilisi.

In the end, though Christian gatherings are visibly real, their essential reality is not subject to social engineering. Church planting as a witness strategy may well be genuinely motivated, yet as a concept it readily misleads. All too quickly it reduces to social engineering, seeking real estate or professionals ahead of living presence and witness among existing populations.

To the extent that the foregoing comments are helpful, for that very reason they cannot be taken as externally applicable blueprints. There may indeed be occasions in which it is appropriate for Christians to form colleges, but merely and fully as colleges! There may indeed be occasions in which it is appropriate to build meeting places for Christians. If, however, they serve as meeting places for what is intended by Matthew 18:20 and the related New Testament passages, what form should such structures take? Once land, real estate, budgets, and professions are in place, the dynamics of the faith community change. In the end we are left with the question: To what extent, and in what ways, can the stream of redemptive history announced in Genesis 12—and flowing from there through many centuries into the full realization as foreseen in Acts 1:8—be reified (made concrete)? Practically speaking, to what extent can Christian ekklesias become embodied as materially-based cultural institutions without jeopardizing their pneumatic integrity?

Much of our Christian scholarship is devoted to comparison and criticism of the paradigms of belief and practice crystallizing within and among our several Christendoms. All too often such inquiries, however informative sociologically, tend to befuddle this fundamental issue. To me, living and working ecumenically in various settings on three continents over half a century, the power of Paul the pioneer apostle's homily in 1 Corinthians 3:10-15 has become ever more incisive. I have met authentic fellow-believers in, and despite, all these varied traditions. On the one hand, "no one can lay any foundation other than the one that has been laid; that foundation is Jesus Christ" (3:11). On the other hand, what emerges from our efforts to promote that cause may turn into mere "wood, hay, straw" (3:12).

The Christian story is reminiscent in this regard of the time of crisis in the life of the Old Testament prophet Elijah. Things had gone badly, and Elijah was about to give up. But God accosted him with a new assignment, encouraging him with the mystery that "I will leave seven thousand in Israel, all the knees that have not bowed to Baal, and every mouth that has not kissed him" (1 Kings 19:18). That instance exemplifies the emergence of the salvation of the remnant that in God's larger providence transcends disaster. Indeed, as yet we have encountered no institutional form or denominational paradigm able to guarantee that all its adherents are authentically Christian!

From Reifying to Sacralizing

Historically, as already noted, this problem became radically acute as the accommodation of the churches to the Constantinian cooptation of the Christian movement set in. Over the centuries before Constantine and since, the faith communities that emerged after the outpouring of the Holy Spirit eventually became sacralized. Many volumes of historical writings describe and recount these complex developments. But at the beginning Paul, the apostle, observed in Romans 10, "Everyone who calls on the name of the Lord shall be saved" (10:13). "So faith comes from what is heard, and what is heard comes through the word of Christ" (10:17). That fundamental dynamic can be neither effected nor destroyed by merely human structures.

From the very outset, beliefs and practices varied. Meanwhile there were teachings, admonitions, and warnings. Erroneous beliefs and practices as well as their protagonists were to be shunned. Some of these differences contributed to the diversities that had to be surmounted by the imperial conquest of the wider Mediterranean world that the Romans were pursuing with considerable success. Enlisting Christianity in support of that cause reduced that diversity and at the same time externally incorporated Christianity into the imperial ethos. Scholars meanwhile, step by step, brokered the doctrinal rationalizations needed for the compromises of Christian teachings that those change required. The world Christians had set out to acknowledge and surmount they were now led instead to bless ritually.

Certain beliefs gradually were accorded sacramental status. About this there has been an enormous and unending debate. Classically, in the Christendom tradition, the grace of a sacrament came to be seen as conferred by the sacrament itself. For this, the Latin phrase, *ex opere operato*, emerged, translated literally meaning "from the work performed." Ironically, the above formula, in seeking to guarantee spiritual reality materially, effectively becomes operative apart from believing commitment of recipients. It tends thus to reduce the transforming grace, in human terms, to mere magic.

The Church as Faith Community

While fundamentally this criticism challenges various Christendom paradigms, simply to condemn or write off these varied histories and traditions is beyond human competence or mandate. Already above we noted the parallels between the emergence of the Old Testament Israelite monarchy and (beginning in the fourth century) medieval Roman Catholic Christendom. Implicit in both instances is the mystery of the stream of God's redemptive agency within the cosmic stream of creation in the finitude of all human responses.

We note here again to the profundity of Jesus' response to human exuberance at the final moment of his departure from the disciples recorded in Acts 1:8. This is not the grand finale, Jesus informs them. Instead, what will happen to his disciples then, and indeed to the end of this age, is that "when the Holy Spirit has come upon you . . . you will be my witnesses . . . to the ends of earth." Jesus' earlier pronouncement (John 14:12) now becomes lucid: "Very truly, I tell you, the one who believes in me will also do the works that I do and, in fact, will do greater works than these, because I am going to the Father."

An Aborted Reformation

Renewal movements have repeatedly surfaced during the history of Christianity and doubtless will continue to do so. At times they have been dubiously, occasionally even heretically, inspired. Given the human propensity for routines to ossify, renewal movements in Christian circles are well-nigh inevitable. Most such movements are of local, regional, or temporary significance. A few, such as the Benedictine monasticism among Catholics, or Pietism within seventeenth- and eighteenth-century Protestantism, effectively left wider and continuing legacies in Western Christendom.

In the context of this book, a glance back at the partly ill-fated sixteenth-century Protestant Reformation is appropriate. Superficially, the story is familiar. What began as reform of the existing church order unexpectedly turned instead into an effort to begin anew. There was little inkling of the ambiguity of a top-down social-engineering diagnosis of the problem. Before the emerging vision of spiritual, and hence moral, renewal could be realized, the social, economic, and political ferment of the time erupted in the revolt of the peasants (Peasants War, 1524-1526). To suppress that chaos, the reformers themselves radically reversed the reform that entailed the loosening of the ties between church and state on which Christendom rested. Luther and his associates abruptly called on newly non-Catholic rulers in German territories to take control of external church affairs—buildings, finances, rituals, and clergy. Thereby princes became *Notbischofs* (emergency bishops), a title that continued in some instances until World War I.

As noted briefly in the preceding chapter, only at the persecuted Anabaptist margin was the vision of radical reform carried through. Historically, the story of that seemingly premature effort has been told principally from the records of the political regimes who took control of external church affairs back then. But finally by mid-twentieth century an organized effort got underway to publish both the legal records and the formerly unpublished writings of sixteenth-century Anabaptism. Thus the inside-out side of that story can now be placed alongside the outside-in readings that had dominated for four centuries. For the first time, the deeper story emerged.

Earlier I quoted Zurich professor Fritz Blanke, one of the architects of that publishing venture. Though himself a member of the Reformed (state church) tradition, he concluded that both the medieval corpus Christianum and the Anabaptism that arose as its alternative are deficient. Finding a third way remains our challenge today.

Today's New Millennium

Historical developments during the half-century since Blanke's reading of the sixteenth-century Anabaptist story—that it came too early and that neither Christendom nor an apolitcal Anabaptism are adequate—render his observations prescient. History has exposed the fallacy (heresy?) that was the corpus christianum—but also the incompleteness of the Anabaptist protest movement's effort to supply the missing dimension of Christendom. Clearly, neither Christendom nor its sixteenth-century alternatives are directly suited to the challenges of the new twenty-first century. Nonetheless, the lessons of the whole Christendom era are profoundly instructive today.

On us as heirs of the now-outdated era of Christendom an enormous challenge descends. We inherit a complex, rich, yet tragically failed legacy. How, then, shall we proceed today? First is the need and opportunity to listen humbly and carefully to the message of that past, or rather to view both past and present anew through the prism of the gospel. Already in 1950, in his book *Christianity and History*, British historian Herbert Butterfield observed that today "we are back for the first time in something like the earliest centuries of Christianity, and those early centuries afford some relevant clues to the kind of attitude to adopt." He based this assessment on the observation that in the twentieth century:

> We can just about begin to say that at last no man is now a Christian because of government compulsion, or because it is the way to procure favour at court, or because it is necessary in order to qualify for public office, or because public opinion demands conformity, or because he would lose customers if he did not go to church, or even because habit and intellectual indolence keep the mind in the appointed groove. (Bell, 1949, p.146)

Today, more than half a century later, these words of Butterfield appear profoundly prescient. Since 1950, though more in Europe than in this country, the older church structures formed in medieval and early modern Christendom have become increasingly irrelevant. In the United States these mainline denominations have also undergone membership losses in recent decades. What Professor Blanke viewed as historically premature in the sixteenth century had dramatically ripened by the beginning of the new millennium.

Again, the Creation/Salvation Symbiosis

As already intimated, given the communality of our humanity, it is in the ekklesia, the gathering of believers with Jesus in their midst by way of the Holy Spirit, that the creation/salvation symbiosis (chapter 13) reaches critical mass. "You will receive power when the Holy Spirit has come upon you; and you will be my witnesses. . . to the ends of the earth" (Acts 1:8).

You will be witnesses, not judges or rulers. It his hardly accidental that the concept of witness emerges at the peak of Old Testament prophecy (see especially Isa. 43). Certain stages of historical human development had to be attained as preconditions for the spiritual unfolding of the biblical story. It is not accidental that the concept of witness becomes pivotal in the farewell words of Jesus to his disciples. Here we are at the heart of the symbiosis of creation and salvation.

The biblical narrative accents faithfulness to the transforming grace in the life and service of those who respond to that grace, rather than social engineering for the world of those who do not. Not surprisingly, this accent again and again has gravitated toward the withdrawal impulse in renewal movements within Christendom. There is seeming scriptural validation for such withdrawal. Paul, citing the prophet Isaiah, writes in his second letter to Christian believers in Corinth (6:17-18), whom he had led to Christ in the first place: "Therefore come out from them [unbelievers], and be separate from them, says the Lord, and touch nothing unclean; then I will welcome you, and I will be your father, and yours shall be my sons and daughters."

Yet to the contrary Jesus himself had said in his high priestly prayer to God the Father, recited in John 17:15-16, 18:

> "I am not asking that you take them [my disciples] out of the world, but I ask you to protect them from the evil one. They do not belong to the world, just as I do not belong to the world. . . . As you have sent me into the world, so I have sent them into the world."

How and why was Jesus sent into the world? By his radical otherness to redeem that world. A dilemma indeed. How can one at once be fully in the world while being not of the world?

The Parasitic Shoe on the Other Foot

By the sixteenth century, in medieval Christendom (as in the Tbilisi episode), that dilemma had become doubly acute. What does it mean when the whole society has externally taken on Christian trappings? The reasoning and formulations of Anabaptism, the sixteenth-renewal movement, may seem unduly harsh. Yet precisely for that reason, the deftness of the key phrase in the Brotherly Union adopted at Schleitheim in 1527, the first group statement of faith by that group, is the more piercing: "The sword is an ordering of God outside the perfection of Christ." God remains in control, thus containing the effects of the default of human partnering in the stewardship of the earth. Meanwhile God has sent Christ and those empowered by the Holy Spirit as God's redeeming initiative.

We may well ask: An ordering of God outside the perfection of Christ? As we noted, Emil Brunner, even though newly inspired by the theological renewal movement of the mid-twentieth-century, objected to the Anabaptist movement. To him, as we saw above in chapter 5, withdrawal from engagement in war by one's country is parasitic. It means leaving the dirty work of the world to others.

Up to a point I understand and respect the Brunner-style reading of that sixteenth-century movement. But after decades of Tbilisi-like experiences, I have begun to wonder whether the parasitic shoe may fit better on Christendom's foot. May it be instead that the average Christendom person who marches off to war is a parasite, leaving the hard work of following Christ, of surmounting war, to others? Or perhaps, more realistically, both camps alike may be vulnerable to parasitism, seeking to avoid the hard work of following Christ.

More helpful may be the formulation of church historian Oscar Cullmann, a Lutheran contemporary of Brunner, but at the University of Basel. At one point he observed this: Paradoxical as it may seem, the concentration upon redemptive history signifies the very opposite of indifference toward the world process, thus of withdrawal from the world. To follow Christ on his redemptive mission in the world is to take Cullmann's world process seriously. We already met precisely this same vision in the words of the English theologian, Gerard Loughlin: "We serve the world by being other than the world." This observation takes us into our two concluding chapters.

Chapter 15

The Sacralizing/Secularizing Duet

Briefly defined, secularization is the process in which religious consciousness, activities, and institutions lose social significance.
—Bryan Wilson

Trying out alternative definitions and testing complexities in the defining process itself may look like typical academic obfuscation.
—Mark A. Noll

All dualism between creation and redemption is here excluded. In the New Testament there cannot be, in addition to the Christ-line of redemption, another and separate God-line of creation.
—Oscar Cullmann

The organizing focus of this autobiographical book is the enigma that arises in the human enterprise between God's manifestation as Creator and as Redeemer. That contrast becomes historic, as we saw in the previous chapter, between the natural order of human community and the community of redemption that we know as church. An example of this ambiguity is the seeming dissonance between the sacralizing and secularizing impulses in human cultures. Notably, however, just as the fullness of that unity is manifest through the threefold presence of God—Creator, Savior, Spirit—so too there is reciprocity in the sacral and secular phases of history. We begin this chapter with a case study of that mystery.

How Conscientious Objection Became a "Human Right"

In the fall of 1940, as war in Europe was heating up, the newly updated Selective Service agency of the United States Congress reactivated the registration of all American male citizens between ages twenty-one and thirty-five. Registrants were grouped into four classes: (1) Able-bodied men available for induction into the armed services; (2) men already engaged in work deemed of national importance; (3) men with family responsibilities that precluded military service; (4) men physically handicapped, conscientious objectors to military action, and others unavailable for whatever reason.

The date set for registration nationally was October 16, 1940. Six days earlier I had turned twenty-two. As a healthy farm lad, I fell squarely into this now-conscripted cohort of young men.

My awareness of the larger picture at that time was extremely limited. As I recall, in 1940 when the United States military draft was reenacted, I registered at the local Elk Lick Township office in Somerset County, Pennsylvania, where I lived and had grown up in my native farm family. Being a committed Christian in the Anabaptist tradition, I registered as a conscientious objector (CO) to military service, a status approved in a visit to the county court house in Somerset. Meanwhile my young journey was unfolding on its own terms. As yet I had little inkling how that registration would eventually impinge on my life. This presumably was the plight of many young men of my age, though individual situations and outcomes differed widely.

In chapter 2, I briefly sketched the unanticipated weaving of my CO decision into my life journey. Then in chapter 5, drawing primarily on the 1993 volume entitled *The New Conscientious Objection: From Sacred to Secular Resistance* (edited by military-sociologist Charles C. Moskos and John Whiteclay Chambers II), I traced the surprising secularization of conscientious objection in the course of the twentieth century. In his introduction to this volume, Moskos credits the Anabaptists with containing "the embryos of modern ideas of church and state." Important parallels appear in the emergence of the secular graduate universities in the United States from what began on a more limited scale as institutes for the training of ministers in churches (see chapter 4).

While my personal experience in this wider story was but a drop in the bucket, it alerted me to the spread from sacred to secular motivations in the renunciation of military service during the second half of the twentieth century. Secularization in this instance meant not the decline of religious influence in human affairs, but to the contrary its cultural infusion and acceptance in the wider society. And while the secularization of conscientious objection to war did not as yet call for the elimination of war in human affairs, it served as a step in that direction. This growing secular respect for the human conscience served as a breakthrough in the evolving human story.

The 1648 Peace of Westphalia

Our familiar words, *secular* and *secularization*, derive from the Latin *saeculum*. Initially that term meant simply a very long time, typically an entire generation. Scholars trace its use in the European languages, including English, to the Peace of Westphalia that in 1648 brought an end to the Thirty Years War. As transliterated into various European languages, secularization came to mean the removal of public affairs from direct religious jurisdiction.

Today that seventeenth-century conflict is viewed as Europe's last religious war. Insofar as the Treaty of 1648 ended the hegemony of the Roman church in monastic land holdings in parts of northwest Europe, secularization is an appropriate term. The process begun in 1648 took classic form more than a century later (1790) in the constitutional separation of church and state in the newly formed United States of America. Accordingly, organized religion has no direct voice in political rule. In that constitutional amendment, the state expressed a basic insight still fuzzy in religious discourse. A recent controversy about a plaque with the Ten Commandments on a public square reached the United States Supreme Court. Moreover, the concept of secularity has been reinforced powerfully in the empirical sciences and consequently in numerous technologies. Particularly instructive in this regard are the advances over superstition and religion in the diagnosis and treatment of human affairs and disorders.

The three epigraphs at the head of this chapter, however, illustrate the complexity of the issues involved in the concept of secularization. Bryan Wilson characterizes secularization as the decline of direct institutional religious control in public affairs, whether viewed favorably or critically. Mark Noll offers a more nuanced reading of the process. Empiricism cannot answer the deeper mysteries of either the human or cosmic dynamics. Finally, Oscar Cullmann fuses the creation/salvation duality into a unified process, seemingly contrary to our observations here. These three perspectives figure basically in the comments that comprise the present chapter.

SECULARIZATION AND SACRALIZING:
OPPOSING PROCESSES?

As now generally employed, these two terms, *secular* (profane) and *sacral* (sacred), serve as simple antonyms in human perception. The secular is that which is not sacred; and the sacred is that which is not secular. However, the restoration of monastic and other church-held properties to the secular order in the Peace of Westphalia was a highly ambiguous process. Judgments underlying that process are similar in nature to the spiritual assessments that informed the sacramental institutions in the first place. Not only was the formation of religiously inspired objects—images, building, land entitlements—informed by religious intuitions, but so was the transfer of such holdings to secular auspices.

In other words, whether our responses to the mystery of the human saga are religious, irreligious, or neutral, they emerge intuitively. Such assessments cannot be proved or disproved empirically. Our human responses do not alter the objective reality to which they respond nor the subjectivity of our ongoing responses.

To put the matter bluntly, secularizing religious ritual does not rid—or deprive—us as human communities of the religious mystery! The concept of secularization commonly entails a one-sided reductionist reading of the more complex processes of human existence to which it refers. The revolutions of modernity, further energized by the eighteenth-century Enlightenment, seem to celebrate the emancipation of human affairs from religious definition. However, those revolutions do not end or exhaust the sacred dimension in the human saga. To some degree they supplant by either adopting or embodying.

We here confront the distinction, noted in passing in the previous chapter, between the *phenomenal* and the *noumenal*. The former term applies to things immediately experienced by the senses, whereas the latter refers to intuitions that are empirically inaccessible.

Strictly speaking, science and technology can deal only with empirical data. But is this to ignore the continuing impinging of noumenal impulses and judgments on phenomenal affairs? Intuitive impulses continuously break into the realm of things phenomenal. Hence secularization in reality is an oscillating, back-and-forth process.

For example, as quoted previously, Gil Baillie in *Violence Unveiled* notes that "What the Enlightenment did was to secularize a wariness about religion that has its roots in the Old Testament prophets, the Gospels, and the letters of Paul. . . ." That is, awareness of the contradiction between the outer shell that was the corpus christianum sprang to no small degree from the vision it was once thought to embody. Thus historical manifestations of the redemptive history (*Heilsgeschichte*) once embodied in this manner, may assume a life of their own in the revolutions of modernity, turning against the perpetual spiritual energy from which they sprang in the first place.

In the remote past, before the biblical story that began with the call to Abraham, empirical adaptations by humans within the realm of nature were as yet little developed. Prescientific conceptions, largely rooted in nature-religions, dominated. Baillie thus rightly observes in the above statement that, seminally, liberation from those primitive strictures was itself in some measure spiritually inspired. Thus historically secularization in some respects is sacredly inspired!

A Second Look at Westphalia

In our reading here of the Peace of Westphalia, the linear view of history that we met in earlier chapters figures heavily. In contrast to most cyclical views of time, linear views see unfolding processes occurring over time. We noted, for example, the contrast between the stages of social development early in the Old Testament and the later New Testament eras. Social configurations in New Testament times in the Mediterranean world appear sharply advanced over the earlier Old Testament tribal times in Egypt and elsewhere. The emerging social threshold announced by the exilic prophet Ezekiel, historically and sociologically speaking, was made possible by the ending of the Judaic monarchy and surmounting it in the Diaspora (Ezekiel 18). Another threshold in linear time appears in the apostle Paul's declaration that "when the fullness of time had come, God sent his Son. . ." (Gal. 4:4). That threshold is clearly implicit already in Jesus' teaching to distinguish the reign of God from family ties (Luke 14:26).

Thus secularization, defined merely as the withdrawal of organized religion from the political process, ignores the deeper historical significance of that threshold. What is primarily at stake is the enhancement of human development. In the long run, the institutional conjoining of religious and political monarchy, whatever the transitional benefit, thwarts rather than enhances genuine human development and responsible freedom. This is not to ignore the positive benefits that otherwise may occur within—and despite—such conjoining.

THE BIRTH OF CIVIL SOCIETY

Historically, the rule of kings created configurations of order over conflicting tribes and ethnicities. Such ordering permitted specialized activities and relations apart from, and transcending, tribalism. Eventually, in our Western world came industrial and scientific revolutions and the emergence of modern democracies. Such specialization permitted and entailed the growth of human settlements as cities. Spheres of human diversity and freedom emerged that earlier were inconceivable. In popular jargon, distinctions between top-down and bottom-up political initiatives emerged historically.

In the course of the twentieth century, the public arena between personal and private affairs, on the one hand, and institutional political control on whatever level on the other, became increasingly prized in terms such as *civil society* and *social capital*. The enhancement and fulfillment of human destiny came to be seen as tied to the vigor of bottom-up activity in that arena. Yet, ironically, it may seem that only in contexts of law and order can civil society flourish. Trust in human relations is possible only where common understandings and commitments can be presupposed.

Given the diversities of cultures and stages of history among the earth's populations, and even in our own American society, a common definition of civil society hardly exists. The Cold War waged during much of the twentieth century (1917-1989) between Soviet Communism and the Western democracies is a dramatic case study in this regard. These competing ideologies both arose in the eighteenth- and nineteenth-century Enlightenment, importantly reacting to each other. Marxist-Leninist scholars viewed the Western scheme as (bottom-up) individualism running amuck, while we in the West viewed communism as (top-down) authoritarian collectivism squelching bottom-up dynamics in human affairs!

The top-down collectivism, built on the legacy of preindustrial feudalism in Russia, suppressed the rise of civil society. When the Berlin Wall came down, the civil society life blood of democracy was scarcely present, nor had it been permitted to emerge under the Soviet regime. Accordingly, the transition to post-Communist polities is proving difficult. A recent visitor to Russia, the former Soviet heartland, found parallels there to the late nineteenth-century robber baron era in United States history—capitalist profiteering before corresponding civil society and legal regulation could emerge. And there are striking parallels to other preindustrial countries seeking access to modernity, most notably China.

Meanwhile, the verdict on the one-sidedness of Western individualism is not yet in. For while civil society flourishes in societies favored by the Enlightenment, nurturing the responsibility implicit in the freedoms we cherish has yet fully to be fleshed out. Meanwhile, with the globalization of world affairs underway in our time, the rich become richer while the poor become poorer. For example, while writing this page I came across a citation by Jonathan Sacks: "The assets of the three richest billionaires are more than the combined wealth of the 600 million inhabitants of the least-developed countries" (*The Dignity of Difference: How to Avoid the Clash of Civilizations*, Continuum, 2002, p. 29). Although the many ministries among the impoverished masses are to be commended and supported, personal responsibility regarding wide disparities in the distribution of wealth leaves much to be desired.

In a word, we are dealing here with the complexity of exponential growth—circumstances where one emerging variable depends on another. A week after Hurricane Katrina struck New Orleans in August 2005, the resulting explosion of gasoline prices at the pump exemplifies the exponential dynamics of what we now describe as the globalization of modernity. The complexities of economic, political, and social developments emerge well in advance of our comprehending and coping responses. As the above quotation of Gil Baillie deftly points out, a merely secular reading of the exponential development processes energized by the Enlightenment misleads. Baillie implies that the forces set in motion by the Enlightenment were indebted to the Judeo-Christian variable, without which it could not have emerged, yet from which it itself is fancied to have been freed.

THE CHURCHES AND CIVIL SOCIETY

Recognizing this fact does not belittle the importance of the secular energies likewise emergent in that process. Far beyond the ostensible fusion of state and church in medieval Christendom, the separation that emerged in the modern era permitted the state to become more fully state and the church more fully church. This is not to claim that either institution reached perfection in the process. To the contrary, new challenges to both arise with the unfolding of civil society.

Nor is civil society monopolized by churches or other religious formations. Civil society can be described as the voluntary sector of society, distinct from the state and the market on the one hand, and from the world of family on the other. That sector is comprised of a host of nongovernmental organizations (NGOs), community groups, social movements, faith-based organizations, professional associations, trade unions, as well as self-help and advocacy groups, including faith communities. While impulses now coalescing as civil society have long been underway, only recently have the normative claims of all social configurations been increasingly relativized. That ostensible triumph is being described as postmodernism.

Intrinsically, civil society is not monopolized by churches, other religions, or religious institutions. The present study, however, focuses primarily on the vocation of the biblical story within that vast historical process. As spelled out in the previous chapter, that vocation takes the form of *witness*, the content of which is the biblical God's saving presence with his human partners. And witness entails directly neither political engineering nor control. Admittedly the boundaries between the three domains—the private, the political, and the public—overlap and remain fuzzy. But as underscored in chapter 7 above, nowhere does Holy Writ foresee or intend the political triumph of Christianity in the course of history itself.

Instead, as Jesus' parable of the wheat and weeds observes, mixtures of good and evil somehow exist to the end of time (Matt. 13:36-39). In the biblical story, after the Deluge triggered by human apostasy, God reformulated his covenant with humankind. There would be no change in the order of nature (creation) despite the fact that "every inclination of the thoughts of their hearts was only evil continuously" (Gen. 6:5). According to the Jewish reading of the story, that reformulation is the covenant with humanity generally. Meanwhile, following the scattering of humans after the presumptuous Tower of Babel episode, came the call to Abram, son of Terah. Salvaging the human enterprise would be effected by the formation of a "great nation" through which "all the families of the earth shall be blessed" (Gen. 12:1-4). The rest of the biblical story is devoted to that process.

When the Unchanging God Changes His Mind

We now meet the conundrum within which the creation/salvation enigma arises. The prophet Malachi, in a brief pronouncement (3:6), summarizes the thematic foundation of the biblical story thus: "I the Lord do not change; therefore you, O house of Jacob, have not perished." We can count on God as unchanging. But then there are the occasions when, seemingly to the contrary, we are told that God in fact changed his mind (for example, Jer. 26:19).

But these occasions are specially and narrowly defined. They occur in God's discourse with us humans, and vary with our human responses. God's own identity and covenant remain unaltered. Yet when the people of Nineveh repented on hearing the word of God's prophet, he changed his mind, not carrying out the punishment of which the prophet Jonah had forewarned them (Jonah 3:10). Likewise, God says that if a nation "turns from its evil, I will change my mind about the disaster that I intended to bring on it" (Jer. 18:8).

Properly understood, there is no inconsistency between God's unchanging character and variation within the sphere of limited human freedom. The possibility of wrongdoing is implicit in the freedom to do right. If God compelled us as humans to act aright, would that not annul the whole human enterprise? Hence the mixture of wheat and weeds in Jesus' parable. Here once more we confront aspects of the complex duality that is the theme of this book. The biblical God is *The God Who Acts,* the title of G. Ernst Wright's mid-twentieth century book, but within the human domain. God's initiatives are humanly conditioned. Within the boundaries of that dialogue, finite on the human side, the unchanging, self-revealing God changes.

As repeatedly emphasized, this mingling of the changeless and the changing appeared starkly in Schleitheim's "the sword is an ordering of God outside the perfection of Christ." God, it appears, built into creation a self-limiting mechanism to contain disruptive conduct, even as subsequently God initiated a healing process, the perfection of Christ, in the human family reaching beyond mere outward containment. Only in becoming fundamentally other than the brokenness permeating human affairs can the human predicament be altered. As Christians "we serve the world by being other than the world" (Loughlin).

Jesus forewarned, however, that such otherness entails friction with the world on its own terms, and this has occurred throughout Christian history. Persecution emerged early in the Christian story, and sporadically has reappeared ever since. As outlined in chapter 7, once sufficiently widespread in the Mediterranean world, both church and empire yielded to the temptation to fuse church and empire, contrary to the duality between them that is at once implicit and explicit between the two in the biblical story.

The freedom of Christians in American civil society today may well be unprecedented, as is the potential for their effective absorption into that society. Ironically, however, our governments are often more wary of churches meddling in political affairs than are the churches themselves. As leaven, as light, and as salt, Christian faith communities lose their reason to exist when, ostensibly in their mission to penetrate, they lose their fundamental otherness. Failure to understand and accept this paradoxical mystery accounts for continuing schismatic confusions within historical Christianity. Success of the biblical story entails seeming external historical failure.

CIVIL SOCIETY AND RENEWAL OF THE HOUSE CHURCH

Civil society was part of the modernization of the Western world. Today Europe and North America are again caught up in the new civil society ferment underway in this globalizing era. Indeed an important new phase is emerging in religion and society in American life. Historically the English (Protestant) Reformation came about later and differently than did its continental antecedent. And that Reformation, by way of New England Puritanism, had more direct influence on the American ethos than did the continental reform. The constitutional separation of church and state in the United States exemplifies the historical free church trend noted above. Yet that separation has yet to be completed, on the deeper plane, in our American psyche and ethos. In various guises the "God and county" instinct still lies just beneath the public surface, all too readily activated.

Retrospectively, in our present civil society era new historic perspectives are emerging. While both free and believers church groups in America were far more bottom-up in their policies than were the Christendom-descended traditions, both Catholic and Protestant, their church definitions and practices remained heavily shaped by legacy of the Christendom against which they emerged. Church tends to mean building, clergy, and ritual. This materialization the turn-of-the-twentieth-century German sociologist, Max Weber, called "the routinization of the charisma."

In the context of revitalization of civil society in the United States, two relatively new church trends appear to be emerging. One is the loss of membership among the older, mostly European-formed, denominations and the American denominations inspired by them. In most European countries these churches survive only marginally. But in a society as tumultuous as ours, why make an effort to remain Lutheran, Presbyterian, Episcopalian, Methodist—and even Mennonite? On the other hand, the very fluidity of our society accents the need for some kind of anchoring. Today's surge of interest in spirituality is a poor yet sobering answer.

More striking in the context of this study is the emergence of a house church movement. Some, if certainly not all, persons exiting older denominations are responding bottom-up in forming independent house churches. These can be seen as corresponding directly or indirectly to the stories of the Christian house assemblies (Greek *ekklesiai*) of the New Testament era. Such groupings began in the Jewish synagogues that had emerged centuries earlier in the Jewish Diaspora, whether colonial or exilic. As the Christian break with Jewish synagogues became definitive, Christian gatherings transferred to member homes. These house churches corresponded to Jesus' metaphors and parables. In dispersion, Christians were leaven, salt, and light—*witness* rather than externally imposed, imperial-like hegemony.

The house church movement deserves an affirmative, if critical, response. The extent to which the house church paradigm of the early Christian generations was coincidentally historical rather than fundamentally normative may not be fully ascertainable. Minimally, this revival stands in sharp contrast to the sacramentally grounded and politically enforced "cathedrality" of Christendom. The house church movement radically resurrects dimensions fundamental to the Christian story that had long since been eclipsed institutionally. It embraces the spiritual reality of God's saving presence in the dialogical gathering of believers (Matt. 18:15-20).

Meanwhile beginning a new denomination as a challenge to obvious incompleteness of the house church movement would merely perpetuate the problem. Here, in the vein of the gifts in the body as outlined in 1 Corinthians 12, I will offer two observations for further consideration, the one particularly Christian, the other secular and general. The first is doubly analytical, the other is historical. These observations will then be followed by one suggested possible course of action. Readers of previous chapters will detect earlier hints in the directions here indicated.

A Doubly Analytical Tool

In the previous chapter I distinguished primary, secondary, and tertiary levels of interaction among Christians. The primary level is the post-Pentecost gathering of Christians in listening and shared adoration of God in Christ through the Holy Spirit within and among them (Matt. 18: 20). The secondary level is interaction or configuration among such gatherings. The tertiary level consists of institutions or agencies initiated or sponsored by such associations of assemblies. One or more additional levels might be possible, each removed a further step from the other. In any event, by the time we reach the third stage we must ask whether we have descended to the natural order of creation.

That primary level almost hauntingly parallels Jesus' hint that the church consists of gatherings of two or three persons with himself in their midst. Less explicit, perhaps, but equally haunting is the fixed church order Jesus sets forth in Matthew 16:13-20. One can more readily challenge the papal institution that scholars have brokered from this passage than the foundational affirmation itself that Jesus makes here. Church is something other than mere ad hoc tinkering with interest groups, buildings, and professionals. Beyond the primary level, configurations and institutions quickly mutate into entities that are merely natural or secular.

An Historical Antecedent

We have just noted the parallels between our analytical tools and the two instances in the Gospels where the key term *church* (ekklesia) appears on the lips of Jesus (presumably in Aramaic). Much of church history has emerged in the tension between these two polarities. At the same time, however, each pole, taken alone, tends to become one-sidedly reductionist. In the one case the gathering tends to dissolve into mere individualism. In the other the outcome is an impersonal and sacramentally implemented institution that functions quite apart from the personal transformation of participants

From the very outset, Christianity faced dissent and heresy. Once the church, as a sacramentally reified and politically enforced hegemony, was achieved, intensification and renewal were channeled into monastic enclaves. Beyond these, varieties of renewal movements that appeared outside these church and monastic structures were often suppressed by them. Eventually the Protestant Reformation emerged, triggered by abuses that flourished in the previous system. Whatever the rampant nature of those abuses, they were but the symptoms or side effects of the mutation of faith communities into top-down structures. The expectation that the miracle of the Holy Spirit's presence could be guaranteed locally by a centralized outside institution was more likely in the end to undercut rather than to implement that very presence.

As already observed, there were inklings of this among the leading Reformers, yet abandoning the structural order in favor of a house-church-like new beginning appeared too threatening. Thus suddenly the Reformers, while reciprocally excommunicated from Roman Catholic Christendom, effectively joined hands with Rome to suppress the "heretical" Anabaptist sectarians.

We noted that the flaw of the Anabaptist movement lay in its coming to soon, before the time was ripe for it. Not only could that movement's intention not be fully realized, but driven to the margins if not underground, its own bottom-up genius became warped. While the space between institutionalism and individualism was far more limited than in today's world, the Anabaptist movement from the outset, like the house church movement today, drew a clear line between subjectivist individualism on the one hand and hierarchical institution on the other.

For that reason, this Anabaptist story (and other believers church experiments) serves an instructive case-study as we wrestle with these same issues in our own time. No, Anabaptism is not *the* true church blueprint, to be copied outwardly by others, any more than were the previous papal or Protestant institutions.

A NEW "AHA" BENCHMARK

A new "aha" benchmark in the sacred/secular duet emerged in the course of the 1990s. World War II must be seen as the traumatic global earthquake that it was. For our United States that catastrophe entailed almost half a million war dead. But that cost was less disastrous than in lands where, along with great numbers of war dead, came physical, economic, and political destruction. Indeed, World War II effectively paved the way for American triumphalism during the second half of the twentieth century. Of all this, the turmoil now raging in the Middle East during the early years of this new millennium remains fallaciously grounded and fomented.

Our American story, as is becoming increasingly evident, is profoundly ironical. The constitutional separation of church and state, the fusion of which had been the linchpin of Christendom, emancipated the energies from which emerged the civil society and social capital that are the hallmark of the United States. But the persistence of the ethos of historic Christendom in the American psyche is fertile soil for political policies and actions such as the invasion of Iraq. Appeals to "God and country" loyalties violate the gospel at the deepest level. Yes, both Iraq and the United States are subject to the sovereignty of God, but as we have repeatedly noted, to be Christian is to enter the healing process that God has set in motion by the Christ event. It is in and through the *witness* that is the shared faith commitment of believers, not through social engineering or social control, that this healing process is implemented.

Politically, the constitutional separation of church and state is consistent with the resulting distinction between the ordering of God on the plane of creation and the perfection of Christ as set forth in the Schleitheim document. Our modern concept of secularity that evolved after the Peace of Westphalia likewise corresponds to that distinction. Peter L. Berger, a self-confessed liberal Protestant and for decades a leading sociologist of religion at Boston University, long championed the triumph of secularity in our modern era. When the published results of a foundation-financed historical study of the Fundamentalist Project in the 1990s began to appear, at first he was disinterested. In terms of the prevailing secular paradigm, fundamentalism was little more than a flawed vestige of the now obsolete Christendom past.

But Berger's second look at the initial published report of the Fundamentalist Project triggered a different response, a shift he now describes as an "aha" experience. Religion today, Berger has come to realize, is as alive as it ever was, and in some respects more so. As implicit in the title,*The Desecularization of the World: Resurgent Religion and World Politics*, his book reveals that discovery. Given the persistence of radical religious expressions in our time, illustrated by the at-times stormy fundamentalisms, perhaps what needs investigation instead is the view of secular elites that religion is merely a vestige of the now obsolete past. What, then, leads intellectuals to ignore this reality and promote instead the totally secular hypothesis? History has moved beyond that thesis, hence the term *desecularization*.

WHERE DOES ALL THIS LEAVE US?

Response to the where-does-all-this-leave-us question depends on who the "us" is. "Us" here refers to persons who are "Christianly challenged"—outsiders intrigued yet also repelled by the Christian faith, and insiders troubled by the mess in which we find our faith communities today—both groups skeptically at the edge of the Christian discourse. This "us" thus includes you, the reader, since you otherwise would never have reached this point in the present volume.

While bewildering, this is a day of extraordinary opportunity and responsibility. Both the need and the possibility for Christian unity may be greater than ever before. Yet these developments may make the organizational or institutional unity among Christian groupings more remote than ever. Increasingly we experience the vulnerability of our secondary and tertiary institutional church structures and the enriching and widening of the primary realities of the faith that we share. There is a burgeoning literature on house church, on informal conversations about transcendent meanings, and on endless forms of spirituality.

To note all these promptings is not to equate or endorse them. Rather this melee is a cry for help that challenges the Christian core today. What we here confront is the vacuum that emerged in the detour in the Christian story that was medieval Christendom. Missing today are helpful guidelines for primary Christian gatherings. Such guidelines would enable them to reach other similar primary gatherings, communicating in the context of civil societies without undermining their bottom-up faith position. The emergence of such guidelines from the biblical texts and early Christian experiences was aborted as Christianity became state-sponsored and sacramentally implemented.

Somewhat similarly, the disengagement of the believing community from Christendom that appeared on the horizon of the sixteenth-century Protestant Reformation has resulted in its partial reaffirmation in denomination-building. Only marginally did such disengagement occur. And in that regard, we must continue to heed church historian Fritz Blanke's call for a solution that supersedes both corpus christianum and apoliticism.

Chapter 16

Being Human/Christian in This Postmodern World

The isolated individual is an abstraction. Historical life is social life.
—José Ortega y Gasset

Moral knowing and being arise from doing, from experience rather than thinking alone.
—Cynthia Moe-Lobeda

History under God both can be and is full of surprises because it exists within the field of force of God's kingdom.
—T. J. Gorringe

Hold to Christ, and for the rest be totally uncommitted.
—Herbert Butterfield

This book has emphasized the communal nature of humans, largely without attention to individuation also presupposed. Only in approaching this final chapter did I become aware of the imbalance. In the end, I must address the question of where all these musings leave us. What should we do? This problem has to be considered before a concluding summary is appropriate. So I include here a brief reflection on the individuation process in the biblical story.

INDIVIDUALIZING OUR COMMUNAL IDENTITY

The achievement and security of individual rights and liberties in American society is widely celebrated both here and abroad. Paradoxically, the excesses and costs of that individualizing are often deplored and even feared. This should not divert us from our recognition of the importance of this achievement in human history or from our efforts to surmount those deficiencies. Practically, how do we as individuals live freely and responsibly (i.e. communally) in this largely relativized and fluid postmodern world? Here we address this question in the context of the symbiosis of creation and salvation as outlined above. As noted, this book has dealt primarily with our communal destiny as humans. Yet that communality unfolds interactively with increasing individuation as well. But insights from lived experience outweigh theoretical or doctrinal sketching. I turn then to two anecdotes, one contemporary, one ancient, with the latter informing the former.

In April 1951, at the end of my fifth year with Mennonite Central Committee in postwar emergency relief and reconstruction work in Europe, two colleagues and I set out from our MCC center in Frankfurt, Germany, on a vacation camping trip through the Balkans. Three countries were on our itinerary: Yugoslavia, Greece, and Turkey. In addition to recreational tourism, we had two focused interests: a glimpse into the communist world (Yugoslavia—at that time, the Soviet Union was hardly accessible) and, more importantly, into parts of the New Testament world north and east of the Mediterranean Sea.

With sleeping bags and other equipment, we traveled with MCC permission from our Frankfurt base but at our own expense, in a Ford Taunus sedan. My colleagues were Calvin Redekop, a young American Mennonite who had joined our MCC team in Frankfurt a year earlier, and Richard Wagner, a German men's clothing merchant in mid-city Frankfurt, who was also a lay minister in a local Mennonite congregation.

We began the trip with a slight detour—a two-day visit to Vienna, Austria, accompanied that far by my wife Ellen, then matron at the MCC center in Frankfurt, and our staff secretary, Dorothy Swartzentruber, a Canadian. After our brief visit there, the women returned to Frankfurt by train. Eastern Austria was still under Soviet occupation. We three travelers to the Balkans drove west. After exiting from the Soviet zone into the American zone, we turned south toward Yugoslavia.

We entered Yugoslavia at Maribor, then traveled east and south through Zagreb, Belgrade, and Smederevo, then to Skopje, and from there to Thessalonica in Greece. Largely for financial reasons—Cal and I were supported but unsalaried MCC volunteers—on this tour we slept in outdoor shelters or under the stars in our sleeping bags. Given our interest in sectarian movements before sixteenth-century Anabaptism, detouring to see the archeological traces of medieval Bogomils in southern Yugoslavia would provide a nonpolitical focus for our travel through this communist territory.

A visit to the appropriate government ministry in Belgrade was informative. The official we met there had been French-educated in pre-Marxist times. However, the roads south of Belgrade were so primitive for extensive stretches that time did not permit us to detour for the Bogomil project.

Following our tour through Yugoslavia, we headed through Greece into Turkey. Then we traveled by boat (with our car) from Istanbul back to Greece, this time to Athens, our final stop on this tour. Memories of the Athens visit triggered the present chapter. Further unexpected delays had turned up in our travels. As a result, after a night in Athens, and because of a previously scheduled MCC commitment back in Germany, I flew from nearby Corinth to Rome, then took the overnight train home to Frankfurt.

Two Personal Anecdotes

For that night in Athens, we found an unoccupied, unkempt spot on Mars Hill, formally the Areopagus, where we could bed down. Presumably this was where Paul the apostle in the first century CE met the philosophers as recorded in Acts 17. Near the spot where we slept, attached to a big rock, was a bronze plate on which was engraved, in Greek, Paul's address to the Athenians who had brought him there. I had studied enough New Testament Greek in college to recognize the plaque with the apostle's brief Acts 17 lecture, but of course, none of us spoke Greek.

Soon after we had unrolled our sleeping bags to settle down for the night, a policeman arrived and presumably ordered us to leave. When he could not get us to budge, the policeman left, only to return soon with two colleagues. Their joint effort to have us move on was also unsuccessful. Eventually, after they chuckled a bit, two of them left. The third stayed all night, likely more for our safety than for the safety of the city. In the morning, he guided us down to the city police station. Redekop and Wagner went in to negotiate with the officer in charge, while I remained with the car. Eventually they succeeded in convincing the officers that we were upright and harmless. This meeting, too, ended with a chuckle, and we were soon on our way.

About a week earlier, the night before Easter, we had arrived at a small town on the eastern border of Greece. We were just south of the city of Edirna in Turkey, where we expected to enter that country the next day. Greece, of course, had been steeped for many centuries in Greek Orthodox Christendom, quite in contrast to what Paul set forth in his appearance on the Areopagus. Arriving at that border town on Easter evening, we obtained permission to roll out our sleeping bags on the flat bed of a parked truck near the town center.

About 11:00 p.m. we joined the worshippers in the town church for the Easter service that climaxed at midnight. Shortly before midnight, the assembly filed out to an adjoining hilltop shrine. They walked between a line of uniformed policemen and soldiers on each side. Once everyone had reached the hilltop, the priest read the resurrection story from the gospel of Luke, ending at midnight with the phrase, "The Lord is arisen!" A shout went up from the crowd, reinforced by gunfire from the military cortege. Christendom at work!

Here we were, nineteen centuries after the apostle's introduction of the Christian story in Greece. Long since, Christianity had become a ratifying rather more than a redeeming and transforming presence in that society. For me, this Easter scene in 1951, like the occasion at Tbilisi, Georgia, thirty-seven years later (chapter 14 above), dramatized the paradox, and hence the challenge, that is Christendom, the challenge that eventually focused my vocation. But this tour helped to dramatize the contexts of the biblical story, especially the shift from east to west in the apostle Paul's missionary pilgrimage recorded in Luke's Acts of the apostles.

Paul's Plunge into the Western World

Not surprisingly, that night on Mars Hill enhanced my interest in the story of the apostle Paul's visit there nineteen hundred years earlier. Today Athens is regarded widely as the birthplace of Western civilization, though its heyday as intellectual bellwether by then was already several centuries past. Paul's visit there was part of his sally into Macedonia, today viewed as his second missionary journey. He had begun his ministry (his so-called first missionary journey) in Asia Minor, the peninsula between the Mediterranean and the Black Seas, today largely comprising Turkey.

There, working always with one or more helpers, he sensed the need in their mission to move more deeply into Asia. But, surprisingly, when he turned in that direction, according to Luke's story, he was rebuffed twice by the Holy Spirit. Immediately thereafter came the night vision, informed by the same Spirit, with the plea, "Come over to Macedonia to help us" (Acts 16:9), a shift in direction from going east to going west. In effect, by this he would introduce Christianity into what became known as the Western world. The boiling of the pot that was the Mediterranean world, triggered by the introduction of Christianity into the Greco-Roman and Judaic mix already present there, began with his visit.

Retrospectively, we can sense in Paul's Greek experience, however faintly, the seeds of our own postmodern era. This unusual traveling apostle embodied the dissimilar yet interacting visions—the native Hebrew and Greco-Roman context, and now the emerging Christian reality—newly percolating in the Mediterranean world. Paul had responded immediately to the Macedonian call he received in Asia Minor, setting out by boat from Troas, on the Asian coast. His party sailed northwest on a short voyage at the edge of the Agean Sea, to Neapolis (today Kavalla), a seaport on the eastern end of Macedonia. But far from the triumphalism that a call from the Holy Spirit might evoke in him, this mission became for Paul an enrollment in the school of hard knocks. Luke, a Gentile convert, later the author of the gospel bearing his name and then of the book of Acts, accompanied Paul on this journey and recorded their experiences.

Moving westward from Neapolis, they arrived first in Philippi, then Thessalonica, and finally in Beroea, beginning their visit each time in a synagogue, as they had done previously in Asia Minor. Though they won a few converts, disturbance followed in each instance, causing Paul and his small team to move on. Finally, from Beroea, Paul was taken south by sea to Athens. Timothy and Silas followed, perhaps by land. While awaiting them in Athens, Paul "argued in the synagogue with the Jews and devout persons, and also in the marketplace every day with those who happened to be there" (Acts 17:17). Some of these listeners brought him to a public arena, the Areopagus, popularly called Mars Hill, where he shared further about his faith. He drew heavily on is native Jewish heritage, supplemented by his radical Christian experience, standing now at the heart of the Greek world that presumed to supplant both.

Athens had long since declined from its golden years (fifth century BCE), while still surviving on that legacy. As Luke reports, Epicurean and Stoic philosophies were still circulating there. Paul was deeply stirred by the extreme religious interest of the leading thinkers of the city and by the polytheistic idolatry evident everywhere.

Paul had been educated by Gamaliel, the noted first-century Jewish leader in Jerusalem. But he had also grown up a Greek-speaking Roman citizen in the cosmopolitan city of Tarsus (in present-day Turkey). While hardly a Greek philosopher, he had some sense of what was going on in Athens and was moved particularly by an altar with the inscription, "To an unknown god." Reference to that altar became the point of departure for his Mars Hill speech. Luke reports that philosophers who earlier had encountered him wanted to hear what this babbler, this amateur nonspecialist, had to say. Paul introduced them to the unknown true God with a discourse on the resurrection of Jesus the Messiah.

> When they heard of the resurrection of the dead, some scoffed; but others said, "We will hear you again about this." At that point Paul left them. But some of them joined him and became believers . . . After this Paul left Athens and went to Corinth. (Acts 17:32-33; 18:1)

Corinth, a city some twenty miles to the west of Athens, had been destroyed in 146 BCE by a Roman army and refounded under the Roman emperor, Julius Caesar, a century later (44 BCE). Thereby the Roman stream had entered the cultural mix of the time.

THE PROTOTYPE OF POSTMODERNISM

But why did Paul leave Athens for Corinth after the Mars Hill episode? And what does one make of his speech on that occasion, and of the mixed response among his hearers? There has been a tendency among commentators to write off Paul's presentation there as a draw or a failure. However, the speech can be read as an appropriate adaptation to the audience and setting—not bad, one might say—Paul reaching out for common ground with the motley crowd of the curious who happened to gather round that day. Yet, abruptly, Paul left Athens for Corinth with no details given regarding the reasons for his departure. Curiously, only once thereafter does Paul in his writings make even a passing reference to Athens.

In Corinth, Paul took up tent-making, having found there a Jew in that craft named Aquila. That city was an important center of commerce in Mediterranean area. On Sabbaths Paul made the Christian case in Corinth's synagogue. After his associates Silas and Timothy arrived, Paul's debates in the synagogue heated up. Facing stiff opposition, Paul shook the dust from his clothes, declaring to the Jews gathered there: "Your blood be on your own heads! I am innocent. From now on I will go to the Gentiles" (Acts 18:6).

Paul moved directly next door to the house of Titius Justus, a worshiper of God—from synagogue to a private home, typical as the meeting place of the early church. Others followed and were baptized. Then one night Paul received endorsement from God to proceed in just this manner. The circle of believers grew while Paul remained in Corinth for a year and a half. Thereafter he returned to his earlier base in Antioch in Syria, the place from which he originally had been sent out as an evangelist (Acts 13:1-3).

How Macedonia Changed Paul

Between Paul's appeal in Athens and his preaching in Corinth, something seems to have happened in his approach to the people. A hint appears in Paul's first letter to the Corinthians, written perhaps three years after his departure from their city. (Contrary to his brief stays elsewhere in Macedonia, he had remained in Corinth for eighteen months.) In 1 Corinthians 2:1-5 he recalls his first tour of the area:

> When I came to you, brothers and sisters, I did not come proclaiming the mystery of God to you in lofty words or wisdom. For I decided to know nothing among you except Jesus Christ, and him crucified. And I came to you in weakness and in fear and in much trembling. My speech and my proclamation were not with plausible words of wisdom, but with a demonstration of the Spirit and of power, so that your faith might rest not on human wisdom but on the power of God.

Nothing but Jesus Christ and him crucified? Why? In Athens he appealed to reason with words of wisdom, seeking common ground with the Athenians. But after his less-than-successful performance in Athens, he changed tactics. At stake here is the symbiosis between creation and salvation (chapter 13 above). The above excerpt from his letter seemingly underscores the radical otherness of the salvation initiative he had introduced at Corinth—in contrast to his Mars Hill seeking of common ground with the philosophers.

Growing in Grace and Knowledge

Meanwhile, as we already noted, another radical change emerged for Paul at Corinth, intimations of which had already begun. Without ending his association and conversations with his native Jews, Paul finally broke with his usual primary efforts at evangelism among Jews and turned entirely to the Gentiles. But once more we must observe carefully. At Athens he already had unsuccessfully attempted Gentile evangelism. Apparently at this early stage, engaging simultaneously with both efforts was too complicated. If now he turned from the Jews, where could he go, if he was to continue to evangelize?

Notice carefully: In a still later communication with the believers in Corinth Paul reported that he long had suffered an unspecified handicap—"a thorn in the flesh"—from which he three times implored the Lord for its removal, only to receive the reply: "My grace is sufficient for you, for power is made perfect in weakness" (2 Cor. 12:9). Once he had accepted this condition, whatever it was, he became "content with weaknesses, insults, hardships, persecutions, and calamities for the sake of Christ; for whenever I am weak, then I am strong" (2 Cor. 12:10). A dramatic persona, Paul apparently concluded, is more likely to confuse and mislead than to channel God's saving grace! Surely this is a message for our time as well.

So now consider again the words from 1 Corinthians 2:2, "I decided to know nothing among you except Jesus Christ, and him crucified." Why did Paul stop midstream with the story of Jesus, crucified but without the resurrection, the triumphant second half? Was this simply a mistake on the part of Luke, the writer? Or did this deficiency reflect Paul's own suffering at the moment? Or again, is this agony the origin of his dynamic vision that to be Christian is to grow in grace? There may be no definite answer. In any event, we have the triumphal note that rings jubilantly in 2 Corinthians 5:17-18:

> So if anyone is in Christ, there is a new creation: everything old has passed away; see, everything has become new! All this is from God, who reconciled us to himself through Christ, and has given to us the ministry of reconciliation.

Only now does the radical thrust of Paul's decision "to know nothing among you except Jesus Christ" come through fully and clearly. Thereby Paul has broken radically with his initial attempts at winning both Jews and Gentiles for Christ by teasing out common ground in these respective traditions. At last, in his eighteen-month stay in Corinth, he has concluded that such an approach is unfeasible.

But what about anti-Semitism? That issue lies beyond the scope of this book. It is appropriate to note here, however, that Paul's decision now to witness first to Gentiles cannot be viewed as anti-Semitic.

Paul's conversion as described in Acts 9 is not a repudiation of the Jewish legacy that shaped him but rather an unfolding of that legacy. In his Damascus Road experience Paul dramatically encountered the reality that the messianic moment foreseen in that legacy had arrived. With it came his personal call as witness to that realization. Paul continued his Jewish relations, though after Corinth his specialized vocation would focus on the Gentile world.

BEING HUMAN, BEING CHRISTIAN

"History under God both can be and is full of surprises," observes T. J. Gorringe, a contemporary Anglican scholar. The emergence of this account of the Corinth epitome of the apostle's call to Macedonia as the pivot of this final chapter came as a surprise to me. Unexpectedly, the Pauline Christian experience in the postmodern-like, first-century boiling pot that was the Greco-Roman world came to serve as a kind of prototype for our own postmodern era. In conclusion I offer only a few broad strokes.

(1) There is a sense in which the Christendom/believers church contest flows from a misreading of the circumstantial differences between the life settings and vocations of Paul and Peter. And indeed, their different entry into and positioning in the Christ event is effectively archetypal and indispensable. Peter participated in the earthly ministry of Jesus, while Paul did not. On the other hand, Paul's post-Pentecostal arrival on the scene dramatized Jesus' own words: "The one who believes in me will also do the works that I do and, in fact, will do greater works than these because I am going to the Father" (John 14:12).

(2) Given God's verdict in Genesis 8:21 that the human heart is incurably evil, why was God's remedial intervention so circuitous and so long delayed? A hint appears in Paul's Galatians letter (4:4): "But when the fullness of time had come, God sent his Son, born of a woman, born under the law." Fullness of time? Might this suggest that history had first to unfold, that sociocultural complexity—the beginning of postmodernity, as it were—was a prerequisite for the emergence of personalized faith communities? In a word, must our cultural anchors, whether ethnic or territorial, be uprooted to turn us heavenward (see Heb. 11:1-3)?

(3) Nevertheless, the gospel is very explicit: "God did not send the Son into the world to condemn the world, but in order that the world might be saved through him" (John 3:17). This pronouncement

is doubly paradoxical. The world, Jesus said, because it is evil, hates and persecutes his followers; and Christians are called to come out, to be separate. That saving impulse is manifest in the charities flowing from Christian churches. But there is ample reason to ask this: What would happen for us as Christians, if by living fully to *save*, that impulse surmounted the impulse primarily to *condemn* the world?

(4) Paul's above-noted "aha experience" in Corinth, when finally he "decided to know nothing among [the Corinthians] except Jesus Christ, and him crucified," underscored the radical otherness of the Christian story in that multicultural world. Nonetheless, Paul remained positively involved in that world. He continued taking his Roman citizenship, his culture, and his civilization for granted. When he was shipwrecked (Acts 27), saving the lives of his fellow travelers took priority over all else. We can describe Paul as world-affirming precisely because his life and mission were world-saving.

(5) Paul equally engaged the fundamental human paradox, intensified in the Christian experience: our communality and our individuality at once as humans. Though inseparable, developmentally, both historically and biographically, the former is the matrix of the latter. Yet only as the former is embraced by the latter, individually, person by person, hence interactively, does human reality come full-blown. Here the contrast, indeed the discord, between the mainline and the evangelical paradigms since the sixteenth century gradually emerge. Christendom, in both Catholic and Protestant versions, though differing importantly, outwardly alike enforce the communality (state churches) at the expense of the individualizing/personalizing process from which the opposite pole emerges. All too often instead a subjective experience of conversion is marketed, with the moral and communal dimensions largely shortchanged or ignored.

(6) Repeatedly over the centuries, efforts to establish communal faith communities have been quickly stunted. Communal elements triumphed, though incompletely, in the monastic communities that emerged within Christendom. Eventual corruption and historical development reach the stage of the sixteenth-century Protestant Reformation. While importantly reflecting the individuating process—the fullness of time—as the parallel wider historical unrest mounted, politically enforced, totalizing communality was implemented anew by the original reformers. The Reformation reverted to state-church status. Meanwhile a minority wing of that movement emerged, initially scorned as varied Anabaptist sects, later labeled as the Radical Reformation, surviving with scars ever since.

(7) Astonishingly, the Western intellectual tradition is relatively static in contrast to the dynamically unfolding biblical story. This distinction was well-captured in the phrasing of Gil Baillie, cited above in chapter 3. Both the secularizing and rationalizing impulses espoused in our modern era indirectly "were products of the Judeo-Christian tradition that the Enlightenment came into existence by underestimating and repudiating." Where biblical thought (Rev.) is linear, Hellenistic thought was circular. Being circular, the latter is without an ultimate end, hence insofar meaningless. The former, being linear, begins and moves meaningfully to an end. The objection raised by the secular paradigms lies in the fact that both beginning and end are enshrined in mystery, the mystery that is implicit in human finitude. Consequently the Christian maxim to "walk by faith, not by sight" is seen by secularists as absurd, as indefensible (2 Cor. 5:7).

(8) In our modern era, the institutional formations of Christendom have increasingly lost relevance. It is here that the wide-ranging interest in house churches in recent decades assumes importance. At this writing Google word search lists 53,000 "house church" sites! The "small groups" listing is far more extensive: 225,000. A recent media announcement claimed that forty per cent of the American people belong to small groups of some sort, whether secular or religious.

What often is all but totally lacking in both the polar opposites, the top-down Christendom traditions and the individualist, conversionist, fundamentalisms, is the communal reality presented in the words of Jesus, "For where two or three are gathered in my name, I am there among them" (Matt. 18:20). House church movements without this component are surely wanting. But they must not be merely ignored or condemned. In our reach to supersede the one-sided polarities of Christendom or mere individualist conversions, house church and small group stirrings must be taken seriously, though without regarding them as the only pattern for church.

The germ of all this surfaces from time to time in the book of Acts, notably in Paul's written farewell message to the church elders in Ephesus, recorded in Acts 20:20: "I did not shrink from doing anything helpful, proclaiming the message to you and teaching you publicly and from house to house." Churches: Are they essentially reified hierarchies and ritual cathedrals? Or small committed faith communities infused by the Holy Spirit, bonded in their shared experiences? Today Spirit-based koinonias are widely supplanted by secularizing institutions. However, we must listen long and hard to the house church voices. Particularly instructive is the contrast between the megachurch movement and its house church counterpart. The distance between them accounts for the all-too-frequent flaw of the house church movement of dealing mostly with emotional needs.

Four Concluding Summaries

The Symbiosis of Creation and Salvation

The midlife course change described in this book emerged from the post-World War II decade that I spent at the interface between the faith community traditions of Christendom and those shaped by the believers church tradition in which I grew up. The particular focus of that engagement was the longtime debate between the just war accommodation of Christendom to the military cause and its Christian pacifist challenge, newly activated by that war and its aftermath. During that decade I increasingly perceived that debate as futile, because the issue thus formulated springs from deeper error.

My own experiences as a conscientious objector during the war; then as a postwar volunteer in relief and rehabilitative service under Mennonite Central Committee in Europe; and finally as a graduate student in several European universities, served as a backdrop for that decade. Others in my generation were similarly involved, leading to generational differences in the postwar ferment in our communities of origin. For me all this brought deeper understandings of both sides in the above debate.

By century's end, as indicated in preceding chapters, I became increasingly impressed with the confused readings of the creation/salvation paradox of the biblical story during the era of Christendom of which the just war/pacifist controversy can be seen as a symptom. In Christendom, salvation history tends to disappear behind the enterprise of creation. In the Anabaptist believers church alternative, creation tends to be eclipsed by salvation.

Moreover, multiple and diverse forces, such as globalization and postmodernity, are rapidly outmoding the legacy of Christendom, both pro and con. We now confront the radical challenge and the possibility of engaging anew the distinct yet interactive manifestations of God's symbiotic presence in our world, first as creator and later as savior in salvation history. But this will entail something far more radical than mere doctrinal or institutional pronouncements.

Faith commitments need bottom-up revamping in experiential Christian understanding. The biblical story needs clear articulation anew. Creation and salvation need each to be understood in its own right within that story. Though confluent within that story, the fusing of these two modes into common fulfillment comes only beyond the present age. Until that time, activities are bound to occur on the plane of fallen creation, many of which are out of bounds to those who have entered the already/not yet stream of salvation. Yet participation in that stream is beyond the reach of those standing outside. Those participating in the salvific stream serve those outside by their being other than they are. Though outwardly remaining in the world, they are no longer "of the world" in its fallen machinations. This effort calls for grass roots reconstitution (study the "in but not of" theme in John 17).

Implications for Faith Communities

We in the Christian faith communities need to learn to distinguish between the primary and the secondary dimensions of salvation history. By primary I mean the life and witness that flows directly from our response to the call to "repent, and believe in the good news" (Mark 1:15). The faith communities thus rooted nurture and sustain those brought together in this way. Our shared faith and practice in life intrinsically is a witness to others (Acts 1:8). By their very nature, faith communities are the base for evangelism.

Yet as Jesus pointed out early in his ministry (Matt. 5), more complex implications follow. He spoke of his disciples as salt, as leaven, and as light in the world. These metaphors point to the tempering effect of his followers in the world along with their direct evangelistic import, once more the "in but not of the world" paradox. Here we recall again Loughlin: "serving the world by being other than the world." In Christendom, where the church had become conjoined to the world, that otherness tended to disappear. Meanwhile, Anabaptists struggling to disentangle the conjoining of church and world basically found no longer any relation to the state (in effect, the world).

As a result, in today's post-Christendom context, we find ourselves largely in uncharted territory. How is "in-ness" but "not-of-ness" to be implemented simultaneously—"in-ness" without assimilation into; "not-of-ness" without withdrawal? Once more the accent falls on living process rather than on one-size-fits-all blueprints. Are there instances where withdrawal indeed is indicated? If so, is participation in war such an instance? Does refusal to bear arms mean political nonparticipation generally? If not, where and how does one draw the line?

Dealing with conscientious objectors during World War I became a messy problem for both church and state in the U.S. because no previous agreements or arrangements existed to deal with them. In the late 1930s, as a new war loomed, memories of those previous difficulties motivated conversations between churches (along with other pacifist groups) and government agencies, to work out arrangements to accommodate COs. Selective Service, the updated military draft agency, agreed to procedures whereby conscientious objectors could be assigned to nonmilitary alternative public service.

Was this operation a compromise between church and state? Minority objections were voiced within the CO constituency to these agreements, by both scattered individuals and small groups, precisely because such cooperation with the military institution appeared to them as compromise. Practically, however, the system appeared to work reasonably well.

I will not presume to offer any blanket answers to such questions. Partly because the military question figured so importantly in the autobiographical dimension of this book, I will simply cite two examples of unexpected yet positive side-effects flowing from alternative service by World War II conscientious objectors. Such examples are rich with cues, positive and negative, as we engage the postmodern, globalizing era now upon us.

The first example has to do with the effects of conscientious objection on human rights more generally. Above in chapter 5 we noted the way in which the witness of World War II conscientious objectors has spread widely, strengthening the secular grounding of human rights worldwide.

The second example is a more recent account written by a psychiatric professional and published by a psychiatric agency on hospital service reforms in that field that sprang from the staffing by conscientious objectors during that same era. These studies do not address issues of an evangelistic nature. Instead they trace the infusing of new energies and procedures by the services rendered in lieu of military activities, forbidden by conscience, thereby the becoming light to the world and salt to the earth.

Implications for Natural Community

We have no way to measure or count conversions to faith as the primary result (the evangelistic fruit) of the pacifist witness. But whatever the primary outcome, the secondary impact of the practices of conscientious objection on human rights in general, and of treatment of mental patients in psychiatric centers, bear strongly on the symbiosis of creation and grace today coming newly into focus. In a sense these two examples shed archetypal light on the "in but not of" paradox we here confront.

Out of the Protestant Reformation came the maxim, *Ecclesia semper reformanda est* (the church is always reforming). Of course, all human institutions, by virtue of their being, always are subject to reform. But with reference to churches, something other than social engineering is at stake. If indeed such gatherings are Holy Spirit engendered and sustained, socially engendered overlays, insofar as merely that, become the more problematic. If they are truly Holy Spirit engendered, (re)forming growth indeed is continuous.

The Biblical Grand Finale

In the growth of the human enterprise, whatever its origin, the need to coordinate the primary groupings of kinship and place quickly emerges. Otherwise conflicting interests appear inevitable as humans multiply. Such coordination will concentrate power. Thereby bottom-up interests and actions are aroused counter to top-down interests and actions, and vice versa. Indeed, unless tempered to the contrary, power gravitates toward top-down institution.

While this tendency is particularly prominent in economic and political arenas, it emerges in religious life as well. But in religious matters, there are added problems. How does one appropriately take into account the noumenal dimensions of experience (God and the human soul) in this-worldly phenomenal terms? This question is fundamental in human experience generally, but it reaches its most acute form in the symbolic, hence material, aspects of religious life.

This appears most dramatically in religious institutions, where the top-down/ bottom-up conflict is inescapable. Commonly this enigma is ostensibly resolved by way of sacrament. Mysterious, supernatural potency is attributed to ritual acts or sacralized individuals and hence to some degree are externally enforceable.

An insightful citation from Hebrews 11:13-16 appears appropriate to end this chapter, indeed nearly this entire book:

> All of these died in faith without having received the promises, but from a distance they saw and greeted them. They confessed that they were strangers and foreigners on the earth, for people who speak in this way make it clear that they are seeking a homeland. . . . Therefore God is not ashamed to be called their God; indeed he has prepared a city for them.

Epilogue

In classic Greek drama, the principal actor might offer an afterword, an *epilogue*. Thereby he might tie up some loose ends in the plot of the play or muse on future happenings. *Plot,* according to *The Oxford Companion to the English Language (1992)* is "the narrative element in fiction and drama." Such works are distinguished from mere *story* by "the causal quality which links episodes, reveals significances, and reaches a planned conclusion." In this vein, chapter 1 in this book drew on Gerard Loughlin's concept of realistic narrative, whereby he maintains that "character, circumstance and theme are nothing without each other and become themselves only in their mutual reaction."

I am adding an epilogue here not merely to tie up loose ends but also because this writing process turned out to be a continuation of the realistic narrative that it traces. Drafting this book in effect became a phase of the narrative thereby constructed. As a participant observer affected by the events described, I the author am further being changed. Writing this book made connections that otherwise would have gone unnoticed. Some of this mutual reaction between circumstance and theme has already been incorporated in the text. In this epilogue I offer further reflection on that process.

A Shattering but Emancipating Experience

I offer once more the Psalm 71 excerpt cited early in this book:

O God, from my youth you have
Taught me,
And I still proclaim your wondrous deeds.
So even to old age and gray hairs,
O God, do not forsake me,

Until I proclaim your might
To all the generations to come.

In important respects, the attempt in this book to carry out this admonition has been for me a shattering yet emancipating experience. I resonate deeply with the psalmist's celebration of God's "wondrous deeds" that he in the years of his life was permitted to witness. But it was precisely those wondrous deeds that expose the infirmity of my human responses. In my case, living vocationally at the margins and walking along roads less traveled heightened that infirmity. Yes, God's wondrous deeds are there for me to proclaim, but alongside are the increasing exposure of my own inadequacies and failures.

Regarding the fundamental mystery engaged here, a further comment appears appropriate. About that mystery, all the way from ancient through medieval into modern and postmodern times, the literature is vast. A useful analytical tool is the conceptual distinction between *phenomena* and *noumena*, between what is material and what is spiritual, between what is accessible to our senses and what is inaccessible to them. For many people the scientific, industrial, and other revolutions of modernity eclipsed the phenomenal and noumenal inquiry and discourse. Yet, interestingly, noumenal (religious) energies not merely survive but continue to unfold. This has been true in my own life. Whatever personal or even group deviations may occur, the God-mystery is not disappearing from the human saga.

Two Reemerging Aporias

We frequently experience our human stories as enigmatic and puzzling. Often, in the end, such puzzles are superficial or fleeting. But others turn out to be aporias, paradoxes that remain irreducible the one into the other. In the course of this book, two such aporias surface. The first is the mystery of the Supreme Being, reflected in all our God-talk. The second, a derivative of the first, is the godly image in our human species that distinguishes us from the rest of the animal world. I do not presume to offer a solution to the basic challenges that thus confront us all. Instead I merely comment on "what [I] have seen and heard" (Acts 22:15) in living with these aporias.

The use of the term *witness* in both the Old and the New Testament (Greek *martures* [tr. martyr] in Acts 1:8) in this connection is revealing. Not laboratory experiments and tests, not social engineering, but "witness to all the world of what you have seen and heard" (Acts

22:15) is presented as the ground for our God-talk. We contact God the Supreme Being existentially, experientially rather than merely theoretically or doctrinally. We "walk by faith, not by sight" (2 Cor. 5:7). As believers we each receive our particular vocation even as we are incorporated into particular gatherings of Christ's one body.

This takes us to the heart of the apostle Paul's messages in his letters to the Corinthians. In chapters 12 and 13 in the first epistle he describes their faith community as a body constituted by members, each with a particular gift. Yet that body is one. The imagery here is inimitable. It accounts at once for the commonality and the particularity of our human reality as restored and renewed in the biblical narrative. Equally inimitable is the summary that comes in chapter 5 of his second letter: "In Christ God was reconciling the world to himself . . . and entrusting the message of reconciliation to us" (v. 19).

Our role as members of Christ is simply to serve and to witness, not to control, enforce, or engineer. Each of us has a particular gift. The "you-will-be-witnesses" phrase, after the Holy Spirit comes (Acts 1:8), captures this miracle well. We speak primarily by whom we are, not by soap boxing. The nuancing in this love-not-the-world dictum that is the biblical story (1 John 2:15) needs careful attention. The reference is not to creation, the material order as created by God, but to the human cultural constructs that are expressions of evil.

Yet despite the language and story of separation, of exile from the world, and indeed persecution by the world in its evil expressions, life and work in the world of creation is everywhere affirmed and frequently celebrated. Jeremiah's admonition to the Israelite captives in Babylon (29:7-9) is often noted. A parallel to that admonition appears in Paul's first letter to the Thessalonians (4:10-12):

> But we urge you. . . to aspire to live quietly, to mind your own affairs, and to work with your hands, as we have directed you, so that you may behave properly toward outsiders and be dependent on no one.

One can even see this echoed in the secular creative writing maxim: Show, don't tell! In a word, our Christian vocation in the present era is to effect world-transformation but not world-control.

My Personal Vocation

As detailed throughout this book, I found myself placed in life at the interface between two contrasting academic disciplines—biblical and sociological studies. I also found myself exposed to two historical paradigms of ekklesia—church as civilization and church as faith communities (believers church). These contrasts were basic enough in my life to trigger an unanticipated, midlife career change.

Each of these two concept-pairs is at once bipolar yet inseparable. Theology is idealistic, setting forth what is there in its biblical fullness. Sociology deals with what is materially constructed in human life together. Similarly the believers church heralds the dynamic that brings about and sustains faith communities. The inclusive, established church simply assumes and misapplies what appears in Jesus' parables of the sower in Matthew 13. Outwardly that church is thought to include everybody, leaving the sorting out to the time of harvest!

The mystery, the aporia, that is the Supreme Being, giving rise to our God-talk, looms perpetually in the background of this book. *Aporia* (from the Greek/Latin *aporos*, meaning impassable, unable to proceed) points to contradiction that can neither be resolved nor evaded. Though always and everywhere behind the real-world scene, God is never reducible to material, empirical terms. We can neither prove nor disprove God. The vital energy flowing from this perpetual tension evokes and sustains believers personally and communally.

An old legend says that Adam, frustrated with Eve, brought her back to God saying, "Here she is. I can't get along with her, but neither can I get along without her." The same might be said of our human God-story. There are atheistic theories that in some instances must be taken seriously. The claim that noumenal (spiritual) intuitions are not directly translatable into phenomenal (material) calculation is in fact materially irrefutable. Logically, it is possible to be a sincere atheist! Existentially, however, does not the predicament of the atheist parallel that of Adam in the above legend? "God, here I am. Logically I can't get along with you, yet humanly I can't get along without you!"

This noumenal mystery persistently haunts all historical cultures. Here we are treading on déjà vu terrain, on ground already covered in chapter 13, "The Creation/Salvation Symbiosis." Yes, in this context aporia and symbiosis appear as synonyms. But whereas chapter 13 elaborates a particular and unique instance of aporia, in this epilogue, the use is generic. That is, aporia occurs more widely in varied forms. And while the following example illustrates that fact, as a derivative of the symbiotic mystery it retains something of that same mystery. Christian vitality flows from the perpetual interaction of God's creating and saving presence as it evokes believing responses from us humans.

The Image of God in Our Human Being

Profound as is the God-mystery, yet there is a sense in which that aporia is but the beginning of the conundrum that it entails. According to the biblical story, God the Supreme Being endows us humans with something of his own "image" (Gen. 1:26-28). In humans there is a dimension of creative indeterminacy that is truly unique. Biologically, physiologically, as humans we are part of the animal world, yet within that world we stand uniquely apart. We are endowed with nature-transcending capacities that do not appear elsewhere.

Resonating with that Genesis account is the well-known Quaker observation attributed to the founder of that movement, George Fox (1624-1691), that there is something of God in every human. That insight, though apt, has also proved vulnerable. Too readily it glides into mere human self-assertion. The earlier noted diagnosis of our fallen human condition in Genesis 8:21 holds that "the inclination of the human heart is evil from youth." How can that verdict to be understood alongside the declaration in Genesis 1:27, "So God created humankind in his image, in the image of God he created them"?

The image of God endowed in us has been marred beyond the reach our self-improvement, an anomaly in its own right. This further complexifies the human condition, another aporia, we might say. As Christians, we are "sinners saved by grace," already but not yet fully! The interrelated mysteries, divine and the human, are inexhaustible in human terms. But likewise they are simple and direct. To their jailer, as reported in Acts 16:31, Paul and Silas announced, "Believe on the Lord Jesus, and you will be saved, you and your household" (Acts 16:31). Yet equally emphatic is the teaching of Paul and other New Testament writers on the need for continuous growth in the "knowledge and grace" of our God and Savior. Thus to conclude with Paul's triumphant ending of Romans 11 seems appropriate:

> O the depth of the riches and wisdom and knowledge of God!
> How unreachable are his judgments
> And how inscrutable his ways!
> "For who has known the mind of the Lord?
> Or who has been his counselor?"
> "Or who has given a gift to him,
> to receive a gift in return?"
> For from him and through him and to him are all things.
> To him be the glory forever. Amen.

The Author

Like most of his generational peers (he was born in 1918), World War II would shape Paul Peachey's life in ways beyond his imaginings. When Selective Service was implemented in 1940, he registered as a conscientious objector (CO), a status subsequently approved. Though growing up in a rural Amish-Mennonite family without high school, he had learned meanwhile that now being beyond high school age, he might enroll in a two-year junior college Bible course at Eastern Mennonite School (EMS) in Harrisonburg, Virginia.

In the fall of 1941 he did so, not knowing what his registration under Selective Service might entail. There he soon learned that "pre-professional examinations," successfully passed in his home state, would qualify him for regular college admission. Two months later came his order for Selective Service induction. When he reported this to EMS, the dean observed that the four-year college Bible course offered there had just been approved by Selective Service as seminary-equivalent. Given the importance of churches in society, and hence of trained clergy, both seminaries and pastors were being deferred from military service.

Mennonites as yet had no regular post-college theological seminaries, hence this substitution. Largely on the spur of the moment, Peachey transferred to that four-year program, but with some discomfort. Though dedicated to Christian service, being a professional clergyman for him was not an option. The four years of World War II, 1941-45, coincided with his college years, both ending in May 1945 After marriage and honeymoon in June, he began graduate school that summer in sociology at the University of Pennsylvania.

In early September, after war's end in Japan, he was invited by the Mennonite Central Committee (MCC) to serve on its postwar emergency relief staffing in Europe. While staffing policies at the beginning of that program did not permit his bride Ellen to accompany him on that assignment, a year later she did join him. Unfolding during those years was likewise the first-time publication of legal records and other writings of Anabaptist movement from sixteenth century. The possibility of historical/sociological studies in the context of that project in the future likewise beckoned.

Eventually he and Ellen were transferred by MCC to the French occupation zone of West Germany, where emergency relief efforts were still peaking. Their stay was extended to 1951. During that time, Peachey also studied at the University of Basel (Switzerland), then of Frankfurt (Germany). With wife and infant daughter he then moved to Zurich, Switzerland, where he completed graduate studies. This included a sociological dissertation analyzing the interplay of social and religious factors in the rise of Anabaptist origins in Switzerland, 1525-1540.

Retrospectively it can be said that for Peachey, these war and postwar years contained the germ of all that followed. Working with MCC, from 1946-1951, among the ruins and the victims of World War II, drew him into the conversations between the Historic Peace Churches" and mainline Christian traditions regarding the Christian pacifist challenges to the prevailing just war reasoning and practice.

Paradoxically perhaps, while those years deepened has Anabaptist roots, they also placed him practically at the interface of the Anabaptist believers church and the mainline denominations of Christendom, both Protestant and Catholic. During the second half of his career, from 1967 until his retirement in 1987, he served as a sociology professor at the Catholic University of America in Washington, D.C. Throughout those years he continued participation in both ecumenical and academic bridge-building efforts in the Cold War and beyond, until the late 1990s. Thereafter, with his wife Ellen, he spent fourteen "retirement" years as cofounders of the Rolling Ridge Study Retreat Community, some sixty miles northwest of Washington, D.C., until their move to Virginia Mennonite Retirement Community in Harrisonburg, Virginia, where they now live.

Printed in the United States
201287BV00005B/4-54/A